W9-BQI-605

George H. Vier

St. Charles College

September 12, 1967

————————OUT OF THE LABYRINTH

Also by Erich Kahler

MAN THE MEASURE
THE TOWER AND THE ABYSS
THE MEANING OF HISTORY

Out of the Labyrinth

ESSAYS IN CLARIFICATION

Erich Kahler

GEORGE BRAZILLER
New York

For information address the publisher:
George Braziller, Inc.
One Park Avenue
New York, New York 10016

First Printing

Library of Congress Catalog Card Number: 67-19871

Printed in the United States of America

Designed by Jennie Bush

Acknowledgments

In the preparation of this book I am greatly indebted to several friends ·
for their help: to Eleanor Wolff and Richard and Clara Winston for
their fine translations of "Art and History" and "Varieties of the
Unconscious" respectively; to Eleanor Wolff and George Brantl for
their assistance in the final version of the texts. Translations, unless
otherwise indicated, are my own.

The essays in this volume are gathered from various sources in
which they originally appeared. For their kind permission to reprint
them, I wish to thank the original publishers:

"Culture and Evolution," *The Centennial Review of Arts and
Science*, Vol. V, No. 3 (Summer, 1961).

"The Forms of Form," *The Centennial Review of Arts and Science*,
Vol. VII, No. 2 (Spring, 1963).

"Science and History," *Homage to Galileo*, ed. by Morton F. Kaplon.
Reprinted by permission of the M.I.T. Press, Cambridge, Massachu-
setts.

"The Reality of Utopia," *The American Scholar* (Spring, 1946).

"The Nature of the Symbol," which originally appeared in *Symbolism in Religion and Literature*, ed. by Rollo May (George Braziller,
Inc., 1960).

"What Is Art?" which appeared in *Problems in Aesthetics, An
Introductory Book of Readings*, ed. by Morris Weitz. Reprinted with
permission of The Macmillan Company, (©) The Macmillan Company, 1959.

"The True, the Good, and the Beautiful," copyright © 1960 by the
Ohio State University Press. All rights reserved. Reprinted by per-
mission of the Ohio State University Press, 164 West Nineteenth
Avenue, Columbus, Ohio.

The essays "Art and History," "Varieties of the Unconscious," and
"The Disintegration of Artistic Form" (Part II) originally appeared
in German journals and are here translated for the first time.

77405

For Lili

Preface

THIS BOOK is not a mere collection of miscellaneous papers on a variety of subjects. It is rather a selection of essays intended to amplify and supplement ideas which were advanced in my previous books. Its unifying aim is to establish the meaning of certain basic concepts that have developed in the course of human evolution, and to examine in what respect they may still be valid in our present circumstances. The essays all deal, from different aspects, with the relation between what may be considered permanent in man and what changes with the expansion of political units, the technological transformation of our ways of life, the unification of our globe, and the enlargement of human consciousness. Doubtful as it is whether intellectual endeavors of this kind can in any way influence the conduct of human affairs, I still desperately believe that to attempt such clarification is our foremost duty today. Every one of us in the intellectual community, however involved in his specialized field, should contribute his share to a conceptual groundwork which should be both comprehensive and generally comprehensible and without which the thoughtless or careless attitudes widely prevailing among people today could not be adjusted to our present reality. For in our closely interrelated world, such maladjustments must inevitably lead to common disasters and to the destruction of what is human in man.

The first part of the book deals more generally with the relation between permanence and change, stability and movement. From an inquiry into the role of culture in evolution, it proceeds with an attempt to delimit the domain of science, i.e., the exploration of physical nature, whose dimensions, beyond the human scope as they are, bring to the fore of human perception mainly a condition of stability and regular recurrence of events which call for quantitative and taxonomic methods of interpretation. This character of science is contrasted with that of the humanistic disciplines whose domain is the realm of man, a realm of consciousness evolving in history. Here, on a level co-dimensional with ours, where a state of flux and change is prevailingly perceptible in the variety and variability of unique phenomena, the quantitative approach fails to yield essential knowledge. In the third essay of this section the transformation of myth is contrasted with its persistence in changing forms; while the fourth deals with a fundamental change in modern experience, the reversal of the meaning of utopia under the impact of the atom bomb.

The second part of the book is intended to demonstrate the special relevance of the interweaving of perpetuity and change—which pervades all forms of existence we know—to the work of art. Here is shown a contrast and an intrinsic unity between the indestructible validity of accomplished artistic form, and the dynamic, often revolutionary nature of true art in its role as the perpetual avant-garde of reality, ever disclosing and indeed creating new reality.

The third part is concerned with the psychic and cultural implications of the same fundamental relationship, implications which lead us into the paradoxical complexities of our present human situation. It starts with a survey of the changes which the indissoluble interconnection of consciousness and the unconscious underwent in the course of human evolution. In the first historical stages, the divinified realm of the unknown and uncontrollable served as an outward projection of the unrecognized unconscious. This divine realm was gradually secularized, internalized, psychicalized, and there developed a clear awareness of an unconscious sphere in man. Finally, in our days, the dispersion of our over-expanded rational consciousness has allowed the unconscious to predominate in the processes of our life. The second essay of this section, closely connected with the first, specifies and exemplifies the disruption of consciousness—which is nothing else than a fundamental awareness of the coherence of personality and its reality—through its ever-increasing ramification into analytical abstraction. The evaluation of the threatening consequences of this trend leads the investigation to the problem of values. In the concluding essay the attempt is made to establish in what way and to what degree the basic human values have changed their meaning for us since the time when they arose millennia ago, and how far they have preserved a core of permanence and can therefore be considered as really basic, indeed constitutional in man.

E. K.

Princeton, New Jersey
November, 1966

Contents

PART ONE

Culture and Evolution

I

THE TERMS "Culture" and "Evolution" are by no means self-evident. They have been understood in different ways, and the variety of these meanings reflects a variety of human experiences in different historical situations. A brief survey of the diverse uses of the words will show how the meaning of the terms kept broadening, and then, as a reactive consequence, ramifying down into more specific connotations.

The word "Culture" derives from the Latin *cultura* and *cultus*, which mean care, cultivation, but carry a variety of implications, from "training," "fostering," "adornment," to "worship," and "cult." Both words were used originally in an attributive, functional sense, designating the cultivation of *something*. In fact, *cultura* occurs first in the composite form *agricultura*, agriculture, tilling, cultivation of the soil, and traces of this origin persist up to the Middle Ages when occasionally the worship of God is referred to as *agricultura Dei*, "agricult" of God. The meaning of *cultura* broadens through diverse applications: Cicero speaks of *cultura animi*, cultivation of the mind, which he identifies with philosophy; but gradually *cultura animi* ceased to be so restricted and came to signify cultivation of arts and letters, of intellectual capacities in general. Thus, the common feature of all kinds of cultivation

3

was brought to the fore, namely control and organization, refinement and sublimation of nature.

In this way, the various attributive, functional uses of *cultura* and *cultus* fused into the general and substantive term "Culture," as we still apply it when we oppose culture to barbarism, or when we call a person a "cultivated man." This change from an attributive to a substantive significance implies a turn from the representation of *cultura*, cultivation, as an *activity* (cultivating something, cultivating oneself—*cultivare se ipsum*) to the concept of *culture as an established condition*, a state of being cultivated.

In this capacity, when it referred to a specific condition of man, a state of being, the term "Culture" became synonymous and interchangeable with other terms, such as *humanitas*, humanity, that is, the condition worthy of a human being, as compared with that of the animal; or *civilitas*, civility, and *urbanitas*, urbanity, the condition fitting a city dweller and citizen, as against that of a peasant, a boor. The Roman Empire, and the Latin countries, which originated in Roman provinces and followed the Roman tradition, issued from and centered on a dominating city. The country at large was considered subservient to the city, and city life was the standard of life, in contradistinction to Germany, where the cities developed late, after and within the framework of a universal empire, and where, due to the persistent rusticality of the nobility, cities never achieved such a predominant position as in the West. Until very late, in fact, Germany never had a capital city. These differences seem to me to explain the eventual prevalence of the term "Civilization" in the Latin and Anglo-Saxon West and of "Culture" in Germany. The German notion and high valuation of culture, *Kultur*, evolved from the concepts of German philosophy. *Kultur* was identified with *Bildung*, the cultivation of inner life, of mental and spiritual capacities, and was held superior to Western "Civilization" which was understood as a complex of outer forms: nicety of manners and development of technological and socio-political institutions.

From the sixteenth century on, a new concept of culture began to form. In the wake of the rise of modern nations and territorial states, political thinkers started to differentiate the various national customs and institutions, and to speculate about the national denominators of such specific customs and institutions. The theorist of the French monarchy, Jean Bodin, in his *Six Livres de la République*, 1576, inaugurated the notion of different forms of republic as *organisms*, growing and decaying like natural organisms and peculiarly distinct according to character and climate. He thereby anticipated the modern theories of Spengler and Toynbee. Later, Montesquieu, in his *Esprit des Lois*, 1748, and Voltaire, in his *Essai sur les Moeurs*, 1757, spoke of *"le génie du peuple"* (genius of the people), its *"esprit général"* (general spirit), its *"genre de vie"* which may be adequately rendered by "style of life" or "way of life." I need not recount the whole genealogy of this notion which in the nineteenth century led up to the concept of "cultures" as specific forms of life of ethnic communities, or of epochs. As far as I can see, the Swiss historian, Jakob Burckhardt, in the middle of the nineteenth century, was the first to apply this concept of *a* culture to specific studies in his *Kultur der Renaissance* and his *Griechische Kulturgeschichte*. Likewise, modern anthropologists have adopted the term "Culture" in this specific sense for the tribal groups which they explore.

The shift from the concept of culture as a general human condition to the concept of culture as a particular style of life of ethnic groups, in short, from culture to *a* culture, involves another important change of outlook. Culture seen as a general state and stage of human existence carried a *value* connotation which it lost when it was understood as just a different style of life. Culture as a value was equivalent to superiority over the state of plain nature, over barbarism and bestialism; it was an intellectual and moral criterion to measure the worth and dignity of individuals and peoples. It meant improvement, refinement, enlightenment, and this, in turn, implied development.

Thus, originally, *cultura* (culture) was *synonymous with development* and—this is most important to note—development in the sense of *progress*, of betterment of the human condition.

II

Here we have arrived at the problem of *development*, or *evolution*. Both words denote fundamentally the same: development means literally unwrapping, evolution means unfolding. There is only one difference: evolution has come to be the more general, development the more specific, term.

In the human domain, evolution passes over from a mainly physical to a mainly psychic and mental level, and that means, into the development of consciousness, which is one and the most prominent part of what we may call history. The realm of history is the realm of consciousness whose development cannot be traced here in detail. Suffice it to recall the main phases.[1]

Ancient thinking and society were founded on a stable image of the universe. The concept of evolution was arrested in the bud; it was itself, paradoxical as this may sound, static. Although, because of his concept of entelechy, Aristotle is held to be the initiator of the idea of evolution and indeed regarded the different realms of organic nature, the vegetal, the animal, and the human, as consecutive evolutionary stages, he considered one as only the essential premise of the other, but did not assume a real transformation of one into the other. To him, any organic being or genus was created separately by a touch of the deity. Nor did there yet exist among the ancients, at least before the Hellenistic period, any notion of an historical evolution of humanity. The Greeks and the Romans did not conceive an actual, integral history, that is, history as that single, unique, and unrepeatable flow of happenings passing through and beyond the individual peoples, history as the comprehensive record of the career of man. To them, the human world was either rooted in eternity, or it was believed to be recurrently created and destroyed, in a cyclic movement. Accordingly, their conception of change and evolution was still very shallow and was limited by the notion of a periodical recurrence of events.

The experience of actual evolution was inaugurated by the Jews, who came to visualize history as the journey of man from a primal state of *unconscious innocence*, which he lost through his fall, to an ultimate state of *consciously achieved innocence* in the Kingdom of God to be established at the end of time. To be sure, this progression of human history may still appear as a circular movement in that it seems to return to the original situation. But, in fact, the situation at which it is aimed lies on a new level, on the level of consciousness. This makes a crucial difference: it establishes the uniqueness of the whole process.

The messianic prophecy of Judaism led up to Christianity, whose belief in a sacrifical help of the divine savior transformed the Judaic road toward a humanly achieved innocence into a road to divine salvation. So, in the Christian era, evolution was equivalent to man's gradual preparation for salvation.

Through the Judaeo-Christian concepts, then, human destiny was dynamized; it was made into one, unique evolutionary process. This evolutionary process made explicit what was merely implied in the ancient concepts of culture: the notion of betterment and sublimation. Again, development meant improvement, accomplishment of a higher and happier state of man.

Finally, when, at the end of the Middle Ages, the rule of Christian dogma crumbled and human reason supplanted God, rationalism inherited from Christian theology the concept of history as man's road to perfection. To be sure, the established definite end, expected in the Kingdom of God, had vanished and was replaced by the *in*definite goal of a Kingdom of Reason: evolution was no longer a road to a distinct redeeming event but became an unending approach to secular betterment and happiness through the rational, scientific, and technological improvement of man's living conditions. The goal was split into gradual steps; it came to merge with the road itself, with Progress explicit, its ends moving along with it. The emphasis shifted from final being to infinite becoming.

Since the late nineteenth century, and increasingly in the twentieth, the belief in human progress began to wane. Or, to be more exact, what dwindled away was the hope that the scientific and technological improvement of *material* conditions would by itself bring about an improvement of man's *inner* condition, that is to say, make him better and happier. Long before the turn of the century, men of vision had seen the dark reverse of our expanding rational enlightenment, the growing collectivization and dehumanization which technological progress was carrying with it. They presensed what was to happen in the great crises of the twentieth century: the abrupt slump of humanity from an overstrained civilization into a new, rationalized barbarism. The hopes of the rationalistic generations turned into bitter disillusionment with progress; and since evolution had always been identified with progress, the notion of evolution went down together with the idea of progress.

There were other factors which brought evolution into disrepute. In the domain of history, it was the hypertrophy of historicism itself that discredited the very idea of history as a coherent evolution of man: it was the overgrowth of newly discovered factual material which obscured the broad lines of development and made historians apprehensive of "generalizations." Or, better, it was not the growth of factual material itself, but rather the failure of historians to integrate the new facts into a general concept of human evolution. This was due to the scientistic ambition and positivistic tendency of modern historiography. As a reaction against the great philosophical and social conceptions of the post-Kantian era, in the first half of the nineteenth century, a sweeping distrust of uncritical speculation set in. Such a reaction was no doubt justified to a certain degree, but, as usual, it was carried to the opposite extreme; it led to an attitude that was just as uncritical. Under the influence of scientistic positivism, all criterion of facts was lost; historical research arrived at what I would call a democracy of facts, a total equality of facts, which invalidated the distinction between the essential and the non-essential. Where could a broad evaluation of facts derive from when no general view was left of the historical process? Any clear statement of a development became impossible; it simply disappeared under its qualifications. Eventually, this tendency resulted in scientistic, basically anti-historical theories of history, such as Spengler's and Toynbee's, which split the process of human evolution into so many "philosophically contemporaneous" cultures in order to abstract from them "laws of history" equivalent to laws of nature. The constructions of these "cultures" or "civilizations" are no less uncritically speculative than the old philosophical systems.

In biology, of course, the concept of evolution, modified though it has been, could never be given up, just as the historical point of view is the only one from which the structure of the earth can be understood in geology. But even in paleobiology anti-evolutionism left its traces. The German paleontologist, Edgar Dacqué, a very learned and imaginative man, proposed a theory that was meant to reverse the whole course of the evolution of living forms. In his book *Urwelt, Sage und Menschheit*,[2] he contended that from the beginning of life there existed different genetically unrelated types or type groups (*Typenkreise*) which gradually developed into the various animal forms. Like these, man too has existed, rudimentarily, from the outset as a distinct genetic type. Of course, Dacqué could not deny that man had to go through various animal stages before reaching his human form. But this he explained by the theory that the specific circumstances and environments of the different paleontological periods imposed on genetically independent types certain seemingly homogeneous structural forms and organs, structural fashions as it were: from the Cambrian to the Devonian the dominant form was fish; in the Permian the various species were wearing amphibian, so to speak; from the Permian to the Cretaceous they changed to reptile; with the Eocene it was mammals; and later the dominant form was ape.* As a residue of the phenomenon, Dacqué mentions the fauna of Australia where the most diverse species of higher mammals seem to imitate the form of a lower type of mammal, the marsupial. The marsupial badger, the opossum, the kangaroo, the phalanger, the Australian bear (koala), all of them appear as different versions of the marsupial form.

But even this hypothesis does not fundamentally invalidate the fact of evolution. The assumption of several original types instead of a single, common line would indicate nothing else than the existence of so many parallel evolutions; and, in regard to the concept of human evolution, it does not make much difference whether one calls a reptile a reptile, or man in the temporary disguise of a reptile.

III

The main source of the trend, indeed the intellectual fashion of anti-evolutionism was, as I said, disillusionment with progress and the identification of evolution with progress. It seems to me that in order properly to understand what evolution means, it is necessary to put an end to this confusion and clearly to distinguish evolution from progress. The first point I want to make is that *there was no progress, but there was evolution.* Progress implies a value statement; evolution denotes a plainly factual process.

Progress means improvement. In the human domain it was understood as an improvement not only of living conditions, but of human life; that is to say, an advancement not only of material circumstances, but of happiness and morality, or, to put it more modestly, of action according to reason. Evidently, these high expectations of the era of Enlightenment have not been fulfilled. Biological theories also identified evolution with progress inasmuch as they took it to be a succession of steps leading up to the

---

* In the paleozoic period, Dacqué says, when the salamander form was the "style of the epoch," even the first reptiles, or better, those types that were on the point of becoming reptiles, appeared in the attire of the salamander. Later, the first flying vertebrates were just winged reptiles.

human being as its peak, if not its definite end. Indeed, Julian Huxley, even today, seems to assume that the human individual is the final perfection of evolution. In the face of our present situation, this appears to me a rather questionable human presumption. So when we speak of evolution today, we do better, I think, to eliminate the notion of progress which cannot be divested of its original, plainly optimistic meaning.

But if not progress, what is evolution? First of all, we should take into account that in science recent experiences and findings have initiated a trend of thought that runs diametrically counter to the fashion of anti-evolutionism. Our picture of nature has become thoroughly dynamic, that is to say, nature no longer appears, as it did to scientists up to the nineteenth century, as a static, eternally immutable sphere; it has revealed itself as a *process*. Not only, as modern physics has shown, does it in its entirety consist of processes; it is in itself and as a whole, and it has always been, a process. Astronomy today considers itself a historical science. I cannot go into any detail of the new dynamic concept of cosmic nature and the hypotheses of an expanding or exploding universe, on the one hand, and of continuous creation, on the other.[3] Biological nature has been seen as a process for a long time, ever since Buffon and Lamarck. To be sure, the research of one and a half centuries has produced a picture of the history of life which makes it appear no longer as a straight-line development, but rather as a tree-like growth of multifarious ramifications. The most important change, however, that has taken place in our scientific views with respect to the problem of evolution is the fact that the gap has begun to close, the barriers are crumbling, between the inorganic and the organic states of nature.

When we take all these experiences together, then the history of the universe, the history of the earth, the history of life, and the history of man, emerge as so many sections and stages of *one* unique happening. This overwhelming happening which started in the universe and has this very moment arrived at the here and now where we sit reflecting about it, this process, viewed in its entirety, shows undeniably a definite direction. I say *direction*, and by this I do not mean a *plan*, transcendental or otherwise. Here again a strict distinction has to be made. A direction in the sense of *trend* does not necessarily imply direction in the sense of *guidance* or *providence* or *design*. I see a direction, but I would not venture to say anything about the origin or cause of such direction. This direction is what permits us to speak of evolution.

But again, what is this evolution? What is the nature of this happening? When we ask biologists, rather than one clear-cut answer, we get many partial answers concerning functional or structural features. George Gaylord Simpson, for instance, enumerates all sorts of criteria of evolution (he calls it "progress"), such as "the tendency for life to expand, to fill in all the available spaces in the livable environments," "improvement in adaptation," "control over the environment," "increasing structural complication," "progress in individualization," etc.[4] In all this, he is very anxious to remain "objective" with regard to man, that is to say, not to look at evolution from a pre-established point of view of man as the goal or climax of evolution. He refuses to accept the criterion of "increasing approximation to man"; indeed, he finds certain partial aspects which show man to be not exactly at the top, for instance: "If one group had to be picked as most dominant now, it would have to be the insects,"[5] which implies a rather narrow, purely physical concept of dominance. However, he cannot help listing man in almost all respects within the highest range of evolution; indeed, he declares on the grounds of evidence: "Man *is* the highest animal. The fact that he alone is capable of making such a judgment is in itself part of the evidence that this decision is correct."[6] Simpson goes even further by stating that man is an animal ". . . in which, although organic evolution continues on its way, a fundamentally new sort of evolution has also appeared," the basis of which "is a new sort of heredity, the inheritance of learning."[7] Actually, however, he stops, as most biologists do, at the threshold of this new kind of evolution, at the point where Homo sapiens began his career on his own plane which is history and which entails psychic, mental, and social developments, entirely new dimensions of development, by far surpassing the heredity of learning. Julian Huxley is more specific in that he does not hesitate, as I said before, to make the bold assertion that the human individual not only is, but *"will continue to be* the highest product of evolution."[8] Evolution he defines as an increase in complexity, ". . . greater control, greater independence or self-regulation, greater, but at the same time more harmonious complexity of organization, greater range of knowledge or available experience."[9]

IV

I will now venture an interpretation of my own, taking into consideration both the biological and the historical spheres, but disregarding the genetical and functional aspects of the problem. When we view the record of the history of life and the history of man from such a vantage point, looking just at the succession of forms up to now, evolution appears as a gradual, but consistent *extension of scope, extension of range of being,* with all the growing differentiation, organization, concentration, with all the variation and intensification of experience that go with it. Such extension of the range of being seems equivalent to a process of *interiorization,* which means transference and transformation of outer functions into inner functions, an increasing incorporation of external and extensive world contents into internal and intensive organism. Actually, the process consists of two processes, approximating what the Stoics called *diastole* and *systole,* distension and concentration. Only through distension can new world contents be appropriated and integrated.

Let me concretely exemplify this assumption. To begin with, life itself is such a concentration, interiorization, intensification of physical elements: the successive formation of molecule and cell. The process continues in the transformation of living forms; in the development leading from sporiferous plants, which multiply through detached spores, to flowering plants, propagating through internal generation, and in the animal sphere, correspondingly, from ovipara to mammals—this, even Simpson stresses as being one of the most firmly established evolutionary traits: "The mammals are . . . the highest animals in this particular respect and the case is clear-cut and indisputable, from the protection and uniformity of internal gestation through most highly perfected post-natal care including provision of nearly uniform and highly nutritious food from the mother."[10] Parallel developments are: the shift of the body supports from exoskeleton (shells, as with arachnids, insects, crustaceans, testaceans) to endoskeleton (inner bone structure of the vertebrates; the bony fishes are the latest among fishes); further, the gradual interiorization of metabolism, and the formation of a central nervous system; the advance from the metamorphosis of metabolic plants and animals to the immediate generation in higher forms. In all these instances, external processes and relations have become inner functions and systems and have been more and more closely integrated in an expanding organic system.

Integration, in this process, goes hand in hand with differentiation—integration, not ony internally, of the various differentiating, specializing parts and organs and of the organism as a whole, but correspondingly, also externally, of an ever wider and more differentiated world. Increasing differentiation of the organic system means correlatively an expansion of scope, an extension and amplification of relationship and control. So we have here a two-way process of expansion and concentration, and it is hardly possible to make out which originated which.

The same development can be shown in the specifically human sphere, the sphere of history, in which this evolution was carried on and carried over from the physical to the psychic, mental, and the more and more predominant social level. External, magical and mythical, relationships of the human being with external, divine powers gradually turned into interiorized connections of rational ideas and concepts; the visually pictured, diversely animate universe of participation and religion passed over into an inner realm of human reason organizing exploratory experiences. External dependencies were replaced by man's growing feeling of inner autonomy, by judgment, choice, man's control of himself and of his world. The rise of human consciousness corresponds to the unfolding of its counterpart, an ever more abundant and diversified world. We see that this again is as much a process of differentiation, the elaboration of distinctive intellectual faculties, as it is a process of integration, of incorporating an ever vaster phenomenal territory.

When we finally compare the state of human knowledge and of man's technological mastery of nature in the first centuries of the modern era with the one we witness today, we notice a further step in the same direction. The mechanistic universe of Newtonian physics was linked together by outer, grossly material, and sensorily conceivable forces; modern physics faces a universe not moved, but perpetually moving by itself and in itself, a universe in which matter is identical with energy, and which is approachable only by increasingly speculative means of understanding. Today, infinitely subtler methods of intellectual grasp correspond to a hitherto unparalleled extension of the objective orbit of human contemplation and manipulation. I need not emphasize the advance of our technological control of nature, which has reduced our globe to a single room as it were, and has taken us to the verge of interplanetary communication. Modern biology and medicine have penetrated into the microsphere of genes and hormones and enzymes, and have begun to elucidate the subtle interconnections within the organic whole; modern psychology has entered into the sphere of the unconscious. A similar process may be observed in the modern arts, in their reaching beyond the range of portrayal of individual, tangibly "objective" forms, of individual narrative, of sensuous melos, into abstract fundamentals of form as such, of phenomenal appearance as such, existence as such, sound relations as such.

V

What I have stated requires, however, some specification which introduces a new aspect into the problem of evolution. This new aspect concerns the *relation between individual and group*, that is, *between different levels of existence*. It seems to me that without a clarification of this relationship it is impossible properly to understand what evolution means in our present situation. My statement must be qualified to the effect that *the tremendous recent expansion of human reach, and the incorporation of world contents into human consciousness, applies to man as a whole, but no longer to the human individual*. When Julian Huxley characterizes evolution as an increase of complexity and organization of complexity, greater control, greater independence or self-regulation, greater range of knowlege, etc., it appears more than evident that this may be said of man, but hardly of the human individual in his present condition. The human individual today shows, on the contrary, a blatant *decrease* of control, independence, self-regulation, and range of knowledge; and this *decrease* on the *individual* level appears to be correlative with the *increase* on the *collective* level.

A. L. Kroeber in his essay, "The Concept of Culture in Science," distinguishes sharply the different "levels of organization" or "levels" pure and simple, the physicochemical, the biological or organic, the social and cultural. And he rightly rejects the practice of nineteenth century science to apply the categories of one level to another or, more specifically, to reduce the terms of the higher levels to the supposedly basic ones of the physicochemical level. "Gravitation," he says, "electrical conductivity, and element valence apply to organic bodies as well as to inorganic ones. But principles or laws such as these are the only ones which apply to inorganic bodies; and yet they do not to any serious degree explain the specific organic phenomena of hereditary repetition, of conception and death, of adaptability. These specifically organic processes *conform* to established physicochemical processes; they cannot be *derived* from them." So the different levels are to a certain degree autonomous while they are still in certain respects ". . . dependent on the subjacent ones and of support to the independent overlying ones."[11]

While sharing this view in general, I am inclined to assume a much closer connection between the various levels of existence. It was utterly wrong, of course, to derive the specific phenomena of one level from those of another level, but if we want to understand the real nature of any entity or being we cannot sharply separate one level from another, we cannot confine ourselves to considering one level strictly apart from its subjacent and overlying ones. We do not live as individuals *in* society or *in* a nation as within an overarching, delimitable space. We *are* this society, this nation to a large degree; we form part of it, and it forms part of us, down to our physical being. We are, all of us, any entity or being is, *existing on different levels at the same time. Existence is a multilevel affair.* As a body, I am a natural organization of lower beings, living, moving, changing, growing and decaying beings, namely the *cells.* Any change or disturbance in this organization, or even in the internal organization of the cells themselves, has most powerful and serious effects on what we may consider the essence or quintessence of the physical system, the *psyche.* This is, after all, recognized in the psychosomatic theory and in recent psychiatry. The psyche, in turn, has a well-established influence on the *mind.* All such dependence, however, does not invalidate the fact that the functioning or operation on each specific level has its own distinct and, to a certain degree, autonomous character. We must also realize that all effective influence between different levels is a two-way process: it works upward as well as downward. There is a mutual interaction going on between mind, psyche, body, and so forth.

A similar interrelationship prevails between individual and group, and this interrelationship is crucial in regard to our specific concern. As a psycho-intellectual being, as a person and an individual, I move in a constantly interactive relationship with social units, with communities and collectives (the fundamental difference between these two kinds of social unit cannot and need not be elaborated within the present context). What matters is that, socially too, I live on different levels at the same time, in closest interdependence and interaction between my self and the various groups to which I belong. In point of fact, I am part of the groups, and the groups are part of my very self. I simply do not exist without them; and whenever anything changes in the groups, my personal self is affected by it. Accordingly, when we study social or psychic evolution, it is no use considering social forms and individual psyche separately, since they both move together and transform together, in constant interrelationship with each other. Whenever the one changes, the other changes with it, and the nature of the relationship changes too. What develops is not the group per se, or the individual per se, but the combination and the relationship of both, and we have to study both with regard to each other. Therefore, we cannot gain a complete picture of human processes if we deal with psychology without considering sociology, or conversely if we study sociology, or for that matter, any human conditions, happenings, and activities, without including psychology.

I said that the individual psyche changes with the change of social forms and vice versa, and that the nature of the relationship changes also. But along with these interrelated developments an even more important change has taken place. Evolution is, as I have attempted to show, a process of extension of scope. Now in the course of this process it happened at certain points that *the emphasis, the point of gravity of events, shifted from one level to another.* Just as with the emergence of Homo sapiens, the emphasis has moved from body to mind and evolution proper has turned into human history, similarly in our age, since the nineteenth century, the point of gravity of events appears to have shifted from the individual to the collective level. And while on the collective level man has immensely expanded his reach, the individual, through this very process, has shrunk in independence, self-regulation, power of control, and range of knowledge. The fact that the technological and intellectual scope of humanity has advanced far beyond the capacity of the individual mind, and that individual consciousness is less and less able to keep pace with the growing extent and complexity of happenings and with what I would call "collective consciousness"—namely, the vast corpus of our present, ever moving, ever changing knowledge—this tragic inadequacy of the individual is one of the basic causes of our human crisis.

VI

How then does *culture* fit into this picture? What role and meaning has it in the process of evolution?

Our historical survey of the term "Culture" has shown us four different concepts: 1) culture as a *human condition*, which implies a *value* (this is what we mean when we speak of a "cultivated man"); 2) the *value-free* concept of culture as a *specific way of life, style of life, of a people*, or, to use Kroeber's definition, as the *totality of customs and ways of life of a people*; 3) culture as an *ethnic entity pure and simple*, in which sense the term is generally used by modern anthropologists; and 4) culture as a *regionally meta-ethnic entity*, a concept that has been introduced by Leo Frobenius and Oswald Spengler and has been taken over by Toynbee for the construction of some of his civilizations.

These different concepts of culture are, as we have seen, manifestations of different evolutionary stages; they reflect the growth of human self-realization. The realization of the diversity, and the diverse organic coherence of ethnic groups presupposes the Judaeo-Christian realization of a common humanity above and in all of them. In the pre-Christian, pre-Hellenistic, pre-Stoic era, each particular ethnic community identified humanity with itself. There is not too much difference between the attitude of peoples like the Zuñi, Déné, Kiowa, who by these tribal names naively designate human beings, and the Greek and Roman identification of strangers with barbarians. Culture, to the Greeks and the Romans, was the antithesis of barbarism, the advance on barbarism.

The ancient concept of *culture as a human condition and a value,*

as an enlightened, sensitized, humane state, a most desirable state
of the human being, as *paideia*, in the Greek sense, is still valid
today; to express it we have no better word. *Culture in the sense
of a style of life or the totality of customs* seems to me a superfluous synonym. Why not say style of life, or customs? This is
simpler, it means what it says. What concerns us closely, however, is the concept of *a* culture, *culture as an independent entity*,
as a being in itself. Here, we have the choice between identifying a
culture with an *ethnic community*, or the positing of *meta-ethnic
cultures* comprehending various ethnic groups.

For Spengler and Toynbee the concept of man as a coherent
entity hardly exists in any clearly stated form. Toynbee at least
substitutes for it his theological superstructure which in a way
unifies, or is expected retroactively to unify, the various civilizations, dead or alive. But both Spengler and Toynbee break up the
coherence of human evolution in history into the isolated units of
their "philosophically contemporaneous," meta-ethnic civilizations.
What remains of a common human quality are the well-known
parallelisms, the historical "laws of nature." (We may leave aside
Spengler's occasional characterization of man as the "technological
beast of prey.")

Careful analysis would show, indeed has shown in critical studies
by a number of scholars, the precariousness of these theories.
Since the whole of nature in its broadest perspective comes to be
seen as an historical process, history proper must be understood as
a unique section of a unique cosmic happening; it must be understood as the history of the organic genus, Man. Accordingly,
we have first to explore the uniqueness of the process of human
history, the uniqueness of its place within the larger, comprehensive whole of nature, and the uniqueness of its stages and
ramifications, before we may be able to recognize the real, the
genotypical homologies prevailing among its different subdivisions
and subprocesses. We have first to establish what specific stage
each subdivision represents within the whole of human history,
and only over against this coherence of historical consecution and

diversity can we try to find out very cautiously what the different subdivisions, or variations, of the one historical process may have in common. If, however, we start from seeking general laws we are prone to crude simplifications and fallacies. An apparently identical phenomenon or institution may have a fundamentally different significance in this and that specific unit according to their different origins, their different relations to the whole, the different evolutionary stages they represent. In studying history, we have to use a method diametrically opposite to that of Spengler and Toynbee; we have to strive for ever more subtle differentiation and grasp of the unique.

The unreliability and superficiality of "general laws" as derived from "philosophical contemporaneity" is enhanced if one chooses as units "civilizations" which first have to be established in order to yield their general laws. Such a procedure carries the danger of begging the question, namely, the temptation to shape the civilizations according to the general laws they are supposed to demonstrate. But apart from this ambiguity of Spengler's and Toynbee's concepts, their views must be considered inadequate in that they confine the historical processes to one single level, whereas, as I have tried to show, these processes move on different levels at the same time, and involve changes not only from stage to stage, but from level to level.

For all these reasons, I would prefer to stick to the units which human evolution itself has developed, the ethnic communities. Here again, I would not be inclined plainly to equate these ethnic communities with "cultures." Culture and community are not exactly the same thing. It seems to me that the cultures and the communities have the same relationship to each other as the psyche or the character of an individual person has to his body. And I would equate the culture of an ethnic entity in its subjective, inward aspect with the *psyche*, in its objective, outward aspect with the *character* of an ethnic community.

There are, however, certain turning points in the historical process when cultures become independent of the place and community in which they originated. When an old people declines, and when, after its climactic flowering and absorption of world contents to capacity, its physical power begins to disintegrate, something takes off; the spirit, the transcending form as it were, the residual character of this people, detaches itself from its specific origins, survives spiritually and fecundates new forces. Only such a transcending form of life that disengages itself from its specific origins and becomes a spiritual being of its own, influencing other units, merging with others, and carried farther by others even after its originator may have died down and dissolved, only such an independent entity may be seen as *a culture*, or *civilization*, per se, clearly distinguished from the people from which it has emerged. As seen in this aspect, cultures are not identical with their originating peoples and historical spheres; they are their offsprings, their spiritual spores as it were. They mature very late and come into being as detached, separate units of history only in the ultimate stages of their originators. In this capacity, as independent entities, intermediate between ethnic communities and Man, they represent and carry evolution.

The first cultures, or civilizations, of that kind, the first that were explicitly recognized as meta-ethnic, were those arising from the Greek and the Jewish peoples: Hellenism and Christianism. The very fact that they were so recognized indicates that they represent historical units of a higher order, involving a new stage, a new level of consciousness. Other examples are, within the European orbit, Latinism, the survival of Roman tradition, and in the Oriental sphere, Buddhism and Islam.

The historical process entails a gradual shift to broader units, and at the same time to higher levels of consciousness. The process starts with peoples. Peoples are the units which, in a relay as it were, carry the evolutionary process and develop, in their inner and outer forms, in their psychic and social forms, man's specific quality and consciousness. Gradually, the widening scope produces new and broader units which later take over and lead the essential process.

In our time, we are witnessing the gradual detachment and independent global spread of what we may identify as our Western civilization. Whether this Western civilization still means culture in the original sense of the term is, however, an open question.

[1960]

Science and History

Lᴇᴛ ᴜs start with a fundamental question: What is all our knowledge for? what is, or should be, the aim of our constant striving for more and more knowledge? It is good, indeed necessary, to ask this question from time to time lest we forget the ultimate end of our intellectual endeavors. Our intellectual activities have become so institutionalized and compartmentalized, and the problems in which we are involved have grown so overwhelmingly complex and besetting that we are apt to lose sight of this guiding aim.

Let us go back to the dim origins. What was the initial urge that stimulated man to seek knowledge? The question takes us to the primeval stage of man in which what may be called "instinct" passes over into conscious attempt. The borderlines are fluid, but we may learn something from the observation of an infant or a little child, trying gradually to cope with his surroundings. The apparently aimless first movements, the groping of the little hands, the wondering eyes eager to take in what happens around him, all this betrays the rudimentary urge of the human being to get to know his environment, to learn how to deal with it. The playing of the child, likewise, is a very serious affair, very different from the adult's playing; it is the continuation, within a somewhat broader scope, of the groping of the infant; it is a kind of training, with quasi-experimental objects and objectives, for the mastery of his world. And so it goes on in the life of the adult, in the life of man, the desire at the same time to orient himself in his environment, to learn how to deal with it, and to put it to use. Curiosity, which is often referred to as the ultimate motive of man's drive toward knowledge, is by no means the original incentive. Curiosity is a by-product of the need for orientation, of man's need for self-maintenance and self-expansion, a by-product which developed rather late into a dominant motive, a kind of *l'art pour l'art* of knowledge, when means became self-contained ends. The range of man's self-expansion widened more and more in the course of fighting, exploring and exploiting his environment, until the conceptual task came to exceed the individual's capacities and called for collective efforts, for instruments and methods of most abstract concentration. But, in all our absorbing explorations at the remotest frontiers, we should remain aware of the original and ultimate end of these endeavors, and that is the maintenance of humanity, of the human being. From the time when man has reached a stage where world religion and the very achievements of science have taught him, or should have taught him, the natural equality of human rights, that is, what I would call the *identity of man*, it is no longer the human individual or any group of individuals, but humanity, the human form and dignity that has to be maintained.

We live today in a more and more scientified world, a world dominated by the principles and methods of science and their application, which is technology. This does not mean, I hasten to say, that the majority of people act according to the principle of science, which would mean that they make their decisions more rationally than before. On the contrary, as far as the conduct of human life is concerned, people are today particularly prone to irrational acts. This is precisely the result and overcompensation of that functional overrationalization—mechanization, quantification, organization, bureaucratization—which is the inevitable consequence of the progress of science and technology, and of the more and more intricate task of regulating the public concerns of a rapidly increasing population and life machinery. People feel their personal life narrowed by this vast network of collective control, organizational and scientifico-technocratical; they do not see why this has to be, and how this hangs together. They are inclined irrationally to cut through the complexities, which they are incapable of understanding, and to restore conditions as they existed before the recent world-shaking advances in science and technology, before the inherent technical interdependence of people and peoples all over the globe.

This is the extremely dangerous situation in which we find ourselves today. The psychic and mental condition of individuals did not keep pace with the speed of collective functional achievements. People have lost their bearings in their world; they are motivated by the expediencies of the moment and of their parochial wants. And this means that they have lost their sense of history, their sense of the evolution of human conditions.

It will be no news to anyone watchful of present trends when I say that ours is an anti-historical, anti-evolutional era. There is, to be sure, much official talk of progress, but what is meant by progress in such talk is the advancement of functional achievements in science and technology. Certainly, it includes social care and legislation, but this is precisely what is opposed by large sections of our population. There is hardly an awareness of the fact that those scientific and technological achievements have a bearing on social conditions. People want to enjoy the advantages and comforts of our increased knowledge and technical skills, but refuse to accept the social consequences. However, in the very methods of their opposition, they cannot help being subject to the influence of the organizational techniques of our time.

So far I have spoken of the people at large. But the anti-historism, anti-evolutionism has taken hold also of considerable parts of our intellectual and academic community, and for two main reasons: the first is the result of our experiences since the First World War that have utterly discredited the belief in human progress, that is to say, in human betterment and increase of happiness. We have seen civilizations crumble and revert to extreme barbarism, humanitarian treaties and charters reneged, and unheard-of atrocities committed by peoples that had arrived at the highest cultural standard. And the follies and frenzies, the anxieties and frustrations that multiply with the inventions of our gadgetries and weaponries, with the whole mechanized apparatus of our life, do not fit exactly into the image of human happiness which our progress-minded forefathers in the eighteenth and nineteenth centuries had cherished. Since the idea of Progress and the concept of human evolution had developed together and were seen as one and the same process, the concept of human evolution broke down together with the concept of Progress. This, in conjunction with the confusing overgrowth of uncovered historical details, resulted not only in a denial of history as a consistent development of man, but in a rejection of the historical viewpoint as a means to explain human conditions and problems. I quote one prominent historian, Geoffrey Barraclough, who writes: "We ourselves have experienced enough of discontinuity to feel renewed sympathy with all those historians who, from the time of Augustine and Orosius, have been more impressed by the cataclysmic than by the continuous in human affairs . . . no present-day issue is, or ever was, intelligible in terms of its history."[1]

But the disbelief in historical evolution is not the only motivation for our present anti-historism. There is another one connected with the first and, I would think, even more powerful. It has to do precisely with the overwhelming influence of science and the scientific point of view on all our life and so, on all our intellectual activities. The predominance of the cyclic view of history, as it is expressed in recent theories such as those of Spengler, Toynbee, and Sorokin, involves in itself a scientific approach, tending as it does to the search for historical "laws of nature." One might men-

tion the typological and taxonomic treatment of history prevailing
in modern sociology—think of Max Weber's "ideal types" and of
the statistical and structuralistic methods of sociology and anthro-
pology in America and in other countries (in Europe, for example,
Lévy-Strauss versus Lévy-Bruhl).

Here we are at the crucial point: the relation between science
and history, which I would characterize as a fundamental difference in their premises and their subject matter, a difference that
calls for diametrically opposite methods of approach.

To be sure, most historians have come to realize that historiography is not a science. The study of history, it is argued, has to
do with a motley multitude and multiformity of singular phenomena—happenings, conditions, personalities, nations—which cannot
be subsumed under general laws. And from the standpoint of
science, Professor Karl Popper in his book *The Poverty of Historicism* supports this view by stating that history is neither amenable to verification through experiments nor to quantification as
a method of research. He refers to such features of history as
novelty, complexity, unpredictability, unavoidable selectivity of
presentation, insufficiency of causal explanation, all precluding
scientific treatment.

We seem confronted with a choice between two antagonistic
notions. On the one hand, history is seen as a chaotic medley of
the most diverse entities and occurrences, in which it is impossible
to discern any order and regularity; indeed historians, just as the
general public, appear to derive a real pleasure from the unre-
strained imagination of the "fortuitous and unforeseen," the discontinuous, the "cataclysmic"—to quote Barraclough again—a
delight in "the most exhilarating testimony to the creative vigour,
the splendid variety, of the human spirit." On the other hand, we
have the strained, quasi-scientific "laws of history," as propounded
by theorists of history.

I for one am inclined to reject both of these views of history
which reflect, in the intellectual domain, the current popular
divergence of overrationalization and irrationalism. I cannot bring
myself to recognize a scientistic regularity of historical processes,

as it is suggested by the theorists of history; nor do I find it possible to agree with historians to whom history is devoid of any kind of intelligible order, and is just an intrinsically incoherent sequence of circumstantial events and human inventions. In the following brief outline I will attempt to show what appears to me the true nature of history and the basic difference between the scientific outlook and an approach accordant with the distinctive character of historical reality.

The methods of science are based on the assumption of the *immutable stability of Nature,* an assumption which, paradoxically enough, is a religious heritage. It originated in the concept of a cosmic order created once and for all by the will of God. Even for Newton the laws of nature were laws ordained by God, and the study of the universe was identical with the study of God's creation. In the course of ever more elaborate research, the image of God gradually vanished into a more and more distant background, but the belief in the stability of Nature remained. Since the innovations of the Ockhamist school in the fourteenth century, this belief began to be shaken in a restricted domain—Galileo's famous conflict with the Church brought this into the open—and the whole history of astronomy, physics, and biology in the modern period is a history of an increasing erosion of the concept of the stability of Nature.

The decisive pushes began at the end of the eighteenth century with the rise of the biological theory of evolution. A succession of great scientists, from Buffon and Cuvier to Geoffrey Saint-Hilaire, Lamarck and Darwin, overcame, against powerful traditional resistance, the old method of mere classification of divinely created beings. These scientists gradually realized the autonomous and consistent development of living forms, and this very discovery opened the way to a true and deeper understanding of organic structures and functions. To be sure, an element of stability persisted in the search for a static regularity of genetic processes. But recently, even the absolute validity of Mendelism seems to be questioned.

In physics, a corresponding development has taken place. Faraday's study of electromagnetic "forces of matter" eventually led to the modern field concept. Maxwell's theory of electromagnetic phenomena was the starting point of the theory of relativity and its invalidation of absolute space and time. The development was quickened by Becquerel's and the Curies' discovery of radioactive spontaneous disintegration of matter and Rutherford's transformation of chemical elements (the "element" has long ceased to be elementary). Finally, Einstein's famous formula, which equates matter and energy, means the dissolution of the old "material" matter. Nuclear physics as well as recent astronomy shows Nature as a process in particular and in general. Astronomy has become a historical discipline.

So, at the frontiers of our presently known universe, the spheres of the particles and of the cosmic bodies, the concept of Nature's stability is shaken. This has altered the character of fact, it has restricted the validity of causality. Such modifications show a certain approximation of scientific views to what I will presently try to set forth as the essentially historical approach and method. But a fundamental difference remains, and will remain, in spite of our new experience of the dynamic character of Nature, a difference which is founded on an insuperable difference of human perspective. To be sure, the advancing research in various fields of science has discovered irregularities and uncertainties which have created serious theoretical problems, and caused modifications like the replacement, in specific domains, of strict laws by statistical laws. But such irregularities occur in regions so remote from the reach of our human immediate perception and practical uses, they are so minute or so huge in relation to human proportions, that they are practically insignificant and may be disregarded. Not only are the laws of classical mechanics still valid for large bodies, not only do statistical laws suffice for a safe practical application even of nuclear forces, but the dimensions of the entities and movements with which our physical research has to deal are such that they cannot be approached by other than quantifying means. Only equal entities or processes can be subjected to quantification. Although some crazy people have gone as far as to attribute free will to particles, it remains unquestionable that individual differences on this level have not reached a degree relevant for the study and application of physical phenomena. A short-lived cell in my body, if it were endowed with consciousness, would probably perceive and count on only the seemingly perennial and thus predictable and quantifiable regularities in the body—breathing, heartbeat, metabolism, and so forth—but would hardly be aware of the major moves and changes on the higher level of the organism, let alone the psychic motions of the person. This otherwise incommensurable, almost metaphorical, example is of course meant only to illustrate the distances between human and cosmic proportions, and the limitation of human perspective, which will forever compel science in its exploratory ventures to use the methods of quantification and an ever more concentrated abstraction. So, just as the realization of biological evolution did not prevent biology from using quantitative methods when it came to delve into the depths of genetics, in the same way physics will have to stick to its methods of high-powered abstraction, which actually presuppose the absolute validity of laws and causality. Science will continue to proceed *as if* Nature were stable.

The essentially human world, however—which started not with the highest apes, the *proconsulidae*, nor even with *pithecanthropus erectus*, that is to say, with man's physical development, but with history, and that means, with the evolution of consciousness—this world is fully noticeable in our own familiar dimensions. While Nature *itself*—not our *concepts* of Nature—has remained rather much the same for us since the inception of human times, our human world, the nature of man's close environment, his ways of life, indeed to a certain degree man himself, have changed enormously. We undergo directly, indeed we actively participate in, these changes and our experiences can teach us to realize the interaction between man and Nature and the perpetual interaction between man's concepts and man's action, between his ever widening scope of consciousness and his ever expanding range of operations and groupings. *This is, in fact, what constitutes history: the interaction, intercreation of conceptuality and actuality, of consciousness and action.* History is not only what we have learned in school, a succession of wars and treaties, conquests and defeats, powers and civilizations, social and technological conditions; it is essentially not that medley of nations, personalities, popular and intellectual movements; it is above all the evolution of a unique, organic genus, the evolution of Man, of which all the political, social, and intellectual happenings are just the manifestations and vehicles. And, being the evolution of Man, history does not represent a repository of a dead past; history is something that stays and lives with us in every moment of our lives, that inheres in all our acts and projects, something whose very result we all are. When we study history, we have to be constantly aware of the fact that we are studying the life and career of the *genus humanum.*

History has the appearance of an incoherent variety of power struggles, cultural trends, and personal creations only when we see it proceeding on a single plane, when we see it *planimetrically,* as it were. There are, however, various levels of history, as there are diverse levels of all reality. All of us live at the same time on different levels of existence. There is a physical level and on that level I am, with regard to my subordinate cells and organs, a genus and generality. There is the level of the person, on which I am, in regard to the superior entity, the community or collective to which I belong, an individual. There is the level of communities and collectives, of families, nations, states, professions, and so forth, which, in turn, are, in relation to the *genus humanum,* particular, individual entities. These levels imply different extents of existential scope. When we compare the range of existence of the physical being, the animal, or the human being as animal, with the scope of the completed person and his consciousness, or the range of a primitive clan with the range of a nation and its cultural and civilizational implications, not only the existential differences, but also the evolutional coherence of history will become evident. Of course, we can notice these differences and these evolutional changes only when we clearly distinguish the different levels of history, when we conceive of history not as "world history" or as "history of mankind," which would mean the history of the sum total of human individuals, but as the evolution of the *genus humanum*. History is not, as a positivistic view has it, a sum total of the acts, experiences, and feelings of all the millions of private individuals that ever existed on earth. The course of history takes place, and can be seen clearly, only on the communal level, and not on the level of the private individual, whose mode of existence derives mainly from the state of his communal civilization.

The disregard of the differences of historical levels is due to the predominance of the scientific requirement of sensory verification. For science the validity of concepts or assumptions is established only if they are verified, however deviously, instrumentally, by sensory perception. The senses are the ultimate instances—the very word "evidence" expresses it.

Science itself recognizes different levels of Nature: to put them roughly, the level of particles, of nuclei, of atoms, of molecules and macromolecules, of chromosomes, of cells, of organs, of organisms; and different sciences concern themselves with the respective phenomena of these different levels: Physics, Chemistry, Biochemistry, Biology, Histology, Anatomy, Physiology, and so forth. Nobody questions the existence of such different levels and evolutionary stages of Nature because their phenomena can be reached by our senses. But such clear distinction stops at the threshold of history, since no strict sensory perception and verification of entities beyond the individual is possible. And yet, the actual unfolding of levels and stages did not cease at the inception of history; it went on, actually and conceptually, that is, in the course of socio-political processes and of the concomitant evolution of consciousness. Since these levels and stages are not perceptible and verifiable by our senses, they are not validated by a scientistic view of history. Until the beginning of our century, scientists were inclined to trace the phenomena of higher levels to those of lower and ultimately the lowest level, to reduce for instance organic structures and processes to physicochemical mechanisms. More recently, while scientists do not deny, indeed they even more deeply understand, the connections between the different levels—the borderlines between inorganic matter and life appear to have almost vanished—they nevertheless came to recognize the specifically novel characteristics arising with every shift from one level to another.

Because of what I would call this *vertical division* of Nature into the different levels of physical reality, a division that has determined the order of specialization of scientific disciplines, science was enabled to maintain an overall structure in its picture of the universe. The different levels of physical reality are, and will remain, recognized as different stages of evolution. We are about to learn the formation of life out of inorganic matter, we know the main lines of the evolution of the earth and of living forms up to the physical completion of the human form, and, because of this structural and evolutional order that science has preserved, it has still, highly specialized as it is, fulfilled the task of man's orientation in his extrahuman world. Conversely, the humanistic disciplines, those concerned with specifically human matters, with psychic, intellectual, cultural, social, political affairs, have developed a rather *horizontal division* into the different fields of human activity and expression. Thereby, in the course of rigid specialization, the sense of an organic coherence of human faculties, indeed of human existence, was lost. Up to the beginning of the nineteenth century, this sense of organic coherence of human life and of human evolution was still prevalent; the belief in Progress and the corresponding study of biological evolution kept it alive. But the increasing influence of scientistic analysis of quasi-stable phenomena, in conjunction with the crumbling of the idea of Progress, discredited the concept of human evolution, or at least shoved it into the background. The specialization of humanistic scholarship took the form of studies of the various human functions, activities and modes of expression: language, epistomological and logical relations, arts, religion, psychic, social, political, economic conditions, and so forth, with their specifically functional developments. Among all these functional sections of scholarship, history has been given its restricted place as a study of past happenings, political and cultural. As a result of such horizontal division of humanistic scholarship into partly stabilized, partly functionalized sections of human life, and of the disregard of human evolution, history as a whole assumed the aspect of a muddle of "discontinuous," "irreducibly particular" phenomena and lost its capacity to afford people an orientation in their immediate, human environment and a guidance in the conduct of human affairs. A general direction of conduct may be derived only from a *stereoscopic* view of history, that is, a view of history as a consistent evolution of Man, which proceeds on different levels, in different dimensions, and in different stages, whereby the different evolutional stages coincide with a shift from one level to another. A first, pre-historic shift from a lower to a next higher level may be seen in the transition from the animal to the human being, which means the transition from a predominantly physical, instinctually guided to a predominantly conscious, mentally directed being. And the most recent shift, which started with the revolutions at the end of the eighteenth century, and whose completion we have witnessed in our own lifetime, is the passing over from the plane of individuality to that of collectivity; from a stage where the individual predominated in the course of events to a stage where the point of gravity has shifted to the prevalence of masses, teams, and organizations, and where immediate action turned decisively into instrumental action.

These shifts are connected with, indeed they are a manifestation of, a gradual expansion of existential scope: of the determinant units of history, and of the reach of human consciousness. On the socio-political plane, this evolution—not to be confounded with Progress, which has a moral connotation—proceeds from the theocratic temple-city to the city and city-state, settling down here below as a mundane community (even the Roman Empire was still a city-state); then, through the intermediary of feudal principalities, which were the first to give the non-urban territory some political weight, to territorial estates; from the territorial estates to dynastical and nation-states; from nation-states to fully developed nations, representing the whole of the people; from the nations to civilizational and ideological power-blocs, whole continents or even intercontinental units; and finally to the technical, technological prefiguration of a "one world," which is psychologically very far from realization, but which looms as the only alternative that science and technology have presented us to their opposite achievement, nuclear or biochemical annihilation.

There is no need to dwell more elaborately on the counterpart: the vast extension of human consciousness, which was alternately the carrier and the result of the socio-political expansion. The advances of theoretical and applied science into remotest cosmic reaches and into innermost depths of organic structures are obvious enough. Knowledge, conceptuality, is awareness. Unfortunately, but inevitably, this growing human awareness, having become institutionalized, has outgrown the capacity of individual consciousness. The corpus of this ever advancing human knowledge, of this ever expanding human awareness of spheres and relations never exposed before, the totality of these "knowns," not knowable by any single person alive, constitutes a kind of *collective consciousness*, which is, as I indicated before, as much of a danger as it is an attainment.

I characterized history as the evolution of Man, consisting in an expanding interaction, intercreation of human structures and human consciousness, of actuality and conceptuality. Since history is perceptible, indeed experienced, life-size as it were, directly in our own human sphere in the entirety of its movements, we are able to observe in it a *complete reality*, which is a blend of change and continuity, of particularity and generality. To a certain extent, to be sure, features and modes of process repeat themselves in the course of history. So there exists a degree of scientistic regularity also in history. But these historical regularities are inextricably fused with particularities; we cannot neatly separate generalities from particularities in history. The diversities are looming too strongly. And therefore it is impossible and fallacious to try and establish "laws of history" comparable to scientific "laws of nature." In extrahuman Nature—which comprises the purely physical aspect of human nature—we are able to isolate regularities, probably because of the disproportionate distances, temporal and spatial, which prevent us from a perception of its complete reality. We are forever condemned to apprehend only a *partial reality* of Nature. In history, our own, co-dimensional sphere, isolation of generalities will always appear strained and inadequate, and historians are inclined to react to their insufficiencies by holding history to consist solely of particularities, and contending that, as a whole, history lacks any kind of order. Thus they are apt to disregard the specific order inherent in history.

This specific order of historical happening seems to me to consist in the *expansive evolution*, which I have tried to indicate, and in the *distinctive levels of existence* which mark the steps of this evolution. A coherence of development can be demonstrated in the course of history, and the historical equivalent of the strictness of scientific laws may be seen in the rigor of this coherence. To make myself somewhat clearer on this point, I have to add a few remarks concerning the meaning of fact and causality in history as compared with their significance for science.

Fact and causality are intrinsically related: causality connects fact with fact. Facts, therefore, to be fit for a causal nexus have to be firmly established and sharply defined, indeed *con*fined. And this is possible only in a static, stabilized order. In a dynamic order, such as the closely observable coherence of historical evolution, both, sharply delimitable facts and strict causality, break down. To be sure, in history too, we have distinctly delimitable facts. It can be established, for instance, when somebody was born and when he died, when a battle was fought, or a treaty was concluded. But such firmly established historical data have a role and character very different from their equivalents in science. They stand alone, causally unrelated with each other and due to this lack of relatedness they explain nothing. They become relevant merely through connections with facts of an entirely different kind, facts that do not stand solidly by themselves, but exist only in combinations, in groups, clusters, chains of phenomena, in which they merge. And this is why they require that so much deplored selection and interpretation, a selection and interpretation which could derive a criterion of validity only from a vantage point on a level higher and broader than the one of the observed and described phenomena. So in trying to understand history we are again led from level to level.

Let us take as an example the French Revolution, which Professor Barraclough would certainly not hesitate to regard as a cataclysmic event of the first order, in which, as he says, the new, "the fortuitous and the unforeseen . . . breaks through untrammeled by the past." Now the French Revolution, a real turning point if ever there was one, was, in point of fact, long in coming and had its origins in a vast variety of places, movements and levels. I cannot and need not in our context detail the story of these preparations, which have been thoroughly explored and described by great scholars. I just want to recall for our purpose what a multitude of preliminaries and preconditions led up to the final event.

In the religious domain, the process of secularization was well advanced even since the end of the Middle Ages. The Calvinist reform with its presbyterian and congregational constitutions had gotten into conflict with the monarchical principle. Its political effects were manifest in the Huguenot wars and in the decisive influence of the Levellers on the English Revolution. Politically, the French Revolution was preceded by the liberation of the Netherlands, the English Revolution, which set the example of a popular execution of a king, and, shortly before the French, the American Revolution, whose impact on the European minds can-

not be overrated. When we look at the social and economic situation, we find that the French government was bankrupt
practically since Louis XIV, and the attempts of Colbert, Vauban,
Turgot and Necker to persuade the kings to a new economic
policy appropriate to the trend of the time were abortive because
of the political and social changes it involved. The peasants, whose
personal services had been almost completely converted into taxes,
were susceptible to revolutionary demands precisely because they
were no longer so desperately downtrodden as to be incapable of
imagining an improvement of their condition. The middle class
had grown wealthy enough to feel hampered by governmental
restrictions on commercial enterprise and to be stirred by the
example of the British industrialists who had just begun to sub-
vert the old guild regulations. In the nobility a mood of ennui,
of self-weariness and slackening self-assurance had taken effect
which opened their minds to the revolutionary ideas of Rousseau,
of the Physiocrats and the Encyclopedists. Materialistic philosophy
had spread, and technological innovations had fostered the belief
in Progress. All such developments were reflected in and reactively
promoted by the arts.

Now this is, of course, a very sketchy picture of the pre-Revolu-
tionary situation. Every single determinant that I list represents
a whole complex of motives and preliminary processes. When we
look more closely into the situation we shall find it impossible
to set apart, and add up, single causes of the final event. Not only
are they innumerable, but they pass into one another, act upon one
another. In scrutinizing the elements of this whole assemblage
of preconditions, we are carried farther and farther, through an
unending genealogy of processes, into the most diverse, spatially
and temporally remote scenes of happenings. We are led to consider the political, economic, and intellectual developments in
the Netherlands, England and America. We are taken back,
through a progressive sequence of philosophical theories and techniques, to the sources of rationalism and empiricism, to the transformations of the concept of natural law; to Descartes, to Galileo

and Copernicus, indeed the Middle Ages. This again is a random selection. The study of the progression of the Revolution itself will draw us into the investigation of the dynastic and feudal mentality, of the counterrevolutionary invasions, which always help to radicalize revolutionary processes, and finally into the background and the psychology of the leading personalities.

The French Revolution was an exemplary turning point in history, inaugurating a shift from one level to another. But in this truly revolutionary event hardly anything appears fortuitous or discontinuous, and what makes it cataclysmic is just the ripeness of the moment, the simultaneous conjunction of the results of long-grown forces and circumstances. History is growth, an all-out continual process, and in it causation is limitless and endless. It is futile to ask *why* something happened, it carries you to the beginning of time. There is no *prima causa*. The only fruitful question is *how* things happened. Wherever we take up a historical investigation, the search for the how may lead us deeper into the understanding of the working of the historical process, if only we keep in mind the distinction of stages, levels and dimensions of history.

What these observations were meant to suggest is that any historical research, be it ever so specialized, should be pursued with an awareness of the distinctive character of history and of the ultimate aim of historical studies. We need a new view of history, keeping clear of the two extreme positions which seem predominantly held today: the emulation of science and the denial of any consistency and evolutional order in history. We need it in order to recover some orientation and guidance in our badly disrupted human world.

[1964]

The Persistence of Myth

Denn wer ist noch unbefangen Formen gegenüber, die einen Namen haben?

(Could anyone feel quite unconstrained in the face of forms that have a name?)   RILKE

To MAKE a historical concept clear to ourselves, it helps to look for its verbal root. The Greek word *mythos,* most etymologists believe, goes back to mü, mu (moo), which imitates an elementary sound such as the lowing of cattle, the growl of beasts or of thunder, and originally meant inarticulate sounding of all kinds: bellowing, booming, roaring (Lat. *mugire,* Fr. *mugir*), murmuring, humming, rumbling, groaning, *mut*tering, or, in humans, nonverbal utterance with closed lips—and, by derivation, the closing of the mouth, *mut*eness (Lat. *mutus*). From the same root comes the Greek verb *müein, myein,* "to close up," "to close the eyes," from which derive *mystery* and *mystic,* the secret rites and teachings. Myth and mystery, then, are connected in their origin.

By the linguistic process that so often turns a word into its opposite—as in the case of the Latin *muttire,* "to mutter," and *mutus,* "mute," which became the French *mot,* "word"—the Greek *mu,* signifying inarticulate voicing with closed mouth, evolved into *mythos,* "word."

And yet the meaning of the root sound carried over into the specialized meaning the Greeks ultimately attached to *mythos.* The poets and writers of early periods used *mythos* indiscrimi-

41

nately in the sense of "word" (Homer, for instance, in contra-
position to *ergon*, "deed"); they scarcely distinguished it from
other Greek terms for "word": *epos* and *logos*. But gradually the
uses became specific: *mythos* became the word as the most ancient,
the original account of the origins of the world, in divine revelation
or sacred tradition, of gods and demi-gods and the genesis of the
cosmos, cosmogony; and it came to be sharply contrasted with
epos, the word as human narration, and—from the Sophists on—
with *logos*, the word as rational construction.

The maturing of human consciousness is reflected in the great
step from *mythos* to *logos*, from the dark tales of the emergence of
cosmos from chaos as told in the early Greek myths, to the Judaeo-
Christian Word of God, through which the Creator by an act of
mind brought into being and shaped the world, and which in itself
contains all creation.

Yet *mythos* has never been completely obliterated by *logos*; it has
persisted through all the ages until today. It can no more be abolished by reason than the deepest, elementary layers of our existence
can be completely penetrated by rational thinking. But myth has
in itself been subject to changes, in which the evolution of our
thinking and our consciousness has left its traces; it has indeed
taken on the forms, methods and results of our rational achievements and has consequently become sometimes difficult to identify.

In the Greek concept of *mythos* we can find all the essential
features and recognize all the transformations myth has undergone
up to our own day. These are the essentials of myth: it deals with
the fundamentals of our existence; it does not explain, but simply
relates; its material issues from an anonymous source, or one that
has become anonymous; its assumptions are unquestioned, surrounded by an aura of sanctity and venerability; it bears with it
a kind of awesome breath from regions unreachable.

In its primary form, mythology proper, the naïve tradition is one
with what it transmits—the genesis of the world and the life of
gods. The past is one with the present; both partake of timeless-
ness in a kind of confluence of the eternal and the immediate. That

means—and it even has a bearing on the operation of myth in our time—that mythology was a form of life and behavior. "There is no gap between thinking and doing . . . In antiquity the ego, and its consciousness of itself, is said to have had the door open to the past which entered into it and in it was re-enacted, was 'there again' . . . In antiquity man found reason enough in the *world* to experience his gods as real. Just so it was his *life* that tended to enter into the creations of his mythology and to verify them."[1] This earliest stage of "living in myth" cropped up again even in Napoleon who "regretted that the modern state of consciousness did not permit him to proclaim himself the son of Jupiter-Amon, like Alexander. But there is little question that at the time of his Oriental enterprise he mythically took himself at least for Alexander, and later, when he settled for the Occident, he declared: 'I *am* Charlemagne.' Note—not 'In me, the world recalls him,' not 'My position is similar to his.' Not even 'I am like him,' but simply 'I *am* he.' That is the formula of myth."[2]

At first, then, myth appears as *given*—born, not made. But soon the human "makers," the poets (from *poiein*, to make, to create) begin to elaborate and embellish it, to interweave it with new fictions. When the work of the poets becomes embodied in the memory of the people and sanctified by tradition, the unquestioned authority of myth is transferred to them and what they tell of. The human beings themselves who had enlarged the myth come to be included in it; they—the poets, the seers, and the sages—are supposed to be inspired by the gods. Their figures and their lives are endowed with mythical traits, as in the case of the early Greek philosophers and the founders and prophets of Oriental religions. Empedocles and Elijah are examples: both—the one flinging himself into Aetna, the other borne up to the skies in a whirlwind—show their connection with a primal beyond, are restored to the depth or height of the cosmos.

Platonic philosophy introduces a rationalization of myth, or, to put it the other way round, shapes the newly-discovered human system of logical thinking into a new mythology. Plato attempted to invalidate the ancient mythical stories of the personal gods and in their place set up a mythology of Ideas as Archetypes, of a world-soul and Demiurge.

Here a second form of myth arises: the mythization of explicitly human thoughts and creations. In Plato, the habit of seeing the world as myth was still so ingrained that his account of the world of human thinking assumed an immediately and involuntarily mythical character. This process, the mythization of human elements, later became more distinct, that is, purely historical: flesh-and-blood people and events, even man-made, rationally planned events, were retrospectively transformed into myth.

Figures, whether of fact or fiction, insofar as they expressed destinies, aspirations, attitudes typical of man or particular groups, were invested with a mythical character. The most powerful of the medieval emperors, Charlemagne, Otto the Great, the two Fredericks of Hohenstaufen, as they weathered in popular memory, took on a mythical coloring and were endowed with all sorts of attributes from the stock of pagan Germanic or Christian worship. They had not died, but lived on in the deep interior of mountains, whence they were expected to emerge at a predestined hour as princes of peace and saviors of Christendom or the German people. For the French, indeed for the whole of nineteenth century posterity, Napoleon grew into a mythical configuration that had little in common with the actual man. For millions, Lenin, the progenitor of a new social order, has long since become a myth. And the miraculous rise of Hitler, his monstrous deeds, his ostentatious "inspiration," his eccentricities, and his habitations in the depths and heights of mountain fastnesses—all this made him a paradigm for mythization. Even while present he had become almost mythical, and in the mysterious circumstances of his traceless disappearance he may well have deliberately prepared his legendary survival.

All hero-worship involuntarily mythisizes. It involves a curious interplay of creating and, at the same time, bridging a distance: people set the hero apart by exaggerating his unusual traits, and yet they seem urged to make him familiar by elaboration of details.

The existence of the extraordinary affects human beings with a deep uneasiness. They seek and magnify and at the same time fear it; they long for a reassuring connection with it; they are impelled at times to enhance their ego by participating in it. Often, indeed, to keep nature within the bounds of rational explicability, they tend to regard the exceptional as supranatural. In reality, nature is strange enough: it contains in itself those fathomless reaches that used to be labeled "supranatural."

Any colorful historical figure, any adventurous career, in fact anything or anybody out of the ordinary in a village or city bears the seed of myth. The shudder that accompanies whatever is outlandish or anomalous may prompt its growth when the historic climate is favorable, that is, when some unrest in a people or a group furnishes the stimulus. The germs of the mythical are present always and everywhere. The people of today, who set such store by rationality and realism, are avid to hear about the personal habits of public personalities and particularly about their most colorful and capricious vagaries; they are not aware that in doing so they are indulging in a rudimentary hankering to mythisize. The newspaper or radio man who reports a movie actress's longing for solitude or a prime minister's longing for lemons is the unwitting successor of the ancient bards.

Figures of fiction, too, grow to be myths: Don Quixote, Don Juan, Doctor Faustus, the Wandering Jew, Tyl Ulenspiegel, Rip Van Winkle, Schweik. In all of them a typical folk character or human attitude, or flavor of a landscape lives as an irrational image, that can only be described, but not explained or referred back any further than exactly that specific appearance and experience. In such figures people recognize themselves; in them they find their timeless ancestors or archetypes, their spiritual progenitors. But while ancient mythologies, in the eyes of men, possessed a direct reality comparable to that of historical events, the reality of these modern myths is only the condensed reality of the symbol.

The Age of Rationalism, to be sure, has made myth illegitimate and denied it all significance for our life. Our world—so it was thought—was increasingly to be constructed and determined by logic and empirical investigation alone. While this goal was being confidently aimed at, a subterranean process of mythization went on unobserved, slipped in from a quarter where it was least suspected: from the rationalistic premises themselves.

The events or acts that in the Enlightenment initiated the modern democratic state: the French Revolution, the American Declaration of Independence and Constitution, and, above all, the ideas and premises on which the new political order was based, Natural Law, civil liberties, the idea of Progress and of the unfailing beneficence of technical advances—all these were subject to an anonymous, unperceived process of mythization. In his book, *The Theory of Business Enterprise*, Thorstein Veblen has shown how the whole of Anglo-American jurisprudence and civilization is founded on the assumption of the sanctity of property as an inalienable Right of Man. Indeed, the doctrine of the omnipotence of reason has itself become a myth.

All this was mythisized by being established, once and for all, as the inviolable foundation of our modern world, by being accepted as sacrosanct. The Enlightenment has become the cosmogony of our civilization. People willingly forget, with all their belief in progress, that human conditions are not stable, but subject to perpetual change, and that the basic assumptions on which their systems rest have to be re-examined again and again if the process of mythization and dogmatization is to be kept from spreading boundless roots and overrunning the original rational meanings. The old vitality of myth, its indestructible claim on human life, is always ready to surge up again. The initial tests of reason do not guarantee an unlimited or permanent validity of principles. Hence arises the paradoxical situation that the assumptions of the rationalistic order have to be questioned in order to meet their very claim to rationality. The indelibility, the mythical immutability of those assumptions must be abolished. And this has to begin with the recognition of the very fact that their compulsion is mythical, that the whole of our life and world is founded on myth and interspersed with myth, that myth has an indestructible hold on human beings, and that it answers an elementary urge in man. In our scientific thinking, we have come to realize today that all basic assumptions in any rational structure worthy of the name are "assumptions," that is, postulates. The "axiom" of old is a kind of myth or partakes of the quality of myth.

Mythization springs not only from human inertia, not only from the steady regeneration of the mythical urge, but also from man's fear of change, from his need to protect himself against the disruption or dislocation of the underpinnings of his life. In the early, religious ages the foundation of life was the divine, in whose all-powerful being and rule the incalculability of all ultimate foundations was openly admitted and the dread of the impenetrable was localized and allayed. Myth was one means of getting hold of divinity, of bringing it closer, making it familiar, establishing a reassuring connection between man and god. Magic, conjuration, was another such means.

Since then, the cosmos and the origins of man and his institutions have been divested of their divinity. The cosmos is open to infinite research, and in his own history man has experienced change, the transformations of his modes of life. He has made reason, its judgments and conclusions, the firm grounds on which he may safely carry on his daily bustling, alterations and material progress. For this purpose, for his ease of mind, he wants to have reason stable, to place it beyond doubt; and this he does unconsciously by mythisizing it. In this way mythization has lost its concreteness; it no longer takes shape in images or idols, but has become a pure function.

Man's dread of fundamental change and of the chasms opened by it, man's dread of himself and his own inner depths, which he prefers to leave undisturbed, are exploited by forces that have a stake in preserving the status quo and are opposed to any far-reaching reform. These "conservative" forces, therefore, purposely cultivate the general tendency to mythisize the foundations of the State and the traditional way of life, and even block where possible the very discussion of them. No matter how rational the original foundations may have been, in becoming inviolable and sacrosanct they assume a more and more irrational character.

The fascist movements drew the final consequences of all this. They simply went ahead and manufactured their own myths for their own purposes: the inspired Führer, the Hierarchy, the Master Race, etc. And even when they formulated this mythology in contemporary scientific terms they openly admitted its irrationality, and on that basis began their campaign against Reason. With the aid of these handy new myths and their statutory inviolability, the Nazis succeeded in undercutting the moral supports of our civilization—supports that in their turn rested on principles which have long since lapsed into the mythical. In this the Nazis did us a service: what had seemed merely desirable they made necessary; we on our part are forced to re-shape the principles of our civilization, to submit them to the test of our present-day knowledge and, on the other hand, to make them effective in our present-day life.

Fascism exposed a basic need of the human psyche, one that the Age of Rationalism refused to recognize. The longing for a fixed, unreasoned ground of existence cannot be altogether extinguished. We do not meet the dangers inherent in this human propensity by denying it, regarding it as overcome or to be overcome, or as the residue of ancient superstitition, but only by recognizing it and taking it into account. In fact, today, such an urge is more justified than ever. Not only does the individual in his everyday life feel helplessly ensnared in a chaotic skein which he is unable to disentangle by reasoning, but even at the most advanced front of human knowledge a situation has been reached where an extreme expansion of man's power at the same time brings him to realize anew the extent of his ancient powerlessness to resolve the cosmos. The limits of our reason become more and more clear, and the rationalistic overconfidence in man's unrestricted domination of nature has been discouraged by natural science itself. In its recent prodigious advances, physics has arrived at a border region that seems to refuse itself to rational penetration. It has pushed forward into depths of reality where phenomena can no longer be pictured, but only schematized, that is, symbolized. It has reached so deep into the innermost structure of the elements that it has discovered their modes of transformation and so has come to recognize the elements themselves as being only specific arrangements, linkages of general energies. It has not only shown the total transformation of matter, but matter *as* transformation, and has even reproduced this transformation and made it a tool of man.

Physics, at a new level, merges the inner and outer world, postulates on epistemological grounds a unity that was taken for granted in early religious periods. Between the observer and the observed there exists a close interaction: one affects and changes the other. The findings of research, by completely dissolving the object into a complex of relations, have led the physicists ever farther away from the realm of sense perceptions into one of abstract conceptions that can only be mathematically symbolized and indirectly verified. Research moves through conceptual operations; and the operating mind, recognized as a factor conditioning what it formulates, comes to be placed inside, not outside the event. In this, physics, starting with the external, corresponds curiously with the theory of psychoanalysis, which, starting with the internal, has effected a merging of the outer and the inner world by seeing reactions that are directed outward as projections of inner situations. Physics has, by its very triumph, stirred in man the primeval shudder in the face of the impenetrable reaches re-emerging at the borders of the outer world; psychoanalysis has revealed man's disguised dread of his inner depths. But physics, as well as psychoanalysis, has shown that these anxieties are functions of each other, that they are one and the same dread of the unknown, which is the true source of myth.

There is a level of events in the universe and in man that rational research itself demonstrates more and more to be inaccessible to reason. A rational control of our world is only possible within certain limits and valid only for limited periods. Nothing can be accepted as final—the final becomes mythical. We have to be constantly on the alert to examine and re-examine the foundations on which we live and not to recoil from rebuilding our systems as those foundations shift. We must become accustomed to living on that floating ground on which science has moved for so long.

[1946]

The Reality of Utopia

This paper was written for a Forum of *The American Scholar* on "Life with the Atom," which was published in the Spring, 1946. It is included in the present collection of essays *not in spite of, but because of* its being behind the times. It seems to me not unimportant to show how our future looked shortly after Hiroshima, and thereby to contrast what the developments in the last twenty years have changed in the outlook, with what, to my mind, they have left unchanged and persistently, indeed even more saliently, valid.

THE APPEARANCE of the atomic bomb has not created a substantially new situation, but it has nevertheless completely changed the world. The state in which mankind finds itself now is no different from what it was before Hiroshima; it is one that long ago crept up on us unobserved. The atomic bomb has simply, at a single stroke, made it acute, peceptible to the senses, and visible to all eyes. What formerly could be considered the extravagant interpretation of intellectuals, or lightly dismissed as pious warnings from podium and pulpit, has now risen up before mankind as unavoidable, menacing reality—not words, but fact. This realization is the only new element introduced by the "Atomic Age." But it is certainly a shattering innovation, for it has reversed the relationship between idea and reality: "Utopia"—the world community—is today the only real thing, and all previous "practical" and "realistic" conceptions—national sovereignty, power politics and the unrestricted pursuit of economic interests—all those, from now on, are obvious delusions.

The paradoxical, indeed fantastic, aspect of this development is that it has resulted not from an advance in human reason and morality, as the optimists of eighteenth-century enlightenment were inclined to expect, but through an improvement of the technical equipment of life, that actually was connected with a retard, even a deterioration in the standards of human reason and morality. The picture presented by the last half century is one of increasing disparity between the rapid development of technical machinery and the lagging ability of man to understand and control the effects of this development. And the very automatism of this technical development has, contrary to the aims of man, made of the unpractical enthusiasts' wish-dream for world unity so urgent and real a necessity that the survival of human civilization depends on its fulfillment.

Let us examine this development. In the Middle Ages, the aim of all thought and study was the interpretation of Divine Creation and Providence. Christian dogma had undisputed authority over human knowledge, hence a measure of authority over human activity. This meant that for people in those days the conduct of the individual was inseparably bound up with the whole of humanity and of the universe—this whole being represented or personified by God. In and through the person of God (who at each moment in the life of man, thanks to faith and the power of the Church, had assumed extreme reality in the affairs of man) the whole was able to burden the individual with a degree of responsibility, and to summon him before a spiritual tribunal in afterlife. The whole, the human and cosmic universe, possessed reality and authority, and man possessed a soul about whose salvation he was concerned.

Both these circumstances are decisive, for they indicate the reality and authority of morality. What mortal dangers, soul-searchings and conflicts beset the scholars in their efforts to establish analytical thought and empirical science; what obstacles to economic development were the Church's ban on interest, and its principle of the "Fair Price"! The state of human affairs was bad enough, but the attitude of the individual was of considerable importance; in his own sphere, a single person had the power to influence events for good or bad.

Since the latter part of the Middle Ages, the power of dogma has been undermined by the disruption of the Holy Roman Empire, the schism of the Reformation, and the forward thrust of economic and rationalistic movements. The empirical exploration of nature and the exploitation of natural forces were given free rein. But when human reason, expressing itself in great philosophical systems, grew more and more autonomous and as the heir of God took over His representation of the whole, the whole was bound gradually to lose its compelling force. Worldly as reason was, it had no sublime, spiritual tribunal before which to hold man responsible for his conduct. Its arguments and decisions were manifold and intricate, and they attained unquestionable validity only where the practical results of applied science gave them concrete and apposite confirmation. Speculative theory, the consideration and interpretation of the whole, weakened and fell into discredit while scientific research, possessing an apparently infallible criterion of truth in its economic and technical applicability, gained exclusive control over mankind. Gunpowder and the compass, chronometers and telescopes, steam power and its teeming mechanical world, the plethora of commodities and comforts that it produced, and later those that came from the exploitation of electricity, of internal combustion, and of electromagnetic waves—these myriad products of applied science became, in the eyes of the masses, the yardsticks, the shapers and dominators of reality, the very goals and targets of human life.

The turning point was the Industrial Revolution. Until then the world was still governed by man and by human relationships. There was time for leisure and reflection, and man was still able to survey the world's spiritual and factual composition. The rationalistic advocates of enlightenment could still hope that the improved means of controlling nature might bring about a perfection of man himself. Living under better, healthier conditions, his toil lightened by mechanical power, man would be able to devote himself to his intellectual and moral betterment. Higher education and greater enlightenment would lay bare his reason and innate goodness which, according to contemporary belief, were latent in every human being and obstructed only by superstition and despotism. And once rid of the tutelage of church and monarchy, man would attain ever greater inward and outward freedom. That was how the future looked.

But something very different sprang from the Industrial Revolution. A huge production of commodities, devices and conveniences arose, swamping the very presence and consciousness of man and hemming him in with a new and much worse tyranny. This was fulfilled by means of two irresistible and inseparable procedures: technicalization and collectivization. Gradually, a technical machinery of life set itself between man and man, installing mechanical links that created between men a natural schism and alienation and a new and artificial relationship. Or, to put it more accurately: it separated the individuals but brought together the masses, establishing connections between the consolidated groups, and thereby transferring the arena of decisive events from the individual to a new, collective plane. This transference meant, of course, an increasing subordinacy and prostration of the individual.

A few examples will suffice. The movies, to a great extent, supplanted the theater. In the theater there arises between the players on the stage and the audience for whom they play, a distinct, momentary, living relationship, a direct mutual reaction from person to person that exercises a particular influence on every single performance. In the movies the actors play in front of a machine, their only medium of communication with a completely anonymous, world-wide, timeless, and placeless mass audience.

Between the customer and the artisan of former days—tailor, cobbler, cabinetmaker—between man and his neighbor, there existed an intimate relationship based on personal confidence. Today, however, between customer and supplier we find the machines of mass production and of mechanical transport; and the inhabitants of a modern metropolis have more in common with the members of their particular trade or profession than with their individual neighbors, whom they scarcely even know. On the other hand, these same machines of mass production, distribution, and communication, have segregated the community into specialized and differentiated producer and consumer groups. And between these groups, between the remotest nations and communities throughout the world, they have established so closely woven and complex a pattern of interdependence that the individual completely loses sight of his place in this vast network.

Entangled in such gigantic mass relationships, the individual sinks to hopeless insignificance, impotence and ignorance. In the tumult of our daily life and business in a metropolis, where press and radio, with their ceaseless waves of urgent news, sweep away even the experiences of yesterday—in this overwhelming turmoil, no sort of connected memories, and hence no coherent knowledge, can be built up. Through the rapid communication and interaction of events, everything occurs much faster than before. In fact, much more occurs, and that more complicatedly; and all that occurs (more even than actually occurs) is perpetually recorded. Even that which does not really occur, but is announced falsely either on purpose or through careless haste, produces by reaction real occurrences. Research and technical discovery have become a gigantic, permanent procedure that constantly injects into daily events a stream of innovations and alterations that touch closely the very foundations of our living. But who knows about this? Who can be aware and keep abreast of all this? What single scholar is capable of keeping in touch with the sciences immediately bordering on his particular field, let alone of achieving a general picture of our whole present-day knowledge? What single man, even in our governments and parliaments, has a comprehensive view even of the momentary situation, let alone of what is looming up from the depth and breadth of daily events to form the future?

This state of affairs has several ominous consequences. Since no single man—be he ever so close to political developments—can

understand or master the total situation, the true course of events
(in spite of all Führers and dictators) has become leaderless, a
pure automatism. In fact, the Führers and dictators are a direct
result of that leaderlessness; they are the immediate makeshift for
the lack of human leadership. The individual, no longer able to
grasp the highly complex situation or to pierce, with the help of
reason, through the maze of overpoweringly material automatism,
feels himself helplessly abandoned. He clutches desperately at some
simplification by substituting for the whole any part that is within
reach. And through this simplification, he becomes prey to latent
irrational and emotional currents, to uncontrolled impulses and
prejudices determined by traditions or by profession, class or property, which he rationalizes after the event. Finally, the individual
succumbs to atavistic paroxysms of violence, and consequently to
the demagogues, those most brutal simplifiers who see in every
form of opposition the primitive personification of enmity. In this
way they unleash all the irritation, fear and panic that the incomprehensible awakens in the individual against the windmill foe, the
other nation, the other race, class or group, and its rascal leaders.
The other group and its leaders, acting and reacting in the same
manner, have always made enough mistakes, have committed sufficient crimes, and so bear enough guilt for the accusations to be
tangibly founded and justified.

The individual human being who, for ease of comprehension
and action, simplifies the situation and personalizes objects, is
completely unaware that he is thereby gradually dismissing his
reason. He simplifies in order to rescue his rational comprehension
of what is otherwise incomprehensible. He does not, however,
perceive that something within him ceases to take reasonable cognizance of the true situation, that his simplifications and personal
projections make him slide back into conventional and emotional
behavior (and today that means collective behavior). He does not
know that at the very point where he fails to comprehend the true
complexity, he falls back on the standardized collective interests,
representations and prejudices that already make up the major portion of his personality.

The collective representations, and the collective wills, through the millions of irrationally or semi-rationally reacting individuals, clash against one another and, by their blind battles, complicate the situation even further. So far, collective will is effective only emotionally; it is as yet in no way rationally organized. No means has yet been found for transforming collective will into collective consciousness. Every form of democracy to this day, and every form of socialism, despite the first Russian steps in this direction, have failed in their task. Such a transformation would signify that the individuals are conscious of their collective conditionings, that they learn to recognize the specific groupings as interconnected parts of a common whole, of that leaderless, automatically advancing whole in whose snares they all are caught. Not even the true scope of this whole is seen. Not only the groups—national, professional or economic—but in the Western Hemisphere even the individuals still believe that they can decide their own lives independently, or at least that they could if only they were not hindered by evil foes. Problems still appear as conflicts.

The development of the last 150 years therefore shows a twofold process. On the one hand, there has been a luxuriant growth of the technical machinery of life and knowledge, separating men from one another as individuals by segregating them in specialized and standardized groups. More, it has made these groups so very closely interdependent in the state and in the world that all occurrences become almost ubiquitous and simultaneous, and the world nears technical unity. On the other hand, proportionally, the individual sinks back into insignificance, impotence, and general ignorance.

It is as though the rational forces had objectivized themselves in the far-reaching and manifold technical processes and become autonomous, independent of man, withdrawn from man. Collective consciousness is latent in technology. For all that individual man may apply himself, in his factories and laboratories, to specialized tasks of utmost rational refinement, the whole of the world recedes further and further from him. And in his relationship to this whole, to the general questions of humanity, he becomes less and less capable of comprehending and of deciding. More and more he reacts irrationally, emotionally, and quite unawares falls prey to the collective currents and aspirations that now, as always, tend toward the primitive state of simplification and personification of the problems.

This trend implies a decline of morals, a moral degeneration. For morality is nothing else but the attitude toward the whole— positive or negative, furthering or hindering and disturbing. When knowledge of and orientation in the whole are no longer possible, then the individual must, in his consternation, be carried away by the nearest wave of impulse or opportunity. To whomever human history and events are no longer a living whole and a oneness, to him the brotherhood of man cannot have any meaning.

These circumstances had long prevailed when the atomic bomb exploded. It was the practical outcome of an exploration into nature that has reached the purlieus of sublime theoretical abstraction and is in the very act of passing from extreme materialism, through the study of matter, into extreme spirituality. The most important aspect of this event is the releasing of atomic energy for practical uses. The atom bomb is only the first stage of this long drawn-out process. It was brought to such rapid fruition by the headlong race between the belligerents for a decisive weapon. And this example illustrates most crudely the state of human affairs here described. The practical exploitation of atomic energy was expedited not for the purpose of solving the most urgent problems of human communal life, but in order to equip with the most murderous weapon of all times the long obsolete struggles for power between groups.

The weapon, however, turned out to be so murderous, concentrating the whole of warfare on a few points and moments of thorough devastation, that humanity, or at least human civilization, stands before the cold alternative of being or not being. The automatism of technology that had long been in opposition to the obsolete ways of human mentality begins to revolt against the destructive misuse that has so far been made of technical achievements. Technology balks, it poses the last decisive question.

And this is but the beginning. What the atom bomb has wrought, the disruption of the international political system, is, in spite of all its vital threat to mankind, negligible in comparison with the effects that the now discovered technical application of atom splitting has yet to produce in its further development. It will not be possible to prevent the harnessing of atomic energy, sooner or later, for economic uses. And when that time comes, humanity will face a change in the established social order compared with which all previous man-made revolutions will appear as absolute child's play.

Technology, in the same way as religion and morality, compels man by offering a promise and a threat. Religion and morality appealed to individual man, and the choice they offered him had reality only insofar as the individual believed in the actual existence of a heavenly world, or a distinctly immaterial, psychic order. For the world of the Middle Ages, Heaven and Hell were just as real as are the amusement park and the concentration camp for the world of today. However, the reality of Heaven and Hell began only beyond earthly life.

As morality came to substitute itself for religion the clear outlines and personal expectations of Heaven or Hell were replaced by a limbo of Progress, a never-never-land located on earth and within human life in general, but in an ideal future, and never to be fully experienced personally. And when eventually the original ideal of human progress degenerated to the promotion of an ever higher "standard of living," and partly lost itself in the mist, partly was discredited by the events, the binding force of morality was more and more restricted to the private field. It became valid only for a rapidly dwindling minority of individuals who had preserved in their souls that criterion of the whole, formerly represented by God—that conscience, that consciousness of the whole—and carried it through life as a part of their personality, as a superego. In the face of the political and economic developments of our century, anyone attempting seriously to apply moral yardsticks to public affairs was derided as a dangerous and unrealistic fool. Plans for a closely united world, a world community, were labeled utopian. And, on the other hand, to whom would it have occurred, even quite recently, that the uninhibited surrender to practical and tactical expedients, the abandonment of all principles, could really bring the world to such a degree of disruption and corruption as we have experienced in recent years?

The promises and threats of morality, then, stood, in the eyes of most people, for a far-distant dreamland of the future. Lacking immediacy, they lacked reality. But now, suddenly, the very instrument of practicality, technology, has erected before mankind a promise and a threat, both imbued with imminent, unmistakable and completely earthly reality. We may have unity and lasting peace on earth. We may even have, in a not so distant future, a world like that depicted by the Enlightenment: a world in which man, through his control of vast new energies, could find both comfort and leisure, and lead a life at once more free and more human. But still closer and more perceptible looms the threat of physical destruction. And this time promise and threat are so closely connected that they ask for a radical decision, one way or the other. Out of practicality itself Utopia is born, and even here, following the process of natural science, extreme materialism turns into extreme spirituality.

There is little interest today in promises. He who has capital and influence has no use for promises, and he who possesses nothing does not believe in them. And their fulfillment lies so far beyond the conceptions and experiences of everybody's daily life that one would not accept a paradise if it entailed a change in the customary network of circumstances in which he is so tightly, deeply and helplessly embedded.

The threat has certainly made impression enough. Its echoes boom on unceasingly from radio, press and platforms. Yet it will scarcely alter the behavior of mankind—at any rate not so suddenly or radically as this inexorable ultimatum of events requires. The tragedy of the situation consists in the fact that the same process that has pushed the moral challenge to the point of technical reality has also driven man to a condition where he is less prepared to meet it than ever before.

The first reaction was paralyzing fear and, as always, an attempt to escape, to minimize and to procrastinate. But the physicists and technicians have blocked one escape after the other. They have established the following points: It is useless to try to keep the process secret. The scientific data of atomic fission are common knowledge among physicists everywhere; the final stages of technical realization of the atom bomb, sole items on the agenda, can be achieved very shortly in other countries and might even be perfected secretly, thus adding to the danger of surprise. The huge cost of the invention is no protection. New results in physical research may offer tomorrow a considerably cheaper method of production. And in Russia particularly the cost today is of no account.

A really effective defense against the atom bomb is inconceivable. "Since the aggressor, in the next war, will have the advantage of surprise," says one technical expert, "I will still have to beg for from one to five years to develop a defense (assuming that I know how) against new ways of delivering atomic explosives. . . . Atomic explosives demand not 90 per cent, but 100 per cent defense. This, we do not know how to achieve."

This, then, is the present state of affairs. The danger can increase immeasurably in the future. A systematically sharpened sense of discovery is today at work in thousands of brains, and the work is being done at feverish speed. The Hiroshima bomb was obsolete when it was dropped. Nations and governments have therefore been so driven into a corner by actuality that there remains but one course of action. Yet no sooner are the first steps taken on that course than the old irrational (one might almost say animal) inhibitions come irresistibly into play.

Here is where the evil is located, at this human and moral point. No matter how strenuously we exert ourselves once more to find a technical avenue of escape, some new preventive machinery which, in the last analysis, will leave everything unchanged, it is all in vain. We are thrown inescapably back to a human and moral transformation, a change in the attitude of mankind toward the whole. Technology itself has once and for all transcended the purely technical stage. Technology itself has become a moral force.

At the Moscow Conference in December, 1945, it was resolved that a commission be set up to examine the problems of atomic energy, and to make appropriate recommendations to the UN Security Council. The main problems are the outlawing of the atomic weapon and the possibility of effective international guarantees against its use. Not until such guarantees are put into effect are the secrets of manufacture to be handed over to the UN. Let us consider for a moment what the commission is faced with.

The international outlawing of the atomic weapon offers against the background of history no guarantee whatsoever, particularly since the group of powers which now wants the bomb outlawed was the very one to introduce its use without prior warning. There is scarcely a single provision of the Geneva Convention that has not been broken in the last wars, so long as there seemed to be any advantage in breaking it and the fear of retaliation was not too great. One might just as well outlaw war in general, and this has often enough been attempted without success.

What is the outlook for the other, technical guarantees? A condition of real security will not prevail in the world until any state that might undertake a surprise attack with atomic weapons may fully expect immediate and automatic reprisals with the same weapons. To make that possible, there would have to be a world-wide network of internationalized, well-guarded and well-protected bomb stores, and an international secret service to uncover and nip in the bud any such plans and to guard the stores.

It seems obvious that such protective measures can be reliably administered only by an unquestionably supranational authority, a world government. The UN is not such an authority. It is basically an alliance of the Big Three, surrounded by their satellites, a constellation whose rival forces and interests can be maintained in unstable accord only by means of repeated compromise. A world government worthy of the name would be a constitution above the sphere of interests of the great powers, and armed with such instruments of control and supreme authority as are at the disposal of a present-day democratic government with regard to its citizens: legislature, judiciary, and executive. Its agencies would have to be delegated by a democratic procedure—that is, by popular election, not governmental appointment—from all nations that show a minimum of functioning democracy. These nations would have to be as equal in their rights and obligations as are the American states within the union, allowing in a similar way for quantitative differences of population. The exploitation of atomic energy tends to further democracy in the international field; sooner or later, it will bring about the political equalization of small and big nations. The days of great powers are numbered.

There is no sense in deceiving ourselves. Effective security cannot be bought more cheaply in view of the present condition of mankind: the constant danger of crisis, inherent in the uncontrolled automatism of world affairs, and the constant latency of irrational collective impulses with immeasurable potentialities.

But in the face of all this how far present-day humanity is from achieving such security! What personal and national sacrifices would have to be made, how many of the prerogatives of sovereignty would have to be abandoned, what responsibility would have to be shouldered for the common weal! What opposition would have to be overcome! And what degree of insight, knowledge, and reasonable self-control would be demanded of man! Thus, step by step, the apparently technical machinery for protection against the danger of the atom bomb points back to such tasks as the purification and rationalization of democratic institutions, a more comprehensive and intensive education, a methodical attempt at a unified picture of our world—in short, to an orientation toward the whole and toward the human community; that is, to an essentially moral task.

The moral transformation is the only course that remains for us, no matter how arduous it may be. In the meantime, we can rely only upon the clemency of fate. The general fear, on which so many people count as a restraining influence, is a very questionable defense. Between fear and its object there exists a menacing and magic interaction which tends to gradual intensification, and eventually to a panic merging of the two. In a crisis, help has never come from fear, but only from calm and careful consideration.

A mother recently surprised her child muttering the following prayer: "Please, God, let us all perish in the same catastrophe!" This prayer by a child in 1945 is the most horrible indictment that can be delivered against our world. It should be posted everywhere, on the walls of every polling booth, parliament, office, and university, to bring men to their senses and remind them of their responsibilities.

[1946]

——————————————————————PART TWO

The Nature of the Symbol

ALL UTTERANCE, be it expression or communication, be it "language" or shaping of objects, tends to expand and eventually to split the being from which it comes. Plain, solid existence is mute.

The most rudimentary, inarticulate form of utterance in sound or gesture is mere *expression*, that is to say, a reaction to the stimuli of pain or joy, want or fear. But even the cry of a hunted animal, the groan of a suffering or starving creature, is a *symptom* of something, it is a *sign* of some motivated feeling. It is, to be sure, only a sign *of* something, not necessarily a sign made *to* and intended *for* somebody; and it is so close to its actuating source that we still feel it to be one with the being itself.

Utterance turns into language when contact with the environment is sought and, through sound or gesture, some kind of *communication* occurs. Communication is directed expression. The wooing songs and warning cries of birds, though roused by elementary urges, are addressed to mates and fellow creatures; they are *signals*. The "wagging dance" of pilot bees goes a step further: it transmits detailed factual information. In all these cases the emphasis has shifted from mere expression to communication. Something new is introduced; the utterance carries a meaning,

67

a meaning for someone else. A sheer symptom, an unintentional, undirected sound or gesture has no meaning, it has a cause; more precisely, it has meaning only for someone who wants to discover the cause. And on the subliminal, physiological level, a symptom, like pain, may be said to carry a warning of organic disturbance, i.e., a meaning, from the body to consciousness. An intentionally communicative utterance, however, is not simply a sign *of* an experience; it *signi-fies* something, it *is* not, it *makes* a sign.

Through communication the living being is carried beyond its sheer existence, much further than by pure expression. It has found a target, indeed an anchorage in the environment. A partner, a counterpart has come into play that will respond to, occasionally counter, and by this challenge reflect on, the correspondent's existence. And in the course of this developing dialogue the means of communication unfold, a vast world of multifarious and multi-level articulation, of words and concepts and universes of discourse, all of which, growing weightier and weightier, ever more objectified and autonomous, come increasingly to split existence into different sections and layers.

The same thing happens in the development of *tools* which, like language, are a means of communication between the living crea-ture and its surrounding world. To be sure, the objects and ma-terials of nature to which tools are addressed are not partners in the same sense as living correspondents of language are. Resisting or complying, they respond passively, not directly to the maker or user, but to the impersonal function of the tool. They do respond, however, and particularly in the higher technical stages, they are induced to answer questions which are put to them through experiments. Here, in the use of tools and machines, communication has assumed the character of conformation, con-formation of objective material to the human being and, retro-actively, of the human being to objective material.

The most primitive tools, anthills, birds' nests, beavers' dams, artificial arrangements for breeding and dwelling, are an "accom-modation"—an adaptation of environment, a special kind of dealing with the elements of nature. The long history of these objectified procedures—from such initial contrivances as artificial dwelling places to the overwhelming machinery of modern technology—shows more evidently still the same features as the evolution of language. A huge realm of apparatus evolved between the human being and nature, which stretched his existence to such an extent as to divide it into manifold strata. The human being came to reside in different spheres at once; and in the broadening and lengthening way of his getting acquainted with ever wider surroundings, the direction of his communication slowly shifted from the immediate to the intermediate; practical means turned into, or brought forth, theoretical ends. So it happens today that the human being, in his capacity as an individual, corresponds with other individuals and uses the complex products of an elaborate communication with nature in a personal way, for the personal ends of his living; and at the same time, in his work and even as a consuming participant in technological achievement, he also lives in the realm of generalized apparatus. Inasmuch as the human being has come to extend his existence over manifold spheres, his communication with his outer world turns into a communication with his self, of his practical with his theoretical mind, and—since the outer expansion reflexively involved an inner, psychic expansion—of his ego with his id, with the lighted depths of his unconscious.

The use of language and the use of tools are deeply interrelated and differ only in their media and points of emergence. Words and concepts can be seen as instruments not merely to reach an accord with fellow men, but to assimilate and integrate ever wider ranges of objective reality and of the expanded self. Tools, conversely, may appear as means of conformation to the world of objects. Concepts are tools; tools and machines (which are more elaborate and rarefied tools) are materialized concepts. Both kinds of communication mutually supplement and support each other.

Even *art* in its beginning was a use of magic as a tool to appropriate other creatures or to influence animate powers. And here again, communication with living forces eventually turned into a discourse with objective reality, visual or psychic, a venture into the depths of outer and inner reality. Art, however, has preserved that original character of magic even in its most advanced and perfected works; it has remained an act of conjuration even in the stage when it has lost its patently magic or cultic intent. Both science and art evolved through expanding communication, which means expanding the reach of human existence. Both became, at least provisionally, self-sufficient: theory for theory's sake, art for art's sake. Science developed words, which are rudimentary concepts, into more complex, theoretical concepts; concepts into formulas, which are intellectual tools; and thus, in its means of communication, science quite explicitly maintained an instrumental character. Art transformed words and tools into organically consistent, representational forms, i.e., images, magic into "imagic." While this implies basic differences of approach in dealing with the objective world, it should not blind us to the fact that both scientific formulation and artistic figuration are exploratory ways to get acquainted with the nature of reality. Science proceeds in a direct manner through analysis and quantitative reduction of reality itself, art indirectly through "imagical" representation of coherent existences or existential coherences. By establishing such independent exemplary entities, art introduces a third mode of utterance: *creation*. In art, communication proceeds by creation.

II

It is against the background of this evolutionary process that we can best understand the nature and development of the *symbol*. The symbol originates in the split of existence, the confrontation and communication of an inner with an outer reality, whereby a meaning detaches itself from sheer existence. Communication starts with signs, with *made signs* and, as has been stated before, only made signs are "signi-fications," that is, carry a meaning. This simple fact that a sound or gesture carries a meaning implies an original establishment of two levels of existence and also of two distinct spheres, the inner sphere of motivation and the outer sphere that is asked to answer, to satisfy this motivation; it establishes them by bridging them.

Any made sign is a *bridging act*, an act of pointing to something or somebody. In the distinctive mating or warning *signal* of an animal species it appears in a somewhat stabilized form, but it has not parted with the living creature and settled down as a separate entity. The word, however, the articulate name of a person or of a thing, is an objectified fixation of the act of "calling" him or "de-signating" it; it is a *frozen* act. It inaugurates what Alfred Korzybski has called the "time-binding capacity" of the human being; it bridges not only spatial but also temporal spheres. This fixation, this consolidation and extension of the bridging act, this settling down of the meaning as a separate entity, and an established junction of diverse spheres of existence, marks the actual beginning of the *symbol*.

The linguistic sign as established in words (and perpetuated in writing) carries a magic spell which was strongly felt in previous ages. The word was not limited to sheer designation, but an aura of influence went with it. The bare name of a deity constituted an invocation, and contained rudimentally the *magic formula* in all its variations and stages. The formal prayer, the liturgy, the litany, all of them are ritually hardened acts of bridging through incantation and cultic service.* Their literal meaning is mostly forgotten or overgrown, it is solidified, contracted, and thereby transformed into a verbal instrument of communication with divine powers.

Thus, in the magic formula the act of bridging turns into *an act of abridgment*, of *contraction*. It is still, however, an unintentional contraction, the result of a long ritual practice of repetition. Subsequently, the broadening communication of man with his surrounding world, this ceaseless questioning and seeking answers, engendered wider and deeper questions and exfoliated

* Greek *leitourgia* derives from *leitos* (public or voluntary) and *ergon* (work).

72 OUT OF THE LABYRINTH

new spheres and levels of existence. The increasing distances between these spheres produced new forms of contraction, *intentional contraction of reality*, which were needed to make man's communication—with his fellow men, with his self, and with nature—more manageable. Such fully conscious, deliberate contraction is *abstraction*, which gained its overwhelming importance when man was confronted with a fundamental change in the nature of his surrounding world.

In dealing with daemonic or divine powers, man faced animate beings of a somehow familiar, organic character on his own level as it were, inasmuch as these powers were believed to respond in the same way, with the same will and the same feeling as man himself. They were indeed projections of man's own forms of existence and therefore accessible to magic influence. When the domain of these powers was gradually pushed back through the broadening of secular experience, there emerged a realm of objective reality essentially different from the nature of the human being. In this vast, unbounded realm it seemed quite uncertain with what entities man would have to deal. Effects were cut off from animate sources. Loose, impersonal energies appeared to be functioning autonomously. Directing its exploratory questions to these forces, the human mind was lured into dimensions far exceeding the bounds of man's organic equals—be it fellow man, living creature, or deity. Such far-reaching, impersonal forces could not be met through magical, i.e., personal, contact. They called for a rational "nomothetic" approach toward certain regularities which were brought into view by the new suprahuman perspective, the disproportionate relation of the human to the cosmic forms. These regularities, which promised predictability, appeared as the only possible media of communication with the forces of nature, and they could only be comprehended through abstraction, an *abbreviating act* of thought which again consolidated in various forms.

The most elementary abstraction is *number*. The conception of number presupposes a twofold capacity: to distinguish different single events as set against the mere recurrence of one and the same event, and to isolate common likenesses from the variety of single events and phenomena. Only likenesses, or entities connected by some identical property, can be numbered.

Number was established in the dim past, far back in the age of cultic communication, and like the word it has carried a charge of magic potencies. (It may even have come to the primitive mind originally through visual configurations to which magical power was attributed.) But its great role began when in the face of an inanimate universe words proved incapable of dealing with impersonal and boundless forces which could be approached only by way of their regularities and common properties. The adequate vehicle of correspondence was number. Being initially an abstraction, it contained the seed of unlimited further abstraction. The relationship of numerical abstractions in arithmetic (from Greek *arithmos*, "number") was generalized, i.e., abstracted again, through the substitution of letters in algebra (from Arabic *jabara*, "to bind together," "to combine"). Calculus, the theories of functions, of aggregates, of probability, etc., are many extensions and rarefications of numerical abstraction. The operation of combinatory and abstractive thought was reduced to pure, general form by logic in its sundry varieties. Along with all such abstracting operations which were built up one upon the other in ever intensified degrees, there evolved the *modern rational formula*, the conceptual tool that helped the natural sciences in their steadily expanding correspondence with the forces of nature. The rational formula, just like the magic formula, is the fixation of an act of bridging, but a bridging of ever widening distances through ever more condensing abbreviations. (The ultimate pragmatic abridgment through contracting abstraction is the computer.) The *law of nature*, finally, in that it establishes samenesses in the functionings of natural forces, is the statement of the conclusive act of quantitative abbreviation, opening up a way for man's theoretical and technological communication with nature.

III

We have traced the genetic line from the *symptom* (undirected sign) through the *signal* (the made sign and the stabilized sign) to the fixed sign, the actual inception of the *symbol*. The signal marks the transition from expression to communication; and all the various kinds and stages of the symbol which we have considered so far, the word, the tool, the number, the magic and the rational formula, the law of nature, all of them are frozen acts of communication—communication, first through bridging, and later through abridgment, contracting and abstracting abridgment.

But anything fixed, anything settled in a steady form, tends to become autonomous; it starts on a life of its own. So any act of designation as soon as it is firmly established no longer merely points to, or "points out," something, it gradually comes to represent the thing it points to. If stabilization of a sign may be seen as the preliminary and fixation of the sign as the first stage of the symbol, *representation* is its second and final stage.

In common language, in formulas, magic or rational, the character of active communication, of designation and bridging predominates. Language always moves toward a human partner, be it even the self, to whom it carries a message. A formula is concerned with, it is "instrumental" in, establishing relations. But when, in our memory or in theoretical contemplation, a name or a concept engenders an *image*, the emphasis shifts from communication to representation; or, to be more exact, communication is effected by representation. So the second stage of symbolization, the stage of representation, implies the formation of an image, which is *simultaneity of meaning*—meaning, not as relation, but as substance.

The capacity to form images, "imagination," is deeply rooted in *the human psyche*, probably even in the psyche of animals.*

---

* The psychiatrist Silvano Arieti, in his book, *Interpretation of Schizophrenia* (New York, 1955), assumes that animals have images: "They seem to dream, and if they dream they must do so with some kind of images. [This is not

Its subliminal, spontaneous operation in dreams has become a focus of attention of psychoanalysis, which uses the term "symbolize" for the unconscious translation of a personal or archetypal "dream thought" into a distinct dream image ("dream element," in the terminology of Freud) and calls the resulting images "symbols." However, they are, it seems to me, rather symptoms than accomplished symbols (i.e., *made* signs or representations), symptoms emerging in images instead of sounds or gestures. If, as Freud tells us, parents in dreams take the shape of emperor and

---

necessarily so, their dream stimuli may be provided by other senses, by smell, sound, or touch, or senses unknown to us.] However, animals do not seem to have the capacity to evoke or reproduce images when they want to, and, of course, they are incapable of expressing them to others. . . ." Then, he raises the question whether animals are capable of the next step: making images into symbols. He writes (pp. 282*ff*): "The comparative psychologist, Kellogg, reports, that his little chimpanzee, Gua, was so attached to him that whenever he left the house she became very despondent. She would go into a tantrum of terror and grief. If, however, he gave her his coverall at the time of his departure, she seemed placated, showed no emotional displeasure, and carried the coverall around her as a fetish. As [Susanne] Langer points out, this fact is extremely important. This is probably one of the first manifestations of high symbolization of which animals are capable. The coverall represented the master . . . it replaced the master . . . it was a symbol, but it was a symbol which was identified with the object it symbolized. Possibly the ape was able to evoke the image of his master at the sight of the coverall, or the coverall reproduced the image of the master plus coverall, or the ape really accepted the coverall not as a coverall, but as an emotional equivalent of his master. . . ." These interpretations of Susanne Langer, with which Dr. Arieti seems to agree, appear to me highly anthropomorphic, or better, logomorphic. Similar experiences I have had with dogs lead me to believe that what went on in the psyche of the chimpanzee was of a very different nature: the coverall was not a symbol, but rather a real piece of the master and part of his presence, which probably was conveyed to the animal through smell combined with associative sensations of touch and vision. Even among certain primitive humans we find the assumption that objects of personal property are parts, or extensions, of the body of their owners. In any case, the chimpanzee did not perform a conscious act of substitution, which alone could be called symbolization. (In a recent private communication, Dr. Arieti has told me that in quoting the example which Susanne Langer took from Kellogg, he was referring not to symbols but to *paleosymbols*. He has expanded the concept of paleosymbols in his forthcoming book *Feeling, Cognition and Creativity in Health and Mental Illness*. According to him the paleosymbol, which is something between the symptom and the symbol, requires for its occurrence an external object, as well as an image evoked by the external object.)

empress and children that of little animals or vermin, if being born is pictured as plunging into water and dying as departing by train,[1] such a process of transformation appears to be a kind of reflex, an automatic projection of inner urges or discomforts into whatever visual material is at hand in the outer world. This is even more evident in archetypal images, where the visual material is not taken from the outer, but from the inner world. C. G. Jung relates a dream of a seventeen-year-old girl in which she saw her mother "hanging from the chandelier and swinging to and fro in a cold wind that blows in through the open windows." This dream had nothing whatever to do with her mother, but turned out to be the symptom of an organic disease of the girl herself. The mother image expressed something going on in her physical depths, for it is, as Jung says, "archetypal and refers to . . . that which passively creates, hence . . . to material nature, the lower body (womb) and the vegetative functions . . . the 'mother' is also a vessel, the hollow form (uterus) that carries and nourishes. . . ." Indeed, the mother image "points to a darker meaning which eludes conceptual formulation and can only be vaguely apprehended as the hidden, nature-bound life of the body. . . . All this is dream-content, but it is nothing which the . . . girl has acquired in her individual existence; it is rather a bequest from the past."[2] Likewise, the Mandala image, a circle with a tendency to combine with a square, which Jung found recurring in dreams, drawings, dances of his patients who could "say very little of the meaning of the symbols," appears as a kind of organic geometry deriving from the inmost form of the living being. Jung sees in it "the archetype of wholeness."

In all such cases, the actual "symbolization" is done, not by the person in whose unconscious the image arises, but by the analyst through inferential interpretation. To him alone these images are meaningful, just as the physical symptom carries a meaning only for somebody who looks for its cause.

Only consciously formed images are real symbols. To be sure, borderlines between unconscious and conscious operation, between sheer expression and intentional representation, are fluid; and as Jung has amply demonstrated, archetypal patterns, which operate in the unconscious, pass over into the conscious work of artists, poets, thinkers, who create cultic images. These images, as far as they are *made* and intended as means of communication with divine powers and their worshipers, are actual symbols, capable even of embodying complex doctrines.

Science, particularly the basic natural science, physics, in its exploratory advances, has gone beyond the sphere of the visually "imaginable"; it progresses by way of mathematical conceptions verifiable through very complicated instrumental questions and reactions, whereby observation itself is achieved only in an inferential, somehow abstractive manner. The natural sciences, however, make use of certain auxiliary images: *geometrical figures* and *diagrams*, pictorial abstractions which are the equivalent, in the visual domain, of arithmetical abstractions with which they combine or in which they result; and *models*, such as the age-old, now obsolete "ether," or the field concept, or Bohr's atom model. In all these kinds of images the instrumental, mediatorial element predominates; none of them is meant actually to represent reality. Geometrical figures are a means to convey and manipulate the proportions and relations of spatial structures. Diagrams are used to clarify phenomenal or rational complexities through exemplary visual reduction; they are a sort of pictorial metaphor. A model, being just a *modulus*, a measure of the real thing, will never permit us to forget its provisional, hypothetical nature; it can never stand for an established reality.

IV

It is only in *art* that representation comes to prevail over the signi-fying act. Here, the act merges in the accomplished form. Ultimately, the image is no longer merely a road to reality, but the very figuration of reality—more than that, it is in itself a new, independent reality.

In the development of such accomplished symbolization, the

religious image, plainly or artistically shaped, has an intermediate role: it is real representation, but at the same time it remains predominantly a sign.

Religious and artistic imagery arose in common. Earliest images, prehistoric cave paintings are not symbols as yet, they are virtual acts of seizure; they do not signi-fy, or represent, they actually *are* the creatures represented. They do not point to prototypes, they are pointed at with the points of arrows. Similarly, the original totemistic idol, as long as the deity is believed to be actually present in the image, is not a likeness of the worshiped being, it *is* the being itself. Only when a difference is felt between the visually present idol and a remote or temporarily absent deity, when the image turns into a mere residue or residence of the deity, only then does the image become a symbol.

Of course, any divine image always tends to evoke the imagined presence of the deity through a mystomagical connection. In Holy Mass, the host and the wine in the chalice, symbolic residues of the body and blood of Jesus Christ, are, through the magic process of transubstantiation, turned into the very presence of Christ. Insofar as this happens, the symbol-character of the image is abolished.

All cultic symbols, though representing accepted reality, are still, just like formulas, instituted acts of bridging distances between different existential spheres. They may be seen as imagic formulas, not discursive or "discoursive," but contracted into simultaneous, embodied meaning. Frequently, they present a *pars pro toto*, that is to say, they signify a sacred being by a characteristic part of it, which may be a mythical or legendary happening, a peculiar divine quality or domain. Or they may use a homologous abstraction of a total form.

The crucifix, for instance, points to Jesus' sacrificial death—even the magic act of apotropaic conjuration is still present in a person's making the sign of the cross. The Indian symbol of the multiheaded snake, called the Remainder, signifies "the residue that remained after the earth, the upper and infernal regions and all their beings, had been shaped out of the cosmic waters of the abyss."[3] The Phallus, or Lingam, originally a deity in itself, later recalls the creative capacity of Greek chthonic gods like Dionysos and the Cabiri ("*Kabeiroi*") or the Indian Shiva. The she-bear or hind of the huntress Artemis indicates her nature and natural sphere. The wheel or hooked cross (swastika) represents the dynamic shape of the worshiped sun-god.

All these forms of symbolic contraction passed over from hieratic to profane uses, from religious cult to the cult of tradition. Royal, official, national insignia, heraldic emblems and coats of arms, point to the origins, the dominions, the aims and claims, of rulers or families or places. The ball or "apple" surmounted by a cross, which a medieval emperor carried at ceremonial occasions, signified, as its name "orb" or "mound" indicates, the catholic globe under his control. The fifty stars in the American flag symbolize the united states. The apothecary pills in the Medici coat-of-arms picture, along with the name of the family, their medical beginnings.

A beautiful example of an immediate, personal message conveyed through an abbreviating image-symbol, a veritable act of poetry, has been related to us by Marie de France (twelfth century) in her poem *Chèvrefoil*. Tristram, exiled by King Mark, wants to indicate to Iseult on her ride to the castle of Tintagel that he is hiding in the woods to get a glimpse of her. He lays a hazel twig on her path, from which she will know that he is near. For "both of them were like the hazel bush and the honeysuckle that clings to it; interlaced they fare well, but parting they both die. So it is with us, beloved one, not you without me, not I without you." The sacred being that is here represented in a contracted form is love absolute, total love between two human beings, of which the story of Tristram and Iseult is the first instance in European tradition—love seizing upon, devouring the whole of existence, disregarding convention and morality, disregarding life itself. Such impassioned, life-transcending celebration of a supreme, if mundane, power is a lived cult.

V

All forms of cultic representation, religious or traditional, are intended to carry on and revive the communication, indeed communion, of present man with his mythical or perennial sources of life. Communication, the sign-character, still looms saliently in cultic representation, not merely where it indicates a whole by a part, but also where it portrays the whole in full, as in paintings, statues, or stories.

Cultic images are made to conjure up historical or canonically sanctioned actuality, which means that representation is not entirely free. The substratum of plastic or poetic depiction is furnished by something outside the creative range, by figures and happenings that are believed to have existed, or to be existent, as such. Mythography and narration only elaborated and adorned them; those who re-lived the events in their tales or pictures were probably vaguely convinced that the vivid additions of their fantasy were true, just as devout medieval painters, while emphatically penetrating into the destinies and attitudes of their saints, must have come to think that this could not have happened otherwise. Creative imagination clustered around a core of reality pre-established by age-old events or by long-grown incarnations of true emotions and drives in the human being.

We know today that Ilion existed and was destroyed several times, we know of Mycenae and the migrations of Hellenic tribes. The princes of the *Iliad* are probably ancestral projections of tribal lords in the Homeric age. Likewise, the Nordic *Edda* fused mythical elements with accounts of early Burgundian and Hunnish campaigns. To a still higher degree the Biblical stories may be seen as historical documents. Thus, the early epics are by no means pure fiction; they are, all of them, based on happenings, either attested as real by historical memory, or sanctioned as real by a long, anonymous process of mythogenesis. (Myths, in their original form, were accounts of the beginning of things or of the deeds and destinies of gods and heroic demi-gods; and their magic rested on people's belief that they were true. This is confirmed by the violent opposition of Greek philosophy to the mythographic epics because of the "lies" they tell the people.)

Cultic images, then, are symbols inasmuch as they are signs; they are not, however, wholly accomplished symbolic representations. A fully representational symbol may be called a plastic or literary depiction that is not designed foremost to revive the human relationship to some cultic reality, but that is *intended* and *created*, from the outset and in its full extent, as a symbolic representation. Just as, in the initial stage, the sign turns into a symbol only when it is a *made* sign, carrying a meaning for somebody, so an image attains its full representational meaning only when it is created in its entirety by the conscious imagination of an artist; when the artist freely *invents* symbols by selecting, or synthesizing, from the immense diversity of life specific "representative" figures and configurations apt to stand for something generally human, or to clarify a commonly human situation.

The transition, in art, from the sign-image to the fully representational image is a result of the same process that turned man from magic to science: the widening and deepening of secular experience and the depersonalization of the forces that determine human life. Less and less were human destinies derived from divine and mythical sources, more and more from the nature and condition of man himself. Communication with external powers changed into communication with internal dispositions, into communication with the human self, i.e., self-representation.

Yet, reading the great works of the cultic ages we sense a kind of symbolism not unlike that of the artistic creations of our modern era. Whether we are believers or not, we do not read the Biblical stories simply as accounts of some remote happenings. We do not read the Homeric epics as we would read any ordinary adventure or travel story. We feel *ourselves*, our own lives deeply involved in all these doings and sufferings. So these great tales seem to fit exactly the pattern of accomplished symbolic representation: they present in singular figures and destinies matters of common human purport.

There is, however, a crucial difference between the representational symbolism of these ancient works and that of modern works of art, a difference which is due precisely to the dependence of the ancient works on pre-established reality.

We have to distinguish between two kinds of representational symbolism: *descending* and *ascending*.

Descending I would call all symbolism in which symbolic representation detaches itself, descends to us, from a prior and higher reality, a reality determining and therefore superior to its symbolic meaning. Genuinely mythical and cultic works are not intended as symbolic representation, they are meant to describe real happenings. It is *we* who, a posteriori, derive a symbolic meaning from them. In the early ages, when all of life moves under cultic or mythical guidance, reality is so monumentally plain, so naturally comprehensive, undisclosed like a bud, that it holds for us a dormant wealth of meaning all but inexhaustible. This is what makes for the grandeur of that primordial actuality. The ancient divine or mythical beings are by no means, as our modern rational thinking would have it, plainly and fully individual figures made to represent something common or general. They are, for all their characteristic personal singularity, inherently generic existences. The Greek gods, daemons, heroes constitute tribes or localities incarnate; the patriarchs of the Bible, the sons of Jacob, *are* their respective clans. They are not products of symbolic representation, they are real beings comprising their progeny.

This intricate difference may be illustrated by the somehow related difference between Platonic ideas and our modern scientific concepts. Like the deities which they replaced, the Platonic ideas were not conceived as man-made terms designating general likenesses in a group of phenomena; they were meant to be quasi-divine absolute entities, not generalizations derived from the divers material of empirical reality, but the pre-existent realities of which empirical forms are mere shadowy replicas. Accordingly, they were not attained through inductive abstraction, but through a process of mental *maiosis*, i.e., midwifery. The medieval controversy between the "realists," who contended that universals, "generalities," are real entities, and the "nominalists," who considered them *nomina*, conceptual fabrications, marks the decisive clash between the ancient and the modern view, between the divinely pre-established "idea" and what was to become the scientifically developed concept.

Jesus in all his capacities, as Messiah, God's messenger, or as God the Son, or Son of Man, was, unlike the patriarchs, a fully and genuinely individual person; he was for original Christianity a thoroughly real, not a symbolic figure. He was seen to be God's actual descent to man, His very real deed of salvation. Accordingly, Jesus' taking upon himself the expiation of man's sinfulness through his sacrificial death was a real, unique act, which it is believed to be whenever it is repeated in Holy Mass. The potential overabundance of symbolism that was contained in this event has been unfolded only by post-Pauline theologians and thinkers. Up to this very day, Catholic dogma considers Adam and Eve as the actual ancestors of mankind, who hereditarily transmitted their original sin to all later generations. In this Biblical story of the fall of man, so simple and concrete, so strikingly palpable, we see today an account of the intrinsic genesis of man, that is, the rise of consciousness through freedom of choice, the feeling of shame, and labor. But to become aware of this vast symbolism, we needed the accumulated human experience up to Hegel and Heinrich von Kleist.[4] The legend of Parsifal was assembled by Chrétien de Troyes quite naïvely from unknown folklore sources; it was not told as symbolic fiction. But afterwards a symbolic meaning has been gathered from it. The grail, *gradalis*, was originally a precious plate on which venison was served at princely carousals. Only later it was turned into a chalice holding divine grace, and as such it became the goal of a quest.

In contradistinction to such descending symbolism that detaches itself for the interpreting mind from a religious, mythical, or historical reality, *ascending* symbolism is a new creation entirely, springing from artistic imagination. Here, no external, pre-existent material is furnished to the artist; no longer is he guided by cultic patterns. He is free to create images which, though being unique, singular forms, imply something commonly human.* In such works the symbol reaches the stage of consummate representation. To be sure, even in such creations the symbol is not completely divested of its sign quality, for they too are intended to convey a message, they too signify something to somebody. But the strained care that such work of free imagination requires, the growing awareness of artistic means, the artistic consciousness and conscience which it has developed, all this keeps the artist's attention focused on the effort to render his vision with utmost preciseness, to such a degree that the communicative purpose is wholly absorbed by the task of representation. The addressee of the message has become an ideal respondent, a postulate, an inner figure, of the artist: the demand of the artist's vision shapes him so that he almost belongs within the work itself.**

* Wherever modern authors, as for instance Gide, Thomas Mann, Giraudoux, Anouilh, Sartre, use Biblical or mythical motifs to elucidate problems of our age, they do so in a completely independent manner. To them these motifs are no longer a true superior reality to be followed, but raw material like any other from which they build their symbols.
** Music is a language of its own, it is the complex articulation of inarticulate sound. The articulation consists in the differentiation of pitch, the rhythmical division of differentiated pitch, i.e., of tones, and the interplay of the different grades of pitch and their sequences. While even the simplest word carries a meaning in that it is a sign designating something beyond itself, the simplest unit of music, the tone, has in itself no meaning, it receives a meaning only through a sequence or group of tones. A word, therefore, is itself a symbol, a tone becomes a symbol only within its sequence or group. The special, dynamic nature of the musical symbol has been most lucidly described by Victor Zuckerkandl: "The key to understanding the processes that made the tones of this melody a melody at all, a piece of music, we found not in the relation of the tones to any particular feeling, but in the relation of the tone e to the tone d. That the dynamic qualities of tone . . . have nothing to do with the expression of feeling, or with the expression of anything whatsoever, follows from the mere fact that they clearly appear even where absolutely nothing is meant to be expressed or stated, namely, when a scale is played. . . . The word and its meaning are independent things. *Here* is the word—a complex of sounds or signs; *there* is what it means. The two are separable; each exists by itself, the word without the thing, the thing without the word. The same thing is designated in different languages by different words. . . . The tone and its meaning, on the other hand, are connected in a far more intimate way. The acoustical event and its musical meaning are in no sense two independent

VI

Ascending symbolism, having originated in profane art, starts from a fully and purely secular plane of situations and destinies which have no factual, but only vicarious reality, which are created for the very purpose of vicarious representation. Inversely, what makes a wholly devised image into a work of art is precisely its quality of symbolic representation. Only when we feel that a story tells us more than just some peculiar happening, that it shows us through the singular story a generally human or epochal condition, when, by its piercing vividness, it touches the human core in us; only when a picture, even a portrait, reaches through the individual form into a conception of the structure of the phenomenal world*
—only then do these images attain to the realm of art.

This in itself implies another, an ultimate degree of symbolism

---

phenomena, existing by themselves. They cannot be imagined separate. To be sure, it is possible to imagine a tone that means nothing, that is simply an acoustical phenomenon; but it is impossible to imagine the musical meaning of a tone, its dynamic quality, without the tone. . . . What tones mean musically is completely one with them, can only be represented through them, exists only in them . . . tones must themselves create what they mean. Hence, it is possible to translate from one language into another, but not from one music into another—for example from Western into Chinese music. . . . Tones too indicate, *point to* something. The meaning of a tone, however, lies not in what it points to but *in the pointing itself*; more precisely, in the different way, in the individual gesture, with which each tone points toward the same place. The meaning is not the thing indicated but the manner of indicating. . . . Words lead away from themselves, but tones lead into themselves. . . . Tones . . . have completely absorbed their meaning into themselves and discharge it upon the hearer directly in their sound." (*Sound and Symbol*, trans. from the German by Willard R. Trask [Bollingen Series XLIV; New York, Pantheon Books, 1956], p. 56.) So while the musical symbol appears to be identical with the act of pointing, or, more precisely, with pointing in action, while it is thus a signifying per se and *in perpetuo*, it still can reach, in the strictly organized "composition" of a fugue, a sonata, or a symphony, a peculiar kind of image, an image of pure form as it were. The dynamism coincides with the simultaneity of perfected wholeness.

* This quality also makes works of cultic representation into works of art. Indeed, insofar as they achieve in their cultic depiction a fresh revelation of the phenomenal form, just so far do they too gain the stage of full representation.

that goes beyond mere representation. For truly artistic representation is not possible without an inherent dynamic quality, which is a drive toward the unknown, the hitherto unseen and unexpressed. Whatever moves us in a work of art, the overwhelming surprise of a suprarational, "imagical" revelation, the intensity and authenticity of vision, the penetration beyond the surface aspects of our life, whatever carries us along with it and kindles in us a feeling of human communion—all this is due to the vital power of the artist to experience reality immediately, spontaneously, and that means, to discover new reality. Inasmuch as artistic representation is not just *mimesis*—the rendering of an already patent reality—but rather an evocation of a latent, heretofore unseen reality, it carries out in its artistic performance a supra-artistic, a human deed of the greatest consequence: *the creation of a new form of reality*. Such coincidence, indeed identity of the artistic and the human act is the supreme reach of the symbol.

VII

It may, finally, be of some help in clarifying the nature of the symbol to contrast it with other forms of representational imagery: *allegory* and *metaphor*.

The borderlines between allegory and symbol are not always easily discernible, and therefore their difference is frequently blurred in common terminology. The reason for this is that they aim at the same goal from opposite ends. The *symbol* is something concrete and specific that is intended to convey something spiritual or general, either as an indicating sign, i.e., an act of pointing, or as an actual representation in which the dynamic division of the sign is abolished: that which points, that which it points to, and the act of pointing have become one and the same. The Greek word *symballein*, from which "symbol" derives, means "to bring together" or "to come together." The symbolic *sign* brings together, the symbolic *representation* is a coming together, to the point of complete fusion, of the concrete and the spiritual, the specific and the general.

Allegory, conversely, starts from something primarily general

THE NATURE OF THE SYMBOL

and abstract, a purely conceptual entity, which it clothes in a concrete body.* Allegory is a rather late product, it presupposes fully developed reflection, indeed an incipient separation of mind and body. Accordingly, its high period is the Christian era. In a certain respect, Plato's replacing divine personalities by divinified thought-images is the inauguration of allegory; and a further advance in this direction may be seen in the doctrine of Philo of Alexandria, which is a synthesis of Judaism and Stoic, Neoplatonic, and Neopythagorean thinking. To Philo, the hypostases, i.e., the powers mediating between God and man, are attributive faculties of God (as for instance justice, grace, etc.), but at the same time they are real angels. Their head and archangel, the Logos, is God's rational power, His thought and creative word, but simultaneously His "first son," His "shadow," the paraclete in corporeal person. What distinguishes the Platonic and Philonic substitutions from allegory proper is the fact that these incarnations of thought were believed to be real entities, indeed *the* true reality, whereas the figures in a perfected allegory, as for instance Good-will, Faith, Piety, etc. in Bunyan's *Pilgrim's Progress*, are sheer conceptions intended as means of presentation.

Dante's *Divina Commedia* is a historical junction-point of allegory and symbol, and of descending and ascending symbolism. Its design is the structure of the Christian universe, which the indi-

* Related distinctions between allegory and symbol have been made by Goethe and Coleridge. Goethe: "Allegory transforms the phenomenon (*Erscheinung*) into an abstract concept (*Begriff*), the concept into an image, but in such a way that the concept can still be expressed and beheld in the image in a clearly circumscribed and complete form. Symbolism transforms the phenomenon into an idea, the idea into an image, in such a way that the idea remains for ever infinitely active and unreachable in the image and, even if expressed in all languages, still inexpressible" (*Maximen und Reflexionen. Aus dem Nachlass*). "We may speak of true symbolism, when the particular represents the more general, not as a dream, or shadow, but as a living instantaneous revelation of the inscrutable" (*Maximen und Reflexionen. Aus Kunst und Altertum* 1826). Coleridge: Allegory is merely "a translation of abstract notions into a picture language, which is itself nothing but an abstraction from objects of the senses. . . ." A symbol "is characterized by a translucence of the special [the species] in the individual, or of the general [genus] in the special . . . ; above all by the translucence of the eternal through and in the temporal" (*The Statesman's Manual*, quoted by René Wellek and Austin Warren in *Theory of Literature* [New York, 1949], pp. 193ff).

vidual man, Dante, traverses. This dogmatic universe with its infernal, purgatorial, and celestial regions and subregions is a suprahistorical sphere of absolute, pre-existent reality, which is symbolically interpreted down to the minutest details. This is descending symbolism. But Dante, on the other hand, the individual person, wandering through the cosmic zones and arriving at his heavenly haven, represents man with his earthly history which is elaborately displayed in its memorable figures and destinies, and thus an ascending symbolism is built in, encompassed in descending symbolism. Likewise, allegory is included in the picture to serve the universal symbolism, and in some places it actually coincides with the symbol. It can hardly be made out for instance whether Reason is embodied in Vergil, which would be an allegory, or whether the historical person, Vergil, represents reason, which would be a symbol. This example shows how difficult it is sometimes to distinguish allegory and symbol.

The *metaphor* (from Greek *metaphora*, "transference") is neither a sign, nor the representational unity of duality, but paraphrase, parallelism, "simile." Commonly, it is meant to elucidate an abstraction by visualizing it, transferring it into an image—however, not in the manner of allegory, through personifying incarnation, but rather by way of analogy.

Our daily language abounds with such "figurative" uses: words and idioms rendering supravisual circumstances by plain, corporeal images. Expressions of this kind have become elements of our daily linguistic commerce without our being aware any longer that they are metaphors. A transfiguration of bodily images into abstract meanings has been growing in an age-old anonymous process along with the increasing complexity and intellectualization of human life. Its residues are concealed in etymology. Who would still connect "management" with Latin *manus*, "hand"; indeed even "handling" with "hand"? Who would still recognize in the word "demand" the Latin *de-mandare* (i.e., *manum dare*) which means in a physically literal sense "to hand over" (to one's charge); or in "differ" the original *dis-ferre*, "to carry apart"? In idioms—as for instance when we say that something "goes hand in hand" with something else, or that "this has a bearing on that"—the metaphor is of course quite evident.

What poets do is exactly the reverse of the anonymous linguistic process: they transfer the intricate, intellectualized, and spiritualized experience of modern man into imagery, either through comparison and paraphrase or, as in our days, through immediate transmutation, which is implicitly a condensation. A subtle interaction takes place between the flaring image and the experience that kindled it, whereby the image is capable of driving the experience farther, that is, of creating new experience. In such a process of intercreation metaphor and symbol merge.

[1959]

What Is Art?

I

IN AN ESSAY on *The Role of Theory in Aesthetics*,[1] Professor Morris Weitz attempts to demonstrate that theory has no legitimate role in aesthetics and that art is not amenable to any kind of true definition because it "has no set of necessary and sufficient properties" on which to base a definition.

His argument runs as follows:

1) There exists a great variety of definitions or theories of art, but none of them is quite adequate or sufficient: "Even if art has one set of necessary and sufficient properties . . . no aesthetic theory yet proposed has enumerated that set to the satisfaction of all concerned."

2) "As real definitions, these theories are supposed to be factual reports on art. If they are, may we not ask, Are they empirical and open to verification or falsification?"

3) According to Wittgenstein's train of thought from which Weitz derives his scepticism, any concept, theory, or definition, based on common properties is questionable, except logical or mathematical concepts which "are constructed and completely defined," and are therefore "closed concepts." If you look at a group of phenomena denoted by a common name, say games, "you

will not see something that is common to *all*, but similarities, relationships, and a whole series of them at that." This is said to be true particularly of art in which we not only find "no common properties—only strands of similarities," but whose "very expansive, adventurous character," whose "ever-present changes and novel creations" make it especially "logically impossible to ensure any set of defining properties." To "close the concept" is "ludicrous since it forecloses on the very conditions of creativity in the arts."

4) In our use of the term "art," there is no clear distinction between description and evaluation. When we say, "This is a work of art," "the criterion of evaluation . . . is converted into a criterion of recognition. . . . Thus, if one chooses to employ 'art' evaluatively, as many do, so that 'This is a work of art and not (aesthetically) good' makes no sense, he uses 'art' in such a way that he refuses to *call* anything a work of art unless it embodies his criterion of excellence."

From all these premises Professor Weitz concludes that "aesthetic theory is a logically vain attempt to define what cannot be defined, to state the necessary and sufficient properties of that which has no necessary and sufficient properties. . . ." "Art" is an "open concept." "In elucidating [it], certain (paradigm) cases can be given, about which there can be no question as to their being correctly described as 'art' . . . but no exhaustive set of cases can be given . . . for the all-important reason that unforeseeable or novel conditions are always forthcoming or envisageable." All we can do and should do in regard to theories of art is to take them as guides for evaluation, as "serious and argued-for recommendations to concentrate on certain criteria of excellence in art," "debates over the reasons for excellence in art." If used in this aspect, they may teach us "what to look for and how to look at it in art" and to find out "what makes a work of art good."

II

Certainly, Professor Weitz has to be given credit for his reminding professional aestheticians of the fact that their discipline is not a science and that their definitions lack the foolproof exactitude and closedness of logical and mathematical formulas. But then, this may be said of all definitions in whatever field concerning reality and not constructed models. If we insist on mathematical exactitude we may just as well give up any inquiry into the nature of a real entity, indeed any serious verbal communication.

Any real entities or phenomena are to a certain degree fluid and "open," structurally as well as temporally. None of the properties, taken separately, is exclusively their own, none of their "set of properties" exhausts their character, none of such combinations of characteristics is *completely* verifiable. No historical personality, or event, is fully defined by their verifiable data, nor is a social phenomenon by its statistics. As to science, we read in the standard work on biology, *Life* by G. G. Simpson, C. S. Pittendrigh, and I. H. Tiffany:[2] "All organisms are classified into species. All sorts of biologists . . . recognize that a species is a very special sort of thing and one with fundamental significance for the study of life. All biologists think that they have a pretty good idea of what a species is . . . yet for centuries biologists have been battling and baffling each other about the . . . problem . . . to produce a clear, fully satisfactory answer to the question 'What is a species?' . . . It is one of the facts of life that an exact definition of a species applicable without question to all sorts of organisms is inherently impossible. . . . Natural populations are not static things that stay put neatly within the confines of rigid definitions. . . . It is a waste of time to try to agree on one, infallible definition of species." But "it is no waste of time to discuss what species are; on the contrary, that is one of the most important subjects in the whole science of biology." Even in nuclear physics, a perfectly valid definition of a particle will be difficult to obtain, although this entity forms an integral part of modern physical concepts and operations. In regard to verification, we have learned that even practical applicability is no guarantee for the correctness of the picture of reality from which it was derived.

What this situation in the real, the incontestably empirical sciences shows is the precariousness, inherent incompleteness, and insufficient verifiability of *all* definition, or theory, concerned with reality, but, on the other hand, the indispensability of these tentative definitions and theories and the necessity to search relentlessly for an approximative elucidation of such intuitively identified entities that form the elements of our dealings with reality.

The dynamic nature of our world is established by now in all fields. Physical, biological, historical, and sociological entities are no less fluid and subject to change than the artistic ones. In all these domains processes of creativity are involved. Nor are artistic creations as imaginatively free and unconditioned as they are commonly held to be; they are in part determined by the human stage, the problems and the techniques of their particular epochs.

Thus, while the general state of our learning confirms Weitz's (and Wittgenstein's) assertion that any stable, entirely satisfactory definition of real entities and phenomena, and so of art, is impossible, we still, I contend, cannot dispense with the search for approximately comprehensive and valid definitions of anything we are dealing with. The terminological confusion, in our disciplines no less than in our conversation, is staggering, and no discussion can be fruitful unless we make perfectly clear from the outset what exactly we are talking about. So when we go about discussing problems of art seriously, this imposes on us the duty to state, be it ever so tentatively and transitorily, what we understand by the term "art." Just as biologists are not satisfied with their vague feeling and consensus concerning the nature of a species, but keep trying descriptively to elucidate this common feeling, so, in dealing with art, we should not give up seeking a clarification of what art really is. If we carefully take account of the artistic achievements and experiences up to our time, we may even reach a less than personally or doctrinally subjective, but a merely epochally subjective, conception; that is to say, a concept that, by assembling the principal features of art as developed up to the present stage, may claim an approximate general validity *as of today*. If we succeed in making use of all the artis-

tic material, all individual and group efforts up to now, such a
concept should be more inclusive than any previous concept. As
to verifiability, we shall see that there exist certain artistic properties that are no less verifiable and documentable than any relevant historical event or personality, all of which are to some degree
liable to interpretation.

III

Let us first test the conclusiveness of Weitz's argument on
three points. The first one refers to Wittgenstein's "Investigations"
which we cannot consider at length in our context; I confine
myself to Weitz's citation. Wittgenstein is quoted as saying with
respect to games: "What we find are no necessary and sufficient
properties, only 'a complicated network of similarities overlapping
and crisscrossing' such that we can say of games that they form
a family with family resemblances and no common trait." "The
problem of the nature of art," Professor Weitz concludes, "is
like that of the nature of games. . . . If we actually look and see
what it is that we call 'art,' we will also find no common properties
—only strands of similarities."

Now family resemblances, being genotypical, not phenotypical
similarities, are genuinely common traits: they spring from common
genes and traditions. That they do not all of them visibly pertain
to all members of the family does not detract from their being
common traits and belonging to a hereditary group essence. Art
is not easily comparable to a family, since its "members" are not
organically grown beings, but works, "artifacts," achievements,
products of consciously controlled efforts. What links them together are impulses or aims, not just origins. And if there exist,
according to Weitz, "certain (paradigm) cases . . . about which
there can be no question as to their being correctly described
as 'art,'" paradigm cases may be found which, unlike members
of a family, and due to the work character of art, assemble all
detectable features of artistic endeavor up to the present time
and may very well serve as natural models by which to demon-

strate the "set of properties" of art. If there exist "paradigm cases," this means that there exists a definite consensus of feeling as to their being true works of art. And if there exists such a consensus of feeling (as in the case of the biological species) we may, indeed we must, ask ourselves what is the substratum of this feeling. It should be possible to express in words what makes us feel that, unquestionably, these works are art.

IV

Professor Weitz wants aesthetic theories to be considered not as explanations of the nature of art, which, to him, is an impossible task, but as "recommendations to concentrate on certain criteria of excellence in art," teaching us "what to look for and how to look at it in art." This in fact is a *petitio principii*. How can we determine what is excellent in art as long as we have not established a clear notion of the distinct character of art? Wherefrom can we derive the criteria of artistic excellence if not from the artistic performance itself? "Emotional depth," "profound truths," "natural beauty," "exactitude"—any of these can also be found elsewhere, in personal utterances and acts, in nature, in science; none of them affords a specifically artistic criterion; none of them taken by themselves, nor all of them taken together, "makes a work of art good."

The attempt to establish specifically artistic values, a distinctive artistic excellence, inevitably refers us back to the recognition of the specific nature of art. Here is where a third point in Weitz's argument comes in which appears to me questionable.

Weitz maintains that in art any possible criterion of recognition is basically a criterion of evaluation. "In every instance of 'This is a work of art' (used to praise), what happens is that the criterion of evaluation. . . is converted into a criterion of recognition. . . . 'This is a work of art' implies 'This has P,' where P is some chosen art-making property."

However, the relation between recognition and evaluation in art is not as simple as it is presented by Weitz. Art is, first of all, *a*

form of human activity. When we ask, "What distinguishes this
particular human activity from other human activities, as f.i.,
craftwork, science, philosophy, all of which are neighboring fields
and have certain features in common with art?" when we try
contrastingly to single out the distinguishing features of this activity "art," what we are seeking is clearly a criterion of recognition,
which does not lend itself to being confounded with evaluation.
Such differentiation is in no way more susceptible to substantial
praise than, say, the distinction between economy and politics.

To be sure, any recognition of the specific character of a human
activity entails potential evaluation. This is true of science, or
diplomacy, or business no less than of art. An act of diplomacy,
a piece of scientific research, is good or bad according to the degree
in which it fills the necessary requirements of the specific task of
diplomacy or science. The more it is diplomacy, or science, the
better it is. When we say of a man "He is a real businessman,"
we mean by this "He is a good businessman." Any human activity
is liable to evaluation inasmuch as it is a conscious act and effort
toward a specific end. A creature or object of nature, being a piece
of sheer existence, f.i., a tree or a tiger, cannot be more or less of
a tree or a tiger. But any human being in his capacity as a consciously willing and acting person is always more or less of what
he intends to be or to do. In his activity a discrepancy inheres
between end and fulfillment. The degree of achievement, of
approximation to his specific task, invites evaluation. But clearly,
it is not evaluation that clarifies the nature of a specific activity.
On the contrary, evaluation is based on the greater or lesser
approximation to a specifiic task. This is true of art no less than
of all other activities. Evaluation cannot help us to a better understanding of the nature of art. Evaluation *derives* from the understanding and the description of the specific nature of art.

V

Let me finally venture a *definition of art,* as precise and comprehensive as possible.

Two requirements have to be observed for achieving a valid definition: (1) The definition has to be *strictly specific;* that is to say, the combination of properties of the entity to be described has to be distinctively and exclusively its own, shared by no other entity. (2) Distinctions have to be made *by centers, not by boundaries** because there is no real entity without fluid boundaries. If we try to establish peripheral distinctions we arrive at conclusions such as those of a modern historian who in an essay dealing with *Europe in the Middle Ages* ended up by stating that there is no Europe and there are no Middle Ages, since no exact confines can be determined for either sphere of existence. Europe passes over into Asia and Africa, and no rigorously fixed data can be established for the beginning and the end of the medieval period. And yet, to deny on such grounds the real validity of these two concepts is equivalent to denying the existence of any discrete physical body which also peripherally mingles with its surroundings.

As has been stated before, art is primarily a special kind of *human activity* that like other human activities evolved historically into a separate, distinct sphere and manner of work. In the course of its evolution it developed an ever-growing *body of work results,* i.e., works of art, a residue that we also have come to denote by the name of "art." Finally, in more recent times when in all artistic fields a commercialization and mechanization of production, a mass production set in, "art" assumed a more restricted sense, differentiating a *special kind of creation* unaffected by mechanization and commercialization from the products and practices of conventional fabrication. It is this restrictive sense of art which inevitably carries a value connotation and invites that confusion of recognition and evaluation which is said to invalidate all definition of art. As will be shown, however, even in this sense a neatly descriptive identification of art is possible.

* This is the error underlying all applications of strict logicity to objects of reality and so that of Wittgenstein. Cf. *Philosophical Investigations* (New York, 1953), pp. 68–70, 77.

VI

When we first contemplate art as a specific human activity, the
very fact of its being an activity implies a sharp distinction between natural and artistic phenomena. The word *ars* itself derives
from an Aryan root "ar," signifying "join, put together," connected
with Greek *artizein*, "to prepare" and *arariskein*, "to put together"
and means originally a "fitting, adjusting, joining."[3] It has commonly been used in contradistinction to nature. Therefore, sentences like those quoted by Weitz—"X is a work of art and . . .
was made by no one" or ". . . was made by accident when he
spilled the paint on the canvas"—are under no circumstances
"sensible and capable of being true." A piece of driftwood or a
sea shell, be it ever so characteristically depictive or charming,
may remind us of art, but is never itself a piece of art, because it
is not made by man through a consciously controlled impulse
or effort.* This is a basic premise of all art.

As an activity, art borders on other human activities with which
it has, in part or as a whole, certain traits in common: craftwork,
science, philosophy, historiography. Painting, sculpture, architecture are connected with handicraft (indeed technology), and
even music and literary work of all kinds are partly constituted by
techniques. With science, art has in common the exploratory

---

* To be sure, a work of art is never completely a result of conscious effort.
A considerable part of creation, larger or lesser in different artists, goes on in
the unconscious. Picasso said of his manner of producing, "A picture comes to
me from miles away: who is to say from how far away I sensed it, saw it,
painted it . . . how can anyone enter into my dreams, my instincts, my thoughts
which have taken a long time to mature and to come out into the daylight,
and above all grasp from them what I have been about—perhaps against my
own will?" (from Alfred Barr, *Picasso*, Museum of Modern Art, New York
1946). Rilke's most rarefied, analytically sensitive poetry erupted precipitately
from a long, almost vegetative process of unconscious or half-conscious formation, of which he had hardly any command. And yet, there was, in Picasso, an
"I" to sense, see and paint, and be about something, however hidden in the
dark of the unconscious or subconscious, and set against his conscious will;
there was a conscious control of what he has found. There was, in Rilke, a most
subtly discerning mind residing deep below the surface of the consciousness
and directing the structure of the poem. Even in such cases—and there are
others where the conscious effort is foremost, as in Flaubert's and Cézanne's
artistry—what is taking place is guided creation, not accidental growth.

character of its work, the intent of ever expanding cognition; with philosophy, its conceptual nature, its concern with ideas; with historiography, its descriptive element. Art differs, however, from every one of these activities by specific variances of mode of these common properties, by its special combination of properties, and by additional properties which are exclusively its own.

Everybody will agree that the aim and activity of science consists in the acquisition of ever wider and deeper knowledge of the nature of reality. The same can be said of philosophy. And it is no less true of art, only here this is not so easily recognizable because another property of art tends to conceal it.

The manner of such exploration varies in the three activities. *Science* deals with a directly apparent, unmediated, surface form of reality, i.e., factuality. It deals with it collectively; the advances made by single geniuses notwithstanding, it has come to be increasingly collective work, teamwork on a grand scale, where the individual works on an ever narrower, ever more specialistic segment of factual reality and is tied up with a rank and file of students of collectively, quasi-objectively developed sets of problems. Accordingly, the kind of knowledge produced by science is always on the move, advancing on a wide and uncontrolled front, always fragmentary, provisional, open to correction and even replacement; it is never at rest, it never reaches an even transient state of completion. *Philosophy* was in previous periods of less developed empirical learning the attempt to integrate the whole of immediate reality, to grasp it by rational means. The immense expansion of the sciences reduced it to the task of investigating the epistemological, ontological, logico-linguistic foundations or premises of knowledge. In general, its analytical explorations have by now assumed a scientistic, if scientific character. But even where an attempt has been made by recent philosophers, as f.i., Whitehead, to search for the links, and in this way integrate the whole of present reality as presented by the findings of the modern sciences, this attempted integration has been concerned with immediate, factual reality which was intended to be grasped by strictly rational means.

Art too is involved in the exploration of reality, the penetration of an ever wider and deeper range and increased complexity of reality, and in this respect it has a demonstrable evolution, just as science has. This is an evolution of the nature and scope of reality rendered, and implicitly of the forms of rendering, the modes of expression. A newly detected reality involves new forms and techniques of expression. "Content" and "form," as it is well established by now, are but two aspects of one and the same thing. New "contents" call for new "forms" of presentation; they are not expressible, they simply do not exist without their new appropriate form. And just as science, through its new findings, broadens and changes the picture of our reality and in this way, as well as through the application of its findings, changes our reality itself, so art, through its reaching into new complexities and levels of reality, extends the scope, and changes the nature, of our consciousness, and by this means of our reality itself.

In science the crucial importance of novelty is quite evident. What else does science seek than additional knowledge, better knowledge, and that is new fact-finding, new knowledge. As far as art is concerned, however, scarcely any explicit attention has been given to the equally essential role which the search for the new plays in it. Here, the search for the new, the impulse toward the new, means even more than additional material, increased profundity and complexity. It implies other properties which we, more or less consciously, sense and admire in any "paradigm" work of art, such as freshness, vitality, vigor, authenticity, expressiveness, precision, truth, and even emotional impact. All such properties and, as we shall see, even more are inherent in that one characteristic of art: its thrusting out into the sphere of the unknown, the hitherto unachieved, "the ground that never a word has trod," as Rilke put it, and we may add, "never a stroke of the brush, or a conventional sound."* For it is this effort to

* The experience of this pioneer quality of art has been expressed by many artists since LUCRETIUS, who writes in his *De Rerum Natura*: "Not that I am unaware how obscure these matters are: but the high hope of renown has

express something heretofore inexpressible, to grasp and to shape something for the first time, it is this *"for the first time"* that gives a work of art its lasting freshness and vitality, its genuineness of language, its convincing vigor, so that ancient works, whose scopes and styles are by now utterly familiar to us and in one way or another left behind by the endeavors of our age, are still fully alive, and we are able to enjoy them as if they were created today. The trace of that ultimate effort that created them persists in them, the longing, the struggle, the suffering, the immediacy of all primal creation. When we feel certain works to be of secondary quality it is because all this is lacking in them; they echo, iterate and imitate the achievements of masters.

---

struck into my heart sweet love of the Muses, thrilled by which now in lively thought I traverse pathless tracts of the Pierides never yet trodden by any foot. I love to approach virgin springs and there to drink; I love to pluck fresh flowers, and to seek an illustrious chaplet for my head from fields whence ere this the Muses have crowned the brows of none: first because my teaching is of high matters, and I proceed to unloose the mind from the close knots of religion; next because the subject is so dark and the lines I write so clear, as I touch all with the Muses' grace" (I, 922–934, trans. by W. H. D. Rouse, Loeb Class. Lib; cf. also IV, 1–5). Other artists felt their frontier venture either as limits or as feats of their strained expression. DANTE: *Divina Commedia, Paradiso XXX*, 31*ff*: "But now my poetic pursuit lagging behind her beauty must halt, as every artist has to at his utmost." ("Ma or convien che mio seguir desista/Piu dietro a sua bellezza poetando/ Come all 'ultimo sua ciascuno artista. . . ."); MILTON in *Paradise Lost* I, 16: "Things unattempted yet in Prose or Rhyme"; GOETHE: "Art is the conveyor of the inexpressible." DÜRER, *On Human Proportion*, III: "For indeed art is hidden in nature; he who can tear it out has it." DEGAS: "There is courage indeed in launching a frontal attack upon the main structure and the main lines of nature . . . art is really a battle." KLEE: "One learns to look behind the façade, to grasp the root of things. One learns to recognize the undercurrents, the antecedents of the visible. One learns to dig down, to uncover. . . ." BECKMANN: "What I want to show in my work is the idea which hides itself behind so-called reality. I am seeking for the bridge which leads from the visible to the invisible, like the famous cabalist who once said: 'If you wish to get hold of the invisible, you must penetrate as deeply as possible into the visible.'" (Quotations of Degas, Klee and Beckmann taken from *Artists on Art*, R. Goldwater and M. Treves, eds., New York, 1949); RIMBAUD, in his *Matinée d'Ivresse* exclaims: "Hourra pour l'oeuvre inouie . . . pour la première fois!" ("Hurrah for the unheard-of work . . . for the first time!"). And STRAVINSKY, in his *Expositions and Developments* declares: ". . . the composition is something entirely new *beyond* what can be called the composer's feelings. . . . A new piece of music *is* a new reality."

VII

It is this drive toward the conquest of the unknown and inexpressible which also makes for the evolutionary and sometimes revolutionary character of artistic activity; which causes the expansion of scope, the growth of complexity, the development of new dimensions, forms and techniques, traceable throughout the history of the arts.

There is a further most important property of art, which derives from the same source. By penetrating into new spheres and dimensions of experience, developing new forms, creating new reality, artists like Masaccio, Giotto, Leonardo, Titian, Rembrandt, the impressionists, Cézanne, Van Gogh, Picasso, or Dante, Shakespeare, Cervantes, Goethe, the romanticists and the symbolists, Flaubert, Proust, Joyce, Kafka, or Monteverdi, Bach, Mozart, Beethoven, Wagner, Stravinsky, Schönberg—to mention only a few of the most decisive figures—such artists did not just indulge in an arbitrary play of their imagination; they were pushed along or guided in a certain direction by the human condition, the stage of perception and experience, and implicitly the techniques of expression, of their specific period; and the new experience of reality, indeed the new reality itself they reached was a reality in the making that lay hidden under the conventions of the epoch. They presented a human condition, they liberated forms and experiences that were to become *the* reality of the next age. That means: whatever they presented was not just this or that individual story, portrait, scenery, phenomenal structure, or combination of sounds; it reflected a human condition in transition. When we admire in a portrait by Titian, Dürer, or Holbein the deep physiognomical grasp of an individual personality, what strikes us is not only the visual elucidation of this specific character, but implicitly the close, meticulous and yet synoptical accuracy of rendering as such, which these Renaissance masters have achieved. Here, likeness represents the last frontier of visual exploration. Again, when we turn from these portraits to portraits by, say, Van Gogh or

Kokoschka, we are confronted not merely with a peculiarly sharpened and intensified characterization of the specific person depicted, but with a new structural and psychic depth of appearance which has been revealed by these artists. New phenomenal vistas have been opened up, uncovering the new reality of our age. The same applies to the progression from a scene or scenery presented by a Renaissance painter to one by Rembrandt, by Claude Lorrain, and by Constable, and further on one by Turner, by Monet, and by Cézanne. What a modern "non-objective" painting expresses in its line-and-color construction is not just this particular formal combination, but implicitly phenomenal relationships of a more general order. In literature we need only trace the corresponding development from the baroque novel to those of Flaubert, Proust, and Joyce; in music the steps from Haydn to Beethoven, to Wagner, to Stravinsky and Schönberg. By virtue of their frontier character, of their acts of revelation, these works bear a generally human significance. Their presenting in, and effecting through a singular selective unit a coherency of the broadest import establishes their *symbolic* quality. Thus the special creativity of art implies an inherently symbolic quality.

It is this symbolic quality which distinguishes art from science. Both activities have in common the search for the nature of reality, their disclosure of new reality. But the manner of this search and the dimension of reality it reaches are characteristically different in one and the other activity. While science deals with factual reality and approaches it in a direct, immediate way, art proceeds in a symbolic or metaphoric fashion. It presents single individual entities carrying a general purport. The abstraction and generalization of science is extrinsic, it seeks to arrive at strict or statistical laws which call for mathematical expression; the abstraction and generalization of art is intrinsic, it shows macrocosmic through microcosmic coherences, and its form of expression is therefore symbolically or metaphorically variable. It is in the nature of this kind of endeavor, which is aiming at the presentation of a whole, that each work of art is complete in itself, or supposed to be complete in itself, and that it is, accordingly, an individual work. This characteristic of art, that each of its works is complete in itself, has blurred the recognition of the fact that art also has a definite evolution.

VIII

The disposition of art to present a whole (reflecting a broader whole) and to advance by works, every one of which is a whole in itself, entails, indeed demands, that strict organization and integration that constitutes completeness. It is the property usually referred to as "organicism" or "perfection" or "harmonization," certainly the one which has the longest record of recognition, having been established by Aristotle. It has been remarked, and so by Weitz himself, that "Organicism . . . can be applied to *any* causal unity in the natural world as well as to art," which is said to eliminate it as a specific characteristic of art. But what this objection ignores is the premise that art is a *human activity* and that therefore the artistic organicity is the result of *work*, not of natural growth—which carries other essential differences between natural and artistic organicity.

In contemplating this artistic property of organic wholeness we touch upon the concept of *beauty*, which is used widely in a rather vague and indiscriminate sense. The clarification of this problematic term would require a separate study. In our context, I must confine myself to a few indications.

First of all, "beauty," in common usage, is by no means plainly identical with "harmony." As far as natural objects are concerned, the term "beauty" may sometimes designate "harmony"—f.i., when we contemplate a "beautiful" body—but in other cases it may mean just the opposite: extreme *dis*-harmony as in the romantic admiration of the savage contrastfulness, boundless expressiveness and elemental grandeur of an excessive landscape or natural scene (as a thunderstorm). Anything colorful, anything sensational, strongly evocative is often called "beautiful."

The same fluctuation of meaning prevails in people's notion of "beauty" in art. Certain works of art strike us as "beautiful" because of their vigorous expressiveness, their sensitive precision of expression; others because of their ingeniously consummate integration, "harmonization" of a rich variety of elements. To be sure, our feelings of "beauty" will be most intense when a work combines both qualities. In speaking of "harmony," it is important to bear in mind that this concept is by no means static; it has, in our modern experience, by far exceeded the meaning of a balance of simple proportions such as the classical ones. Art has, in the course of its evolution through gradual expansion of scope, in width and in depth, and inclusion of more and more, and ever more diverse elements of reality, broken through the bounds of traditional "harmony." The breaking of these bounds, the dissolution of the old "harmony," necessarily meant disharmony, overemphasis of newly discovered elements at the expense of other elements of reality; and these new disparities and dissonances had to be reintegrated in a wider and deeper, more comprehensive "harmony." Indeed the whole evolution of art may be seen as consisting in an alternate progression from dissolution of a worn harmony to formation of a new, more comprehensive harmony, i.e., in ever recurring stages of expressiveness and integration. Therefore, the prevalence of expressiveness over integration in certain works of art appears to be an intermediary stage on the way to the formation of a new, more comprehensive harmony.

Philosophy, inasmuch as it also attempts interpretatively to synthesize the reality of our world into an integrated whole, is distinguished from art by its rational dealing with immediate reality. Art operates extra- or suprarationally, not by argument, but by vision. What it wants to achieve is rendering a whole through visional simultaneity. Even in the dynamic arts, those compelled to representation by flux, such as drama, epics, poetry, music, the ultimate goal is the grasp of an entity as a visional whole. In music too, in spite of its apparently purely motional character, the final, intrinsic intent is the visional (not visual) unity of a structural piece. This visional character of art is implicated in its symbolic or metaphoric quality.

What distinguishes art from *historiography*, where the two

border on each other, is obviously again its symbolic or metaphoric quality with all that it implies. And it is the same symbolic quality, particularly its source, the conquest of new reality, that marks the difference between art and *craftwork*. Craftwork, good or bad, is routine work adapted to practical uses, and whatever innovation it carries is purely technical. To be sure, technology and techniques also change our reality, but these changes are just the external exploitation of the findings of science and the ventures of art. They lack all cognitive purport.*

IX

With the distinction between art and craftwork we have reached a point where the boundaries between description and evaluation seem to become fluid. We have up to now considered art as a human activity clearly and describably differing from other human activities. However, as has been stated before, the mechanization and commercialization that has seized upon all human activities has given rise to a distinction between art and craftwork *within* the domain of activity that is commonly regarded as art; that is to say, a distinction between art in an uncompromisingly strict and restricted sense, and the routine production of novels, plays, poetry, paintings, or music, the best-sellers and "hits" that flood the markets.

A concept of art derived from such distinction alone would indeed be most precarious, and in this case the suspicion that the criterion of recognition is actually a criterion of evaluation would be entirely justified. Few people who have acquired some familiarity with art will deny that Joyce's *Ulysses* is a work of art, but a

* *Architecture*, due to its regard for practical uses, is particularly involved in craftwork and technology, but within these limitations all that has been said here of the properties of art also obtains of the art of building (cf., in this connection, Erwin Panofsky's admirable study on *Gothic Architecture and Scholasticism*). In previous, non-technological ages (and in rare cases of modern artistic handicraft), a piece of craftwork could also be a work of art inasmuch as it was (or is) individual work, and the dictate of practical uses and arbitrary commercial fashions did not so strongly prevail over the formal expression of a style, or idea, of life.

story of Mickey Spillane is not. But even in such a case of striking evidence this evidence cannot easily be substantiated without applying a criterion of art that has been established beforehand on more solid grounds than just a vague feeling of "excellence" whatever that may be interpreted to be.

In the present investigation I have attempted to show that an approximately reliable recognition of the nature of art is very well possible when we consider art as a human activity characteristically different from other human activities. We have found that the special creativity of art consists in the discovery, and that means implicitly creation of new reality, reality that has not been raised into our consciousness before, that expressing something for the first time is a crucial feature of art which appears to be the primary source of other qualities, less strictly identifiable and rather felt than clearly recognized, such as vitality, authenticity, precision, truth, etc.; that art reaches the new reality in a suprarational, visional, metaphoric way, and that accordingly the reality it presents is a microcosmic whole reflecting a macrocosmic whole—which establishes the symbolic quality of art; that this very same manner of proceeding and presentation calls for another crucial property of art: its aiming at organic wholeness, integration, "harmonization" of an ever more complex and discordant reality. In those works of art which, by venturing into new spheres and dimensions of reality, break down worn, conventional harmonies, the emphasis is on intensity, vigor and accuracy of expression. Such works are the pioneers, preparing the path for other works which attempt to rally these gains in a new, more broadly balanced whole and to achieve completion and perfection on a larger scale. The correspondences and convergences of parts, elements, and symbols which constitute such a work of art are amenable to accurate demonstration, which means a, however limited, verification of art.

Equipped with these distinctions we should be able to safely recognize a true work of art and distinguish it from current and futile craftwork even within the domain of artistic performance.

As a summary definition of art I propose the following: Art is a human activity which explores, and hereby creates, new reality in a suprarational, visional manner and presents it symbolically or metaphorically, as a microcosmic whole signifying a macrocosmic whole.

[1958]

Art and History

ARTISTS AND art historians have a long-standing quarrel—inevitable and irreconcilable to this extent: that it is a quarrel between two extremes.

Art historians take the history of art's forms and motifs—that is, of styles and iconography—to be their proper subject; of this the history of artists is a component. They have become adept at making the subtlest distinctions within periods, places, and ateliers; upon this and the flair that results from it they base their connoisseurship, their *expertise* in the attribution and authenticity of a work of art. In taking this outlook, they are from the very first led away from the consideration of a work of art *qua* art— that is to say, the evaluation of artistic quality seems to them secondary. Insofar as they bother at all about artistic values these enter in, for them, not directly upon the sheer observation of a work of art, but detour-wise on the recognition of authenticity.

The artists take the opposite stand and often go so far as to deny that art historians have any sense whatever of artistic quality. Artists in looking at a work of art have in mind solely the requirements, the experiences and purposes of their own work, and what is important to them is what inspires them, what offers them the most intense stimulus and incitement. Nothing comes between

109

their professional eye and what they are looking at; they see there not just the completed form but, behind it simultaneously, the creative process, the hand, the eye, the impulse of the creator, the effort that gave rise to this form. They can tell in a flash what has life and what has none, what is imaginative and what is routine. And they maintain that this quick glance that regards artistic quality alone is indeed a glance to the quick, and a far surer criterion even of the authenticity of a work than the minutiae of historical research.

From this they go on to draw a radical conclusion which, though stemming from very different grounds, coincides nonetheless with a common and deep-rooted opinion: that so far as artistic quality is concerned, it makes no difference where or when a work of art originated; that the history, the development of art has nothing to do with the artistic quality of a given work, indeed that properly speaking there is no such thing as the development of art. The artistic quality of a work is, they claim, independent of time and place; the "Venus of Milo" and Manet's "Olympia" bespeak quality in the same way, and to gauge it one can, indeed one should, entirely ignore the historical and cultural meaning of the work.

Well, this much is incontestible, that while scholarly work is always incomplete, always in progress, always open to being expanded, corrected, indeed supplanted by subsequent knowledge, the work of art is forever contained and complete in itself, always sufficient in and unto itself. Even though in one period or another its effect may be greater or less, and in any case different, nothing that is done later can take away its validity, can touch its artistic quality, which is the quality of a consciously created whole, a unity, manifold in its aliveness, multiple in its relations and interrelations. With respect to this fundamental characteristic of art there exists, then, no difference of time and place, and to this degree certainly the criterion of art is independent of historical development and cultural milieu.

But artistic quality has another ingredient, one that I hold to be quite as essential to it, and this, precisely, has to do with historical development, with the development of human consciousness and outlook, with which art is in the highest degree involved.

Art is one of man's forms of expression: *what* is expressed—consciously or unconsciously—is the *condition humaine* as of a given moment; *how* it is expressed is the result of an ineluctably personal mode of grasping that condition. What is seen and how it is seen cannot be separated, but are one and the same. Art's statement does not simply consist, as is so often thought, in an especially complete, especially successful reproduction of something that has already been seen, but rather in the creation of something not yet generally, not yet clearly seen, something that is only drawing near, potential, pre-existent in the undercurrent of the period, and that art brings to actuality, to existence. This "creation" of an existent out of the latent—precisely this is the creative process; and the very things that often appear to be arbitrary fantasy or mere subjective representation will prove a thrust of discovery.

All great art brings a new reality into being, a new world that it teaches us to see. It widens and deepens the space of our vision, our consciousness. Certainly this is not always accomplished by a single powerful advance—as in the case of Nicolò Pisano, Giotto, the Van Eycks, Breughel, Rembrandt, Cézanne; often it is done by many gradual steps and variations, many different flashes of insight on the part of many different artists, very personal conceptions that only later, in retrospect, become recognizable as having contributed to a total transformation of our world. Among artists there are those who are the explorers, the experimenters, the conquerors, who make the decisive breakthroughs; there are others who occupy the territory that has been won, who cultivate it, make it fruitful, who work out in an infinite variety of detail what has as yet been only broadly conceived. But in them too the element of innovation, of transformation of seeing, transformation of reality, is an integral constituent of their artistry and of the artistic quality of their works.

But what is it that gives life to a work of art, what makes the difference between it and some conventional product, technically excellent as it may be? Simply that immediacy of perception which is only possible when something is seen *for the first time.* The man who merely follows or exploits tradition is repeating in a superficial degenerated form what the masters before him had exerted their utmost effort and inmost potentiality to generate. Repetition necessarily becomes mechanical, lazy, shallow, tedious, falls behind what had formerly been initial, origin-al. The spurt of life is always happening for the first time. The creative impulse acts right at the forefront of the inexpressible, to wrench form out of what has hitherto been formless. Where tradition works upon him, the true artist extends and transforms it. And a work where we feel that pulse, that impulse toward the initial and initiatory, with its self-surpassing labor, its self-surrender and self-forgetfulness, is the only work that can still move us in a world that has far outgrown the one from which it emerged.

Classical periods, those periods of art enjoying solutions, that is, having reached a perfection of forms, a resting balance of elements, have no immediacy for us today, they are rather remote from our present feelings. Ours is a world of deepest cleavage and desperate perplexity; we are in the midst of a struggle for new and vaster unities. What particularly concerns us are dynamic periods and personalities, situations of open problems and passionate conflicts. The primeval and early Christian periods are closer to us than is fifth-century Greece, Greco and Grünewald closer than Raphael, Breughel and Rembrandt closer than Holbein. And yet these latter have as much validity for us as the former, and when we find a quiet moment in which to immerse ourselves in their work, we feel in it, right now, today, behind the layers of its somehow worn-out glory, that living source and process of all art's first-time conquests; whereas the hundreds of avant-garde epigones who keep filling innumerable art exhibitions with their own little Picassos, Kandinskys, and Jackson Pollocks, strike us as belonging more to the past than the artisans of the Middle

Ages. Whatever was once truly living—truly, that is, newly creative —that, and that alone, remains alive forever.

Innovation, then, is an indispensable element of artistic quality. Artists, for their part, may well maintain that one can see this element of innovation right away in the liveliness of a work, without having to look for any specific content of innovation in it. The personal freshness of a painter's brushstroke, the peculiarity of his color scale, the whole structural conception of his picture, would in themselves evidence the newness of his seeing. Up to a point this is true, where relatively static cultures are concerned, cultures so bound by tradition that they have been "arrested," as Toynbee describes them, in a specific stage of development. The art of "primitive" peoples, for example, is tribal art; the individual is scarcely developed as such, and remains anonymous. Certain basic forms are repeated over and over, but this is a kind of repetition very different from the one that bores us in modern works. Here art is not yet a specialized form of expression, it is a magic function of life, directly nourished by existential fears and visions. What speaks out of it, what is expressed in it, is essentially the tribe and its relations to the powers of nature, and in each person who gives shape to its conjurations and its visages, the tribes' arousal is reproduced afresh. So repetition in this instance is kept from becoming mechanical; on the contrary, here repetition has an enhancing, literally entrancing effect, and may indeed even give the impetus for individual transcendence of the common ritual bonds. Thus in these essentially still unhistorical ways of life, in the eternal present in which that life is lived, the customary, the constant, becomes a new thing each moment, and as there is no separation between what is initial and what is traditional, most of the artistic quality of these works can be gathered from their sensible form. Even here not all, but most. The remainder is easier to discern in the great cultures of the East.

These great cultures, too—Chinese, Persian, Indian, Japanese, and so on—are relatively stable and undynamic by comparison with our modern West. They too were very much bound by tradition, and until recently, before the whole earth had been inundated by the technological civilization of the West, remained in a phase of human development where the whole of life is conditioned by a religious attitude. In their art, however, developments and alternate periods are perceivable, though these are slower and extended over greater stretches of time than in the West. There are times of growth and flowering, and times of decline, when forms become schematized, mechanized, petrified: the art of Chinese bronzes, for example, flowering in the Shang and late Chou period (1523–1027 B.C. and 473–256 B.C.), or the curve of Chinese painting's development from the preparatory pre-T'ang era (up to A.D. 618) to the high point of T'ang-Sung (from 618 to A.D. 1278) and the falling off in the Yüan and Ming–Ching eras (from 1278 on); in Islamic miniature painting those centers of its mature style—the Abbasids' in Bagdad, the Fatimids' in Cairo, those of the Mongol princes in Tabriz, Samarkand, Herat; the Shaybanids' in Bukhara, and especially that of Shah Abbas the Great in Ispahan. In many instances—in China, Japan, Persia—stylistic advances are already connected with specific artists whose names and works have come down to us.

Certainly here too, in the art of these great cultures, a work's artistic quality will to some extent be directly apparent in the freshness and genuine energy of its inspiration. But whereas what strikes us in "primitive" art is predominately its magnificent expressive power, oriental art has attained the maturity of artistic equilibrium. The unity of its creations extends not only into the dimensions of our senses, however, but beyond them into a peculiarly spiritual dimension; and in the religious stages of human development—medieval Europe no less than the oriental cultures in general—the role of symbol, the pervasion of every single form by symbol, the specific treatment, interpretation, integration of this symbolism, contributes something essential to the artistic quality of a work. It is hard to see how Chinese painting in particular can be fully evaluated by a Westerner without knowledge of Taoist and Buddhist teachings, without the sense of a Chinese person's attitude—so basically different from our own—toward nature and his place in nature.

But in our dynamic West it is an utter impossibility to grasp a work's artistic quality without some sort of historical premise. Here the development of man's consciousness and of his view of the world has run its full course up to the present, and in this process of conceptual and actual transformation the arts have played a considerable part. In the West the arts have evolved into a special sphere, an autonomous secular mode of expression distinct from life in general. The specifically artistic or aesthetic function—to bring to completion an everlasting artistic integrality—and the generally human function of art—here this can only mean an evolutionally dynamic function: to bring to birth an ever-changing human reality—these two functions of art, which are in fact indissolubly bound together, seem, in our era, to be breaking apart. The thing is to see them as one again.

In Cézanne, the two were still united: the heightening of pictorial form, the deepening of vision. Afterward we find a painter like Matisse primarily occupied with pictorial form, and his opposite, Picasso, entirely absorbed in the exploration of new structural relations within the visible. For Picasso the conquest of a new visual reality is sometimes more urgent than any aesthetic perfection, for which, hard pressed by the force of his exploratory impetus, he has little time to spare. To reproach him with this occasional shortcoming as some painters do is sheer pedantry. His advances are formidable: not only new visual areas and dimensions, but also his creation of a new sort of symbolism, begotten of the horrors of our time. His very mistakes have been of far-reaching consequence.

So deep a cleavage makes plain the twofoldness, or rather the double aspect, of the artist's task. It shows how impossible it is, in evaluating an occidental work of art, to exclude its evolutional quality, its substantive stylistic advance. We need only imagine Titian or Dürer, both of them pictorially very wise artists, in front of paintings of Van Gogh or Picasso to gauge how much of the human contents of our epoch is involved in these works, and how much one has to know, if one is to grasp these works, about the happenings—factual, spiritual, and visual—of the past century.

But the reverse experiment is also instructive. The art of fifth-century Greece, like that of the High Renaissance, does not, as I indicated above, quite come home to our present-day feelings, and precisely for people of lively sensibility more problematical works will have greater appeal—not just because these are closer to the world we live in, but also because outworn stereotype aesthetics have made classic art seem insipid to us, have dulled our perception of it. If we are fully to recover the beauty of these forms, then the directness, the responsiveness of our vision must be restored, and this can happen only if we try to relive the birth of this beauty, its emergence from the impediments and entanglements of the preceding era, only if we learn to recognize it as the unique outcome—vitally enduring in this very uniqueness of its time and place—of a struggle of human consciousness. Its human meaning must help us fully to repossess its aesthetic meaning.

If then, as it seems to me, the artists are not entirely justified in contending that we require no presuppositions whatever to evaluate artistic quality, it must on the other hand be admitted that the art historians' outlook does need broadening—in the artists' direction just as much as in directions already pointed out by men of imagination like Wölfflin, Dvořak, Worringer, and Kenneth Clark. Expertise as to styles and attributions is not enough, nor is iconography, the genealogical study of motifs and symbols, however valuable and fruitful it certainly is. A work of art is after all a work of art, and cannot be treated in quite the same manner as any historical document or instrument. To grasp the specifically artistic quality of a work in all its complexity takes an ever alert and all-responsive eye.

As this essay tries to show, artistic quality includes not only the element of a work's timeless perfection, in and of itself, within its own structure of motifs and relations, but also that other element: its unique creative vitality, and that means its re-creation, its transformation of the world we see. Thus history of art in its broader meaning is the history of the way people see, of man's sense of his world; as reflected in vision, it is an essential part of the history of human consciousness. And artists as well as art historians, in fact anyone who wants to grasp the full significance of a work of art, must see the two components of artistic quality, perfection and innovation, together.

[1954]

Translated from the German
by Eleanor Wolff

———————————PART THREE

Varieties of the Unconscious

We are such stuff
As dreams are made on, and
our little life
Is rounded with a sleep.

I

DESPITE MORE than half a century of psychoanalytic research we can, to this day, find people questioning the existence of an unconscious. The unconscious, they say, is not a proven fact but a hypothesis. Positivists and behaviorists among the opponents of psychoanalysis are particularly given to this stand. In reply, we might pose a question of a sort positivists disdain: Just what can be accepted as indubitable fact? In that most exact of the sciences —physics—the whole concept of factuality has become beclouded by doubt. Facts have revealed their unfathomable complexity, their nature as "events." While we have not yet reached the point of regarding "facts" as sheer assumptions, they more and more appear to be at best transitory, extremely limited and conditional states.

Physics deals with physical phenomena. Because it is the fundamental science, it is the source from which the rest of modern science derives a common criterion of physical verifiability. Only the "factual" is regarded as "true," and the factual is equated with what manifests itself to the senses. It is what can in the final analysis be reduced to sense-perception—at least through instruments—and as such has become measurable, quantifiable. All efforts to find "laws of nature" in *human* events come down to

121

seeking measurability, which is to say congruence and extensiveness. For only things that are congruent and have extension can be measured.

That is our difficulty with the data on which historical and sociological laws are based. For purposes of measurement such data have to be wrenched out of their living contexts. They form, in phenomena which are not directly perceivable, that portion of an event which can be given extension. In other words, they represent, as it were, an abstract materiality. Thus, in the realm of the psyche, only externalities are subject to measurement and exact evaluation, only mental reactions to external stimuli, to which category the functions of the intellect belong. The inside of the psychic processes cannot be evaluated, only inferred. The threshold from extensive behavior to intensive feeling and imagination cannot be crossed at a bound, but only circled around. It is significant that behaviorism, which eschews psychic experience and observation, has been fruitful only in animal psychology and at best in child psychology: that is to say, where the psychic elements remain entirely or largely caught within the soma, where thought and individuation are not yet fully developed.[1]

For investigation of what is essentially psychic, that is, not purely physiological or functional, we have no means of "verification" other than elusive human experience and observation. We cannot experiment with this part of the psyche as we do with physical phenomena, where animals can serve to illustrate certain organic processes and provide answers to our questions about the structures and functions of the body. The producing of artificial neuroses in rats or cats seems to me to contribute scarcely anything important to the understanding of human psychological problems. The dimensions and proportions of animal and human life, and the corresponding degrees of complexity, remain too far apart.

But if scientific verification of the unconscious seems hardly possible (perhaps the closest we can come to it are the recent studies of dreams and preconscious memory processes by electrical stimulation of the cortex, a matter to which we shall return) we nevertheless possess centuries, in fact millennia of testimony that men have experienced an unconscious psychic stratum. Indeed, the gradual awareness of the unconscious, and the emergence of a clear concept of it, is as consistent an evolutionary process as any other we know, and marks the different phases of man's growing self-knowledge.

This evolutionary process can only be seen in its full scope if we take the concept of the unconscious in a much wider sense than it has for psychoanalytic doctrine. By the *unconscious we mean here that realm of the human self—i.e., intellect, psyche, and body—whose functionings are not distinctly apprehensible to man.* Our discussion will show how vast and varied this realm is.

We must start with the indissoluble and paradoxical connection between consciousness and unconsciousness. The unconscious presupposes consciousness, and only by the development of consciousness could man become aware of the unconscious within himself. Although "there is a vast amount of historical fact which indicates that almost since the dawn of civilization man has had an inkling of understanding that mind activity outside of our waking consciousness does truly exist,"[2] there had to be a discovery of consciousness, a becoming conscious of consciousness before a distinct concept of the unconscious could arise. Actually then, the development begins with the dawning consciousness of consciousness, and this could arise only from observation of the conscious mind in motion, that is, engaged in its activity—which is thinking. In the course of a prolonged process, there separates out of this consciousness of consciousness an awareness of the unconscious as the bedrock of the human psyche. This cognizance steadily gains in clarity and sharpness until, in Freudian doctrine, it finally receives its first empirically based theoretic formulation. That first specific and detailed apprehension of the unconscious signified a reaching out of consciousness into the depths of the unconscious, and hence an extension of consciousness. The connection between the two strata of the human psyche proved to be exceedingly close, exceedingly complex.

II

The differentiation of consciousness and the unconscious may
be traced to two distinctions that impressed themselves on the
Greeks at the beginning of secular thought: a vertical distinction,
so to speak, among *body*, *soul*, and *mind*; and a horizontal distinction between *man* and *universe*, or (for this is what it became
later on) between *subject* and *object*. It is true that Greek philosophy, which despite its opposition to the mythic popular religion
never entirely broke away from its fundamentally religious concern,
did not draw a clear line between these antinomies. Thus, for the
Greeks, mind and soul did not mean simply the mind and soul
of the human person; rather, the mind and soul of the individual
appeared as parts of a cosmic substance, a mind and a soul which
permeated the entire universe and, therefore, individual human
beings also. Consequently, the relationship of body, soul, and
mind (although already distinctly perceived) in a sense accorded
with the relationship of the individual human being to the substantial principle of the universe. In his singleness, separateness
and mutability man represented the body; in his soul and his
reason he shared in the all-permeating principle of the universe.
Even in the doctrine of Aristotle, that most rational of the Greek
doctrines, which already acknowledged the metaphysical validity
of the mutable individual, the close connection between the two
distinctions persists. The divine cosmic principle is the form
(*eidos*) which in individual things and therefore in individual
human beings has mated with physical substance (*hyle*) to make
reality. But in spite of this essential indivisibility of matter and
form, the mind and psyche of the individual are still considered
to form part of the universal cosmic principle. In fact, wherever
religion prevails, and especially in persons of mystical temper, the
tendency remains to blur the boundaries between the two distinctions. To the Christian also, man's mind and psyche appear to
share in the divine essence. Moreover, and for our purposes this

is the important fact to be noted, to the believer, in his mystical ecstasy, God's presence is tangible and dazzlingly visible, but the divine cosmic order and providence are *not knowable.**

The three creators of Christian doctrine in direct line of descent, St. Paul, St. Augustine, and Luther, drew an ever sharper line between body and mind, transforming the distinction into a profound dichotomy. The body, as the source and seat of all sins, was opposed to the mind or spirit, which was seen as the seat of the true life touched by divinity. Hence the body was rejected and repressed. This caused a crucial displacement of the psychic equilibrium; we may go so far as to say that as a result the unconscious, in religious prefiguration, was established as a fenced-off area of the psyche. From the principles of taboo all the way to the commandments of the Judaic God, individual man's relationship to the daemonic or divine powers operated within an external cosmic space. What mattered was active obedience by way of "works" to divine commandments; the unknown and unknowable was subject

---

* The *Upanishads*, especially the *Mandukya Upanishad*, thus early contain a clear distinction among the four states of the psyche, but in an entirely different order from ours, which is oriented by rationality. The ascending order is as follows: *wakefulness* (corresponding to our "consciousness"), which is shared to some extent by the higher animals; *dream*, a subconsciousness in which contact with lower reality is lost and the psyche already perceives a beyond (the lower animals are permanently in this state); *dreamless deep sleep*, the stage before highest perfection, liberation from all desires and worldly cravings (this is the state of vegetable and mineral creatures); and finally the state of *supraconsciousness*, which is attained by yoga, that is, by uttermost—or rather, innermost—effort: concentration. In this state complete cessation of the vital movements coincides with supreme vital illumination; complete withdrawal from all relations with the environment isolates the innermost self—which, however, becomes one with the all-permeating cosmic self, the world soul, Brahma. In Indian doctrine, therefore, the ascent to the world soul is equated with a descent into the unconscious—which thus acquires a metaphysical character totally at odds with our Western sequence. Western and Eastern mysticism have in common the striving toward union with the world soul, but the paths differ. Western mysticism, the Neoplatonic as well as the Christian versions, seeks to achieve union with the external power of divinity by way of the mind. Indian mysticism is inclined to induce harmony and illumination by physical concentration; what is above and beyond the senses is likewise beneath the senses, below the existential level. In Zen Buddhism the opposition to thinking is quite overt.

solely to the will and pleasure of the spirits and gods.* The "tempter," too, is an external power that can be resisted by unswerving loyalty to God, by abstaining from prideful miracle-making or blasphemy, and by ascetic exercises. Ritual is a strong scaffolding, to which one can cling firmly; and grace transmitted by the Church washes away sin. The command of *faith*, however, transfers religious worship to man's inner life and thus accords man the privilege of deciding whether or not he is pleasing to God. That is Luther's "Freedom of Christian Man." Man can no longer pay his spiritual debt by works; faith is what justifies him, and faith is within the psyche itself, hence an unsteady mainstay, apt to prove shaky as soon as the mind fixes attention upon it.

The history of medieval heresies and scholastic disputes illustrates the gradual disintegration of dogma and ritual under the dual pressures of corruption of the Church and the operation of human reason. And when dogma and ritual decayed, the serious Christian, left to his own decisions, began more than ever to feel his rejected body as the source of all the impulses and passions which escape intellectual grasp and psychic control: as the dark realm in man, in which uncontrollable, diabolic forces wreak havoc and threaten the calm, blessed spiritual existence. Thus the devil took up residence within man.** Luther's Passion, his lifelong struggle against the devil within himself, is a vivid example of the nameless presence of the unconscious in medieval man. Not only the abuses within the Church, but also young Luther's experience with his inner self, taught him the dubiousness of ritual and penances. Asceticism brought him no peace, but only excited his evil

---

* In the eighteenth century Lichtenberg wrote: "I wonder whether our concept of God is anything but personified incomprehensibility." And drawing an analogy to man's unconscious, he added: "Man is in the rational intellect, God in the passions." Later, in the nineteenth century, Eduard von Hartmann described God as the "Unconscious and Supraconscious" which creates a consciousness of itself in the individual.

** Incidentally, in German mysticism God also took up residence in the soul of man, in the form of the divine spark. Previously, the center of gravity of divine and spiritual being lay outside, in the world above; man strove to have his soul partake of it. Now the center of gravity moved inside; God partook of the human soul.

instincts. He could not forget that absolution was imperative even for sins committed unknowingly, i.e., unconsciously; and he tormented himself and his father confessor, the theologian John Staupitz, with endless searches for unconscious sins. Only the Pauline injunction to trust in faith reassured him; but by his doctrine of justification by faith he threw wide the doors to the era of doubt. The Puritans who followed him were permanently tormented by scruples and constantly rummaged through their souls for traces of an infection from contact with sinfulness.

III

We see, then, that views held until the close of the Middle Ages recognized two essential foreshadowings or incipient stages of the unconscious: one *spiritual*—the unfathomable presence of the divine, all-embracing World Soul within the individual soul, and the other *physical*—the deep-lying, uncontrollable drives and passions of the body.

Alongside these, however, we possess vast evidence for premonition or observation of an unconscious realm as revealed by various human conditions, sleep, dreams, fainting, fits, epileptic seizures, etc. The chief of these—indeed, unique for that early period—are the anxiety-filled observations to which St. Augustine was driven by his intense religious zeal. He was still enough of a pagan, in his personality and his philosophical training, to experience the spiritual struggles of a Christian as constitutional conflicts within the human soul. Thus his passionate striving for spiritual perfection pushed him to the limits of self-control and of consciousness. In his ponderings about *dream*, in his astonishing description of *memory* and the processes of association, he implicitly developed an initial analytic psychology:

[These erotic images] haunt me, but strengthless, when I am awake; but in sleep not only so as to give pleasure, but even to obtain assent, and what is very like the act itself. Indeed, so far does the illusion of the image prevail, in my soul and in my flesh, that false visions persuade the sleeper to things to which truth

would never bring him when awake. Am I not then myself, O
Lord my God? . . . Where is reason then, which awake resists
such suggestions, which remains unshaken if the things themselves are urged on it? Is it closed with the eyes? Is it lulled
asleep with the senses of the body?[3]

He confronts the same question even more earnestly, and discusses it in greater detail, when he considers memory and its
functions:

Great is this force of memory, exceeding great, O my God; a
large and boundless inward chamber! Who ever sounded the bottom of it? Yet is this a faculty of my mind, and belongs to my
nature; nor do I myself comprehend all that I am. Therefore is
the mind too strait to contain itself. And where then could that
be, which cannot contain itself? Is it outside it, and not within?
How then does it not contain itself?[4]

How, he asks further, did it all find its way in there, everything
that is stored up in "the enormous inner court" and in "the many
secret and inexpressible windings" of memory, "to come forth,
to be called forth again, whenever needed?" Physical images and
sensations enter, he understands, through the senses, through eye,
ear, nose, tongue, touch. But what of pure concepts which "lie,
as it were, in a place more remotely within the self, a place that
is not a place; nor do I hold within me the images of these concepts, but the things themselves."

Whence and how did these things enter into my memory? I
know not how. For when I learned them, I did not give credit
to another man's mind, but recognized them as mine; regarding
them as true, I recommended them to my own mind, and stored
them where I could fetch them out again whenever I desired.
Therefore they were in my mind before I ever learned them, and
yet they were not in my memory. Where were they, then? Why,
when they were spoken, did I acknowledge them, saying, "So it
is, it is true," unless because they were already in my memory,
but so far off and as it were crowded so far back into certain

secret caves, that had they not been drawn out by another's suggestion, I might have been unable to conceive them. . . .[5] But if I were for some short space of time to stop calling them to mind, they again become buried, and sink down as it were into the remoter inner spaces, so that they must once more be thought out [excogitanda] and brought out [cogenda], in order to be known. . . .[6] I remember also the act of remembering. . . .[7] Yet, behold, I am not able to comprehend the force of my own memory—even though I cannot so much as call myself myself without it. For what shall I see when I see clearly that I remember forgetfulness? Shall I say that what I remember is not in my memory? Or shall I say that forgetfulness is in my memory in order that I should not forget? Both would be most absurd. . . . How did forgetfulness write its image in the memory, since by its presence it blots out whatever is registered there? . . . For my part, Lord, I am sore oppressed with myself; I have become a field of hard toil and much sweat.[8]

Luther, the Augustinian monk, felt the unconscious to be nothing but a sink of corruption, the bottomless pit of sinfulness within himself. He clung to faith and the text of Scripture. But for St. Augustine, long before him, the pressure of conscience had led to searching consideration of the unconscious processes. For Augustine, the unconscious had already become a problem; his questions circled around the margins of this realm of the psyche; he tormented himself with the paradoxes of the transitions, but could not think the matter through. Augustine was beginning to guess how closely body, soul and mind are interconnected; he was beginning to guess the physical limitations of the psyche, the psychic limitations of the mind: the power of reason is curbed not only by the power of the drives and their images, but also by the restricted range of the ego. For him, however, the unconscious still blends with the unknowable of divine providence, in which he finally takes refuge. Not until a clear demarcation had been made between divine intervention and the functioning of the cosmos did it become possible to grasp the phenomena of man's inner life as an independent entity.

IV

Complete consciousness of consciousness, I have said, as achieved by the investigation of consciousness in its activity, i.e., thinking, had to precede a clear conception of the unconscious. First consciousness had to be discovered and its workings analyzed before the territory of the unconscious could be scanned in its entirety—not just glimpsed along its frontiers—and the full inventory of its contents taken. The long evolution of reason, of scientific and artistic development, was essential before we could penetrate into the structure and activity of the unconscious to the extent that we can today.

Awareness of consciousness as thinking begins with the Greek "Know thyself," with the dialectic of Socrates and the logic of Aristotle. For these Greek thinkers, however, the discovered laws of thinking still represented a microcosmic reflection of the metaphysical laws of being.

Clear differentiation and thus true recognition of the active consciousness made its first clear appearance in the wake of that general movement of secular emancipation which we call the Renaissance. This revolutionary movement revealed beyond all masking the downfall of cosmic unity, which had been so long in the offing. The unitary divine power which had hitherto permeated the universe, disintegrated into two equal forces, *nature* and *human reason*; and this dichotomy utterly transformed the relationship of man to his world. *Previously,* the human mind seemed to participate in the all-embracing universal substance, to be part of the hierarchically ordered divine cosmos, in which individualized physical being was only one state of existence, and a lowly one at that. *Now,* however, a wholly secularized human mind, understood as sheer *ratio,* confronted a likewise secularized nature. And nature, in turn, no longer belonged to a cosmos, but had become a purely material "object" of human domination, investigation and exploitation. Thus there emerged that antithesis of *subject* and *object* which has become the theme of modern epistemology. The vertical distinction of body, soul, and mind was henceforth sharply set aside from the horizontal distinction between ego and outside world. A conflict arose between an inner realm—psyche and reason—and an outer, phenomenal realm—nature or human environment.

This great change—which in fact marks the beginning of our modern era—was definitively and characteristically formulated in the philosophy of Descartes, whose ideas influenced all subsequent intellectual developments down to the present day. They therefore remain as relevant as ever to any consideration of the relationship between consciousness and the unconscious.

Descartes, of course, is the father of pure, extreme rationalism. That is to say, he installed reason as the base and quintessence of existence. The famous formula *Cogito, ergo sum,* is not so much asserting a conclusion, as stating an identity: "Thinking, I am," or: "To the extent that I think, I exist."* This Cartesian doctrine, an extreme manifestation of self-consciousness in the sense of "consciousness of the thinking self," represents the final transfer of cosmic authority from God to human reason, which is to say, the shift from the Christian to the secular era. God still exists, but only by grace of reason; the ontological proof has deduced Him from the concept of Him, and other logical grounds have corroborated this proof. For Anselm of Canterbury, this proof of God was purely subsidiary; he essayed it for the first time by way of placating rebellious Thought. That is, the existence of God could *also* be proved; but Anselm regarded God's existence as dogmatically unassailable anyhow. The principle was *Credo, ut intelligam,* not the converse; and God and the universals were real, above and beyond the intellect and indeed normative for the intellect. For Descartes, on the contrary, everything begins with that spur to all thought: doubt. The old Christian tendency to denigrate the physical world remains in Descartes, but with a new

---

* *"Ego sum, ego existo, quoties a me profertur, vel mente concipitur, necessario esse verum"* (Meditat. II). *"Ac proinde haec cognitio: ego cogito, ergo sum, est omnium prima et certissima"* (Princ. Phil. I, 8).

significance: non-human creatures have neither soul nor consciousness, since they do not think; like things, they merely have
extension, are consequently comprehensible only in physicomathe-
matical terms. Organism is mechanism.

In championing the sovereignty of reason Descartes develops,
in rudimentary form, a certain conception of the unconscious.
(Herein lies what is important for our discussion.) To Descartes,
all ideas and "perceptions" which come to man from the external,
physical world, all "adventitious ideas" (*ideae adventiciae*) are
deceptions of the senses. Truth, that is to say, the concord of idea
with reality, rests exclusively upon the faculty of thought. But
since Descartes held that no clear knowledge can come from the
external world, he had to assume the existence of an inner criterion
for truth within the human mind. This criterion would consist of
ideae innatae, "inborn ideas," which were originally conferred
upon man by God, but which "of necessity arise by themselves
from the mere capacity of the mind for thinking" (*a sola facultate
cogitandi necessitate quadam naturae ipsius mentis manant*). God
himself would be one such "inborn idea," by means of which He
has, so to speak, proved himself. (Descartes was here linking his
own thought to Kepler's innate archetypes and to the later, eclectic
Stoa's, especially Cicero's doctrine of *notiones innatae*; but he was
the first to draw such radical conclusions from these ideas.) Of
course, we ourselves are not distinctly aware of these innate ideas;
they come from an area beyond our consciousness. They are a
preliminary answer to Augustine's fruitless inquiry into the foundations of the mind which the mind itself does not comprehend.

The conception of inborn ideas has been adopted and elaborated
along various lines by later philosophies, and out of it modern
epistemology has emerged. There is no need for us here to trace
this development in detail. It suffices to point to a recent offshoot
of the Cartesian philosophical concept which is most relevant to
our investigation: the theory of Hermann Broch who, equally influenced both by Kantian and post-Kantian epistemology and by

Freudian psychoanalysis, assumed and described an *epistemological unconscious*.

V

In his account of a personal experience, however, Descartes revealed—for the first time, so far as I can see—further aspects of the unconscious which are even more germane to the findings of modern psychoanalysis, but which have largely gone unnoticed by its present-day practitioners.

At the age of twenty-three Descartes passed through a severe crisis—an individual embodiment of the crisis of his age, out of which the system of rationalism was born. The problem was the liberation of the sense of truth, of the "spirit in its nakedness" (*esprit tout nu*); Descartes was concerned with freeing the mind from the entanglement of "prejudices," that is to say, credulities— a process in which he "had to suffer no less than if it had been a question of stripping himself of his self" (*se dépouiller de soy-même*). His conscious intellectual efforts did not lead to clarity; clear understanding came only as the result of three successive dreams during the night of November 10, 1619.[9]

The preceding day, a glimmering that he had "that day discovered the foundations of the admirable science [i.e., mathematics]" had so filled his depressed mind with agitation and enthusiasm that he was thrown into "a state receptive to the impressions of dreams and visions."

The first dream was tormenting. Descartes felt that he was walking in the street, with difficulty heading toward his destination. Hampered by great weakness in his right side, he had to turn on his left side in bed. But now he felt a violent wind which whirled him around three or four times on his left foot; at every step he thought he would fall. Seeing an open school, he wished to enter the church of the school in order to pray. But then it occurred to him that he had passed by an acquaintance without greeting him; he wanted to turn to pay his respects, but was forcibly thrown back by the wind, which was now blowing

toward the church. At the same time he saw standing in the
middle of the schoolyard another person, who called out to him
in a friendly way, addressing him by name. He was astonished to
see that this person, and the people around him, were standing
firmly on their feet, although he himself was swaying and staggering. As the wind diminished, he awoke with a sharp pain which
made him fear that the whole thing had been the work of an
evil spirit that wanted to seduce him. He prayed for protection
against the ill effects of the dream and of his sins, turned back
on his right side, and fell asleep again.

The second dream was brief, and the most frightening. It
consisted of a thunderclap, at which he immediately awakened
in alarm, imagining that he saw a great many sparks scattered
over his room. By blinking a few times he convinced himself that
these were a sensory deception. Reassured, he glided into a *third,
peaceful dream* which brought the solution.

He found on his table two books, a dictionary and a collection
of classical poetry, *Corpus Poetarum Latinorum* (which had
actually been published a few years before). Opening it, he came
upon a verse from an idyll by Ausonius: "*Quod vitae sectabor
iter?*" ("What way of living shall I follow?"). At the same time
a man he did not know pointed out to him another poem beginning with the words "*Est et Non*," a paraphrase of the Pytha-
gorean "Yes and No" (*nai kai ou*). And now there occurred
something highly singular: in the dream he asked himself
whether this was a dream or a vision. He not only decided that
it was a dream, but he also began interpreting this dream as he
continued to dream. He decided that the dictionary must represent a collection of the sciences, while the *Corpus Poetarum*
stood for the wisdom of the poets, which sprang from enthusiasm and imagination. The verse posing the question of
what kind of life one should choose seemed to him the good
advice of a sensible person. Awakening, he continued this
interpretation, applying it to the phrase "*Est et Non*": this must
mean the distinction between truth and falsehood in human
sciences. The felicitous way in which these meanings all fitted
one another encouraged him to believe that the Spirit of Truth
had wished to open to him, in these dreams, the treasures of

knowledge. He was convinced that these dreams determined his entire future and everything that happened to him thenceforth. The lightning, whose thunder had so frightened him, was, he believed, the Spirit of Truth descending and taking possession of him.

These dreams of Descartes are extremely important in two respects. The third dream is the earliest evidence I know for the experience of *different strata of the unconscious.* It clearly differentiates between a set of visual figurative images and the capacity of the unconscious to draw inferences. For the dreamer Descartes is aware that he is dreaming; in fact, he decides whether his experience is a hallucination or dream and recognizes the dream as a dream. Here is evidence for the degree to which consciousness merges with the unconscious: the borders are fluid.

But the series of dreams proclaims something else. Descartes himself ascribed them to intervention "from above." In the first of the dreams, he is troubled by "evil spirits" which want to keep him away from the church. But in the end it turns out that the "Spirit of Truth" victoriously takes possession of him. No clear division has as yet been made between God and the Spirit of Truth; the transition is blurred. But from his fitful apprehension, in the waking state the day before, that he had seen into the mysteries of mathematics, and from the high significance he ascribes to these dreams, it is evident that the "Spirit of Truth" is Reason, which from that time on assumes its dominating position in his thinking and his system.

To Freud the element of "from above" was a sign that these dreams had been largely preshaped in consciousness, and that only a small part of them came from the deeper recesses of the unconscious. He took the dreams to be manifestations of a conflict of conscience arising out of sexual lapses. Freudian analysis, based as it was on pathological data and aiming at therapy, concentrated at the outset exclusively on the sexual substrata of the psyche. The uncovering of these substrata was its revolutionary achievement. But that procedure resulted in far too narrow a picture of the unconscious. We have since come to recognize the unconscious as an immense reservoir of life in which our conscious impulses and actions originate and end, through which all our experience sooner or later passes, and which includes within itself many layers and provinces.

These dreams of Descartes, with their aftereffect upon his life, seem to me to reveal still another property of the unconscious which later was to be widely experienced and testified to. That is its *creative powers*. When we are much preoccupied by an intellectual undertaking or a project, when we try to solve a difficult problem, absorb, clarify or sublimate experiences, grasp insights which we feel hovering before us, then it may happen that these efforts continue in the unconscious while we sleep or are consciously engaged in something else. Such processes often find their resolutions in dreams. The British theologian and philosopher, Ralph Cudworth remarks in his *True Intellectual System of the Universe* (1678):

> It is certain that our human souls themselves are not always conscious of whatever they have in them; for even the sleeping geometrician hath, at that time, all his geometrical theorems some way in him; as also the sleeping musician, all his musical skills and songs; and therefore, why may it not be possible for the soul to have likewise some actual energy in it, which it is not expressly conscious of? . . . There is . . . a more interior kind of plastic power in the soul (if we may so call it), whereby it is formative of its own cogitations, which itself is not always conscious of; as when, in sleep or dreams, it frames interlocutory discourses betwixt itself and other persons, in a long series, with coherent sense and apt connections, in which oftentimes it seems to be surprised with unexpected wiseness and repartees, though itself were all the while the poet and inventor of the whole fable.[10]

May I offer a few examples of the operation of this *creative unconscious* in various states and fields of creative work? We begin with that famous passage from a letter of Mozart, wherein he describes in the most ingenuous terms the process of composition. What he is describing here is one aspect of the creative unconscious—that mystery known as "inspiration." It is characterized by a continuous flow of the unconscious process into the conscious; receptivity to the inner current passes smoothly into the formative labors of the wide-awake mind.

> When I am quite by myself and in good spirits, say traveling in the carriage or strolling after a good meal and at night when I cannot sleep, ideas come to me in a flow and most easily. Where they come from and how, I do not know, and can do nothing to help them along. Those I like, I keep in my head and may hum under my breath—so others have told me, at any rate. If I hold on to these, ideas keep popping into my head on where this or that scrap could be used to make a pasticcio out of, according to counterpoint, to the sound of the various instruments, etc., etc. That then inflames my soul, when I am not disturbed, that is; it grows bigger and bigger; and I spread it out more and more widely, more and more brightly; and the thing truly is almost completed in my head, even though it is long, so that afterwards I can see the whole of it in my mind, like a beautiful picture or a good-looking person, and hear it in my imagination not one thing after another, as it must come later when it is played, but as if it were all sounding together. What a treat that is! All the finding and making happens inside me as if in a fine, strong dream; but the hearing it all at once that way, all together, is the best thing of all.[11]

Paul Valéry traces the same process of inspiration with more exactitude:

> There are two states: the one in which the person who is doing his job as a writer (*qui fait son métier d'écrivain*) is pierced by a kind of lightning-flash; for after all this hardly passive life of the mind is made up of fragments; it is composed of extremely short-lived elements which one nevertheless feels to be extremely rich, which do not illuminate the whole mind, but on the contrary indicate that there are completely new forms which it will surely be able to seize on with a little effort. I have sometimes

observed the arrival of such a sensation of the mind, a flash, lighting but not enlightening. It serves to announce; it suggests rather than illumines; in short, it is an enigma which carries within itself the assurance that its solution can perhaps be deferred. We say to ourselves: "I see, and tomorrow I shall see more." Something happens, a special sensitization; soon we will go into the darkroom and see the picture emerge. . . . Enthusiasm has no place in the darkroom. It would only spoil the plate. . . . You have to work like your own hireling, your own foreman. The boss has provided you with the spark; it's up to you to make something of it. . . . The new thing that forms in our mind depends upon a certain momentary sensitivity which may either have seized upon it or provoked it—we cannot say which. . . . I wonder whether the effect of intellectual work is not to promote some sort of increase in sensitivity. The work in itself would not lead to the solution . . . but . . . it might momentarily make the artist an extremely sensitive sounding-board for all those episodes of consciousness which may serve its ends.[12]

Rilke's kind of creativity is an extreme example of work proceeding and being completed almost entirely within the unconscious. His poetry, an analytics of feeling pushed to the point of abstract sensibility, was often produced in sudden bouts after long periods of apparent incapacity in which he felt he would never again be able to write anything—I myself watched him suffering such a period toward the end of the First World War. Meanwhile his creative works were growing slowly, as it were vegetatively, subliminally. All at once, several of his great poems, like the *Orpheus* sonnets, would burst forth from him in rapid succession on one and the same day. When they did appear, it was in final form—he hardly changed a word. To be sure, during the times he was dominated by feelings of impotence, he continued to keep up his correspondence and it is very probable that the labor he devoted to his letters furthered that relaxation of the sensibility, that intensification of receptivity, which spills over into creativity, as Valéry experienced it. Only the result in Rilke's case was not a flash of inspiration which was then to be developed by sober-minded work in the "darkroom" of consciousness. Rather, it would seem to have been an extended process marked by feelings of impotence which took place in the true darkroom of the unconscious until the work had come to ripeness.

Here, finally, is the account of one such underground creative process which—much like Descartes'—was released by a dream. The example is taken from the sciences. It is the astonishing story of Otto Loewi, the biochemist, who was granted in a dream his great discovery, and thus the Nobel Prize:

> As far back as 1903, I discussed with Walter M. Fletcher from Cambridge, England, then an associate in Marburg, the fact that certain drugs mimic the augmentary as well as the inhibitory effects of the stimulation of sympathetic and/or parasympathetic nerves on their effector organs. During this discussion, the idea occurred to me that the terminals of those nerves might contain chemicals, that stimulation might liberate them from the nerve terminals, and that these chemicals might in turn transmit the nervous impulse to their respective effector organs. At that time I did not see a way to prove the correctness of this hunch, and it entirely slipped my conscious memory until it emerged again in 1920.
>
> The night before Easter Sunday of that year I awoke, turned on the light, and jotted down a few notes on a tiny slip of thin paper. Then I fell asleep again. It occurred to me at six o'clock in the morning that during the night I had written down something most important, but I was unable to decipher the scrawl. The next night, at three o'clock, the idea returned. It was the design of an experiment to determine whether or not the hypothesis of chemical transmission that I had uttered seventeen years ago was correct. I got up immediately, went to the laboratory, and performed a simple experiment on a frog heart according to the nocturnal design. I have to describe briefly this experiment since its results became the foundation of the theory of chemical transmission of the nervous impulse. . . .
>
> The story of this discovery shows that an idea may sleep for decades in the unconscious mind and then suddenly return. Further, it indicates that we should sometimes trust a sudden

intuition without too much skepticism. If carefully considered in the daytime, I would undoubtedly have rejected the kind of experiment I performed. It would have seemed likely that any transmitting agent released by a nervous impulse would be in an amount just sufficient to influence the effector organ. It would seem improbable that an excess that could be detected would escape into the fluid which filled the heart. It was good fortune that at the moment of the hunch I did not think but acted immediately. . . .

In fact, the nocturnal concept represented a sudden association of the hypothesis of 1903 with the method tested not long before in other experiments. Most so-called "intuitive" discoveries are such associations suddenly made in the unconscious mind.[13]

VI

Descartes, then, uncovered three regions of the unconscious. His predicate of innate ideas ushered in a long line of philosophical speculation that ultimately led to the concept of an *epistemological unconscious*. His interpretation of the dream within a dream revealed a stratum of the unconscious which might be called *half-consciousness*. Finally, his account of his dream experience, and of its effect upon his whole life, was the first clearly recorded observation of the phenomenon of the *creative unconscious*.

The epistemological unconscious is closely related to that *physiopsychological unconscious* which has figured in the views of thinkers ever since the rise of empiricism and materialism at the end of the seventeenth century, and which was later investigated by science. Both regions harbor processes that constructively influence the vital functions without our being aware of them. If the epistemological unconscious houses the prerequisites for the thinking processes, for consciousness in action, we may say that the physiopsychological unconscious is that dark, unplumbable domain in which organic processes take place—the latter extending all the way to the physicochemistry of the body. Normally we are not conscious of these complex, many-layered processes; it takes a pain or a functional disturbance to call our attention to the underpinning which we constantly and carelessly ignore. The further back in organic evolution an organism is, the more it lives in the body, the more concerned it is with the physical processes, so that plants and animals are in their dim fashion even more aware of these physical processes than man. Consciousness in the full sense means: to live on a plane above the physical processes.

From the eighteenth century on there developed, along with ever clearer distinction among the vital functions and vital strata, a greater perception of the fluid borders between the strata. Thus, there arose—in the development of philosophical theories from the English philosophers to Kant—a sharp distinction between epistemology and psychology, and then between psychology and physiology; but at the same time, and especially in recent times, the connections between these separated strata showed up more and more plainly.

In 1748 the British theologian and philosopher David Hartley wrote: "The white medullary Substance of the Brain is also the immediate Instrument by which Ideas are presented to the Mind; or in other words, whatever Changes are made in this Substance, corresponding Changes are made in our Ideas; and vice versa."[14]

We see here an anticipation, going beyond mere "psychophysical parallelism," of knowledge which today is available to us thanks to fascinating and momentous experiments with electrical stimulation of the cortex. It has in fact been determined that the changes in our thoughts and feelings, or more precisely the content of thought and emotion, are connected with movements of electric currents which travel along the nerve fibers in the white matter of the brain and flash out here and there in the network of the nervous system; and this implies a connection between brain and mind. Some experimenters, taking their cue from effects observed in brain surgery, study the sources and functions of memory; they thus are concerned with a region of perpetual passage from the unconscious to consciousness, or rather with the building up of consciousness out of the unconscious. This is not the place to discuss their findings in detail. But let us note the important conclusion implicit in the words of the anatomist C. Judson Herrick (1955):

> The mind-body problem will never be solved by ignoring the troublesome factors, either those of spirit or of matter. The enquiry cannot be limited to either the conscious or the unconscious factors, because what we are looking for is the relation between the two. . . . Traditional materialism (the crude variety) and classical spiritualism (or, more reputably, "idealism") both involve neglect of a vast wealth of human experiences, including common sense and refined scientific knowledge. We cannot choose between materialism and spiritualism. We must have both.[15]

This trend toward a sharper delineation of the vital strata, even as their interactions are more appreciated, may be seen operating in another modern development: the increasingly physiological slant given to epistemology. Leibniz developed further the Cartesian conception of innate ideas. By postulating a pre-established harmony between internal and external processes, he was able, to a still more radical extent than Descartes, to omit the external world from his considerations. On the other hand he classified the innate ideas more precisely, describing some as *intellectually inborn* and the others as *sensually* or *perceptually inborn* ideas. *Perceptions* are for him dark, "unnoticed"—what we would term "unconscious"—mental processes in man; they grow dimmer and duller by degrees in animals and in the "sleeping monads" below the level of animals. As a result of consciousness or reflection in man (*réflexion qui nous fait penser à nous-mêmes*—that is, indirectly or directly, through self-awareness, "self-consciousness") they become *apperceptions*. An apperception is a higher degree of perception; it is perception which has risen to consciousness; the boundaries are fluid. But perceptions do not grow into apperceptions singly; this transformation happens only through their connection with other perceptions. Apperception is composed of a multitude of "unnoticeable little perceptions" (*perceptions in-sensibles, petites perceptions*);[16] and in the form of clear conscious-ness—i.e., self-awareness—apperception reflects the monad of man's entire soul. The feelings registered by our senses likewise consist of such little perceptions which, taken separately, are vague, and clear only in their complex ensemble (*claire dans l'assemblage, mais confuses dans les parties*). This theory of Leibniz's can be viewed as the first explicit representation of the unconscious; as such, it later influenced many types of philosophical expositions, all the way to Herbart's theory of inhibition and Eduard von Hart-mann's philosophy of the unconscious. Kant's distinction between "dark" and "clear" conceptions plainly stems from Leibniz:

> To have conceptions and yet not be conscious of them seems to be inherently contradictory. . . . Yet we can be indirectly conscious of having a conception, although we are not directly conscious of it. The latter conceptions are then called *dark*; the others are *clear*. . . . The field of our sense perceptions and feel-ings, of which we are not conscious although we can indubitably conclude that we have them, i.e., the field of *dark* conceptions in man . . . is immeasurable; it is the largest within the human body.

Clear conceptions, on the other hand, contain "only infinitely few points [of the dark conceptions] which are exposed to con-sciousness." Kant goes beyond Leibniz to the extent that he suggests the conflicts between the two:

> Often enough we are . . . the plaything of dark conceptions which refuse to vanish even though the understanding illumines them . . . and our understanding cannot save itself from the absurdities into which the influence of these notions casts it. . . .[17]

Kant keeps his psychophysiological observations separate from his epistemology. Lichtenberg begins to tie the two together:

> We become conscious of certain conceptions which do not depend on us; others, or so at any rate we think, do depend on us; where is the boundary? We know only the existence of our feelings, conceptions and thoughts. Perhaps we should say, *It*

is thinking, as we say: it is lightening. To say *cogito* is already too much, as soon as we translate that by *I think*. To assume, to postulate the ego, is merely practical necessity.

In our own time, finally, in the careful investigations of Gestalt psychology as well as in the theory of Alfred Korzybski, the epistemological unconscious has been virtually merging with the physiopsychological unconscious to form a unity. Korzybski assumes that the most important processes of abstraction and integration take place in two mutually interacting neurophysical layers which he calls "silent levels." These processes cannot be verbalized, and are therefore unconscious. They comprise what Korzybski calls the *structural unconscious*. Korzybski believes that "life, 'intelligence' and abstracting in different orders started together. Without abstracting, recognition [the elementary form of cognition], and therefore selection would not be possible."* Here we have a portrait of Lichtenberg's "it" which thinks.

VII

During the last decades of the eighteenth century, the second great landslide of the modern world swept away at once the feudal powers and the autocracy of Reason; it brought to the surface both the lower classes of the population and the subliminal layers of the psyche. The movement had begun among the nobility with a "malaise" and general dissatisfaction with reason. These tendencies appeared simultaneously in French and English bourgeois literature. They were the basic elements in schools of sentimentality and enthusiasm over nature: Rousseau, Hamann, Klopstock, Herder and the Storm-and-Stress group, and terminated in Romanticism, to which all Europe succumbed. The movement was

* Alfred Korzybski, *Science and Sanity*, 2nd ed. (Lancaster, Pa., 1941), p. 507. A parallel to this doctrine from the philosophical point of view is Hermann Broch's analysis of the epistemological unconscious. Cf., his treatises: "*Werttheoretische Bemerkungen zur Psychoanalyse*," "*Das System als Weltbewältigung*" and "*Uber syntaktische und kognitive Einheiten*," *Essays*, Bd. II (Zurich, 1955); see also Erich Kahler, *Die Philosophie von Hermann Broch* (Tübingen, 1962).

accompanied by a growing interest in dreams and dreamlike states, hallucinations and hypnotism (from Mesmer, Bertrand and Braid up to Charcot, with whom Freud studied). There arose what amounted to a cult of irrational forces, with strong emphasis on the part played in human affairs by genius, imagination, feelings and passions, as well as such imponderables as historical, national and ethnic origins. All this meant that the unconscious suddenly acquired new importance. Hitherto it had been regarded, when noticed at all, only in the clear light of reason, as a kind of extended Hades, a dark framework around *ratio*. Now it was hailed, not only as the equal of reason, penetrating and affecting many of the vital functions of consciousness, but in fact as the *Urgrund*, the ultimate ground of all manifestations of human life. Revelations from exploration of this "inner Africa," as Jean Paul called it, were eagerly awaited. One example of the new viewpoint is Goethe's famous statement to Riemer on August 5, 1810: "Man cannot linger long in the conscious state, or in consciousness; he must ever and again take refuge in the unconscious, for there are his living roots." And Schiller wrote to Körner on December 1, 1788:

> In a creative mind . . . it seems to me, the intellect has withdrawn its guards from the gates. Ideas come rushing in pell-mell, and only then does the intellect survey and scrutinize the horde. You lordly critics, or whatever else you call yourselves, are ashamed or afraid of the momentary, transitory frenzy which is found among all creators. What distinguishes the thinking artist from the dreamer is the longer or shorter duration of that frenzy.

The first theoretical, epistemological version of this radical reversal of perspective is to be found in Fichte. First of all, Fichte banished the physical world and sense-perceptions so thoroughly from his system as to arrive at solipsism. Leibniz, to be sure, had by his assumption of pre-established harmony already relegated physical, material processes to a lower rank, that of mechanical necessity; but at any rate, he had acknowledged their independent

existence and at least granted sense-perceptions accessory importance as stimulants to the development of innate idea-disposi-
tions. Kant, too, had not questioned the real existence of an
inaccessible world of "things in themselves." To Fichte, however,
our entire world is "posited" by the "ideal" (epistemological) ego.
"Everything that exists exists only insofar as it is posited in the ego,
and outside the ego there is nothing." The ego posits itself, is in fact
identical with "self-positing," with active consciousness of self.
Thus it is nothing static, but an act: "To posit the self and to be
are, as used by the ego, absolutely the same." (The ego might
say of itself: *Ago, ergo sum,* or *Sum agens.*)

In order to delimit itself, the ego must implicitly posit a non-ego,
and this non-ego, the objective world, even "things in themselves,"
are conceptions which can arise only out of some unconscious
conceptual activity. Since the ego, consciousness of self, can only
define itself by its opposite, the non-ego, all consciousness is
secondary, derivative, and points toward an unconscious which
gives it content. Whereas for Leibniz the unconscious was only a
muffled rudiment of consciousness, growing ever dimmer and
duskier in the animal and vegetable realms, for Fichte it is the
proto-deed, the proto-act, the proto-function, from which all higher,
conscious activity springs. In fact, what is expressed in the unconscious is a proto-instinct (*Ur-trieb*) which finds its continuance
in conscious *striving.* The positing of the non-ego, this unconscious
conceptual activity, is only the initial step to an endless activity of
the ego; that is, to an endlessly self-impelling ego which forever
posits new barriers for itself in order to overcome them: an autonomous, endless act in itself.

The genesis of Schopenhauer's system from Fichte's is apparent.
Fichte's "autonomous, striving deed in itself" becomes for Schopenhauer "will—the only thing-in-itself." Will has neither cause nor
goal; it is "blind urge and mindless striving," a "dark driving force."
It operates not only in plants, animals and man, but even in the
streaming of water, in all elemental forces of nature. Indeed, will
is equivalent to force itself, to vital force. (For Schopenhauer the

body is as for Fichte the objectivation, the *Objektität*, the visible expression of will.) Herbart, too, regards the will as a craving and as "the most inward thing in man." Similarly, for Nietzsche, the "will to power" is "the innermost essence of being," "the fact to which we ultimately come down," the agent in all organic and even in inorganic processes. "Protoplasm extends its pseudopods not out of hunger, but out of will to power."

VIII

The pre-Romantic and Romantic movement brought about the first breakthrough of the unconscious, the first value-shift from Reason to the subrational, in both the arts and philosophy. New insights bloomed, though still somewhat capriciously and confusedly. Their very speculative subtleties were fired by an enthusiastic feeling of liberation. Even at this point there appears a paradoxical mutual interpenetration of the newly hailed unconscious and rational consciousness.

The Romantic movement had arisen out of weariness with Reason. It was a reaction against the hegemony of *ratio* and its precepts. But the revolt itself, in Storm-and-Stress and in Romantic critical theory, in Novalis and in Friedrich von Schlegel particularly, utilized the powers of the intellect that had been sharpened by rationalism. This first and still speculative effort to promote the irrational, the subrational and the transrational lapsed into concreteness, into more and more detailed studies in the sciences and arts which would eliminate rationalism by exact observation of the empirical reality. In literature and the plastic arts, the resistance to the nebulous sentimentality of an already decadent Romanticism took the form of Realism and Naturalism, which aimed at an ever more faithful description of life's surfaces. This realism, however, which came closer and closer to scientific analysis, was, like that analysis, still permeated by rational methodology. The so-called psychological novel (*roman d'analyse*) of Paul Bourget, for example, drew up model psychic conflicts, whereby the functioning of the psychic life was shown to proceed from social, hereditary, physiological concatenations. The motivations of feelings and actions, which the writers traced and the public demanded, had to be logically comprehensible; a character or act had to be rationally cogent if the reader was to accept it as convincing and credible. The new advent of the subrational was the doing of the great Russians, who stopped showing neatly constructed conflicts *in vitro* and instead revealed the true inner life of man with all its wild complexity and emotional crosscurrents. Dostoevsky's *Notes from Underground* expressed in its very title the violence with which these novels plumbed the unknown, the way they rent surfaces and disclosed inner disorders. Since then there has been a growing understanding that the vital processes of the psyche do not at all follow plain causality. Rather, these processes involve different, far denser combinations, direct to the point of short circuit, whose "causes" lead into such vital depths that they are scarcely to be sorted out into logical elements. Lightning-like associations flash between the most distant regions, swift as electrical contacts, paradoxical unions of rationally contradictory elements; and in the midst of such momentary ignitions the spark is released which is man's ultimate, truly poetic truth.

The same change may be seen even more plainly in the new lyric poetry which sprang up at the same time as the new epic prose, in Mallarmé, Rimbaud, Hopkins and others, and has become more and more pronounced in the course of the twentieth century. The new idiom is characterized by the breakdown of rational sentence structure, by abruptness, lack of transition, sharply contrasting and compressed images, by the coexistence and intertwining of extremely remote and contradictory matters. What is trying to emerge into the light are interconnections of the innermost, obscurest kind, which could not be reached by directed thought. Nevertheless, these things *are* trying to emerge into the light, which after all means into consciousness. This is, then, an extension, albeit undigested, of consciousness.

In 1887 the French symbolist Edouard Dujardin, in a novella otherwise of small importance, introduced the narrative technique of the "stream of consciousness"—even while William James in America was quite independently supplying the theoretical basis for it in his investigation of the "fringes" and "gaps," the "free water" and "current" of consciousness. In the stream of consciousness, experience is no longer narrated; it is lived aloud in its formless, raw state, along with the feelings and thoughts that accompany it (for example, Schnitzler's *Lieutenant Gustl* [1900]). The next step was the use of "free association," which we may call "stream of subconsciousness." In the stream of consciousness, inner experience is kept within the context of a "plot"; it is linked with a coincidental, partly external process taking place on the margin of consciousness. In the stream of subconsciousness, however, the inner experience abandons itself to abrupt, subliminally conditioned combinations (for example, Molly Bloom's chaotic torrent of thoughts in Joyce's *Ulysses*). The term "interior monologue," which is wrongly employed as a general term for the various narrative forms which include the unconscious, should be limited to those specific works in which the succession of emotions and ideas rising to the surface are constantly accompanied by a deliberate intention to order them, a striving for clarity (for example, Broch's *Death of Vergil*).

This same tendency to penetrate into regions beneath the surface, beneath what is known and shaped by reason, may be seen in the plastic arts: in the development from Realism through Impressionism, Expressionism, Futurism, Dadaism, and Surrealism to Abstract Expressionism. Abstract Expressionism has nothing to do with abstraction; the painters who are considered to make up the group object to the label, and with justice. Their goal—if we can speak of any goal at all—is the transmission of unconscious processes with maximum immediacy, to the point of total undirectedness. They distrust all control by consciousness. That is, they stand *inside* the painting that is being created and let themselves be directed by its undifferentiated stimulus. Thus Jackson Pollock declared:

When I am *in* my painting, I'm not aware of what I'm doing. It is only after a sort of "get acquainted" period that I can see what I have been about. . . . The painting has a life of its own. I try to let it come through. . . .[18] When you're painting out of your unconscious, figures are bound to emerge. . . . Something in me knows where I am going and—well, painting is a state of being.[19]

And Mark Rothko:

I'm interested only in expressing basic human emotions.[20]

And Franz Kline:

The difference is that we don't begin with a definite sense of procedure. It's free association from the start to the finished state.[21]

A somewhat parallel development may be observed even in the empirical sciences. In all of these, a host of details has been brought to light by analytical research. Indeed, in some of the disciplines the search has been pursued so far beneath the surface of phenomena that only the most elaborate apparatus can render the results comprehensible in perceptual form. The subtle scientific mind, sharpened by the specific techniques, can extract stupendous conclusions from such collections of details. Yet this development of highly specialized forms of consciousness is on the whole linked with an atrophy of theory; synthesis is sacrificed to more and more exacting determination of facts. The amassing of data can be routinized; indeed, this end of things is already being undertaken by mechanized robots. Digestion by thought, however, must be the work of the individual mind—so that we find in general an increasing fragmentization and functionalization of thinking itself. Consciousness expands impersonally, faceless and leaderless; in the concrete, individual mind, however, consciousness more and more shrinks to impotence. This ominous development assumes fateful proportions because the unconscious avails itself of the cleverly trained, functionally specialized forms of consciousness to carry out irrational acts. The consciously organized, highly technological character of the atrocities is what distinguishes the crimes of the Third Reich and the cold planning for nuclear and chemical warfare from the horrors of earlier times.

Thus, in all fields of intellectual activity (to say nothing of politics), even as the collective consciousness increases to utterly unmanageable proportions, the power of the unconsciousness swells. This is the dialectic of our time. Whether we call this counterforce the emotional element, whether we call it the functional element—however it may be rationalized, it is gaining ground over genuinely rational, cognitively controlled consciousness.

The first impulse in this direction, the Romantic movement, arose, as we have said, out of weariness with Reason. In the nineteenth and twentieth centuries, with the extensive and intensive expansion of technology, science, administrative and social organization, and with the excessive growth of analytical approaches in art and research, the intellectualization of the world markedly increased. This meant an advance of consciousness into all regions. But this overintellectualization of life in general, this overstraining of consciousness with an ever growing plethora of rational procedures and tasks, created powerful pressure for a dangerous reversal. People, even the intellectuals, became less and less capable of meeting the daily demands for rational conduct or of thinking through their problems, which were forever splitting off into new ones. Nietzsche had predicted it: "Growing consciousness is a peril and a disease." During the world wars the disease entered an acute phase; there was a catastrophic plunge into blind emotional excesses—that overwhelming of consciousness by the unconscious which can be felt everywhere today.

IX

Thus we have come to the pathology of the unconscious, that is, to the *reactive* and *repressive unconscious*. As we have seen, and as has been discussed more elaborately in another context, the very overburdening of consciousness throws man back into the unconscious; he relinquishes the effort to understand the overly complex, overly extended relationships; he resigns himself to short-cut, irrational solutions. By personalizing the problems, by projecting the obstacles upon an enemy, he can at once ease his bonds and "rationalize" his drives. No doubt the unconscious has always acted up this way in men's personal lives when they could not master a complex of problems. The reaction has been exploited in political life by demagogues, who in difficult situations soluble only by patient rationality have brusquely appealed to the violence of the aggressive urges. (We have so recently witnessed this spectacle, with horror, and continue to witness it every day.) But this particular aspect of the unconscious emerged less commonly in earlier, undemocratic and untechnological ages, in which every individual was not pressed day after day by intellectual demands. At any rate, its pathological significance was not so clearly recognized. Today it is a universal phenomenon, and has certainly contributed to the psychotic outbreaks all over the globe.

The *repressive unconscious*, that is, the set of drives morbidly distorted and displaced by repression, has also grown steadily under the impact of modern modes of organization and civilization. To be sure, people had been far more aware of it, in various guises, than of the reactive unconscious, although it remained for Freud to show its full implications and to make it the starting point for a first clinically based description of psychic structure. Even the Christian ascetics, locked in struggle with their drives, had to take cognizance of the discharges of unconscious "sinfulness." Devils are nothing but repressed drives, and we remember Augustine's troubled question, whether in dream he is no longer himself, and where his reason has vanished to, since he does things with phantoms which in the waking state he would never permit himself to do with real people. In this question, the bare existence of the repressive unconscious is noted, though not understood.

In the nineteenth century Karl Fortlage boldly pronounced consciousness a product of the inhibited unconscious: "The capacity of a being for consciousness . . . coincides wholly with its

capacity for inhibition of its drives. . . . The drives are not
annihilated or paralyzed during their inhibition, but the mode
of its operation has merely become a different one . . . while the
process continues."[22]

A somewhat similar position was held by Carl Gustav Carus.
Although he was hampered by his romantic and religious views,
Carus in the middle of the last century raised the fundamental
problem of modern psychoanalysis—the pathological aspect of the
relationship between the unconscious and consciousness—but he
ultimately came to a very different conclusion. He found that:

> One may not speak of disease in the primitive and absolute un-
> conscious. The concept of disease implies that within an or-
> ganism, alongside the vital principle which conditions the very
> nature of this organism, another and alien principle has rooted
> itself, blocking and disturbing the life peculiar to this organism.
> Such a concept of disease presupposes a certain degree of free-
> dom to depart from the charted course of its life, to deviate
> somehow from a path no longer marked out by iron necessity.
> Precisely this is the reason that the further back we go along the
> scale of things, the further we take leave of the concept of free-
> dom, the less incidence we see of disease. Among all the
> creatures we know, man has the sad privilege of being able to dis-
> play the greatest variety of illnesses. In the animal realm, the
> frequency of illness and the multiplicity of diseases already
> diminishes; in plants there is no longer any trace of the prime
> forms of disease found among the higher animals, fevers and in-
> flammations. . . . Thus to the measure that the principle of life
> raises itself to consciousness, and thereby also to freedom, the
> disposition and the actuality of illness likewise increases; for al-
> though destruction, dying, is the fate of all organisms because
> they belong to time and not eternity, the lower organisms do not
> die of disease any more than a man dies of disease when he is
> crushed by a fall of rock or in other ways loses his life by
> violence.[23]

According to Carus, all infectious diseases, that is, illnesses
caused by outside agents, would belong in the category of "losing

life by violence," or at any rate being threatened with such loss. What he has in mind are organic, in fact originally psychogenic illnesses, since "consciousness really determines the disease, and the absolute unconsciousness knows nothing of disease." In his faith in salvation through the unconscious, Carus ventures to ascribe to it not only curative powers, but moral regulation; he transfers the "superego" to the "subego":

> In regard to consciousness, we shall find that underlying all clearly apprehended and felt ideas is something dark, but most definite and fixed, unerring—what we significantly call "*conscience*"; in reference to those deviations which are called Evil it consistently points to the right and pure mean. Similarly, unconscious organic being, which in itself knows nothing of disease, underlies everything that is directed against illness and constantly endeavors to restore health. . . .[24]

A child of his period, Carus saw the facts and the relationships in too simplified a fashion. He failed, for example, to consider that in man, and especially in modern man, the unconscious itself is distorted by a great many traditional, conventional, collective pressures, and errs a great deal, so that on the contrary healing can come only from greater and higher consciousness. Nevertheless, he did thus early suggest the close relationship between the "superego" and the "id."

Freud, too, regards the superego as the superior authority of conscience, the "successor and representative of the parents (and teachers)." The standards imparted to the child by this influence are "internalized," "depersonalized"; "within the ego is formed an authority which, observing, criticizing and forbidding, opposes all the rest."[25] The superego can transmit many kinds of standards, religious, national, social, hereditary; it can emerge out of consciousness, but also seep into the unconscious. In any case, it is closely, and in a highly complex way, connected with the unconscious. It presses upon the ego from "below" as well as from "above," from the unconscious as well as from consciousness; from a lower "above," in the unconscious, it presses upon the drives, and represses them; its principal task is, after all, "restriction of gratification." According to Freud, "neurotic illness is a means to self-punishment." "The neurotic must behave as if he were dominated by a guilt feeling which requires for its gratification sickness as a punishment."[26]

Simon-André Tissot (1728–1797), a French-Swiss physician, was the one among the forerunners of psychoanalysis who came closest to the views ultimately held by Sigmund Freud. Tissot showed by clinical documentation what psychic and psychosomatic disturbances arise as a consequence of suppression of the sexual instinct. He was already aware of the sexual origin of hysteria (Freud's theories had stemmed from a similar insight), and discusses the matter at length in his *Traité sur les Nerves et leurs Maladies*. The worst effects of sexual abstinence, he writes, are "greatly concealed." Irregularity of menstruation signifies its repression, he suggests, and can therefore be both cause and consequence of psychic illness.[27]

All these predecessors in no way diminish the epoch-making achievement of Freud, who for the first time systematically described the operations of the repressive unconscious and thus threw open to our sight the immeasurable reaches of the unconscious. However his theory may have been amended or extended by his disciples and successors (Adler, Rank, Jung, Sullivan, Fromm, Szondi, the Existentialists and many others), and however many variations of it may develop in the future, all are outgrowths of his conception. From it we have learned to see how precarious and narrow, how permeated with the unconscious our consciousness is; and this very knowledge has enormously enlarged our consciousness.

X

Let us in conclusion review the course of our study and consider the multifarious varieties, strata and provinces of the unconscious which we may discern from our present degree of acquaintance with it. We started from a situation in which man directed his awakening consciousness toward an external, divine, and cosmic principle. The unconscious was synonymous with the unknown, which rested upon the inscrutable will of the gods or the unscrutinized, mysterious substance of the universe. Even the kind of reflection which began among the Greeks, the examination of consciousness in action, i.e., while thinking—which represents the beginning of man's clear self-consciousness—even this kind of reflection did not yet distinguish between the order of thought and the order of the universe. The cosmic principle permeated the human psyche; in examining ideas and the laws of thinking, man concurrently explored the structure of the cosmos. With religious justification shifting from salvation by works to salvation by faith, and with, finally, the emancipation of reason from dogma, the separation of thought and universe became complete. The cosmic order became secular "nature," with which man as an exponent of secular reason is confronted. As early as Luther the *unknown* separates out from the *unconscious*, even though the latter is still personified in the form of devils. (That God shades into the devil is characteristic of this turning point. In the course of his first Mass the terror-stricken Luther was, as he himself described it, in doubt whether he was standing in the presence of God or the devil, that is, the ruler of worlds or his own turbulent psyche.)

The problem of knowledge is inherent in the clear opposition of subject and object. With Descartes an investigation was opened into the nature of liberated thought, with special reference to the mental and physical prerequisites for human comprehension of the universe. Consistently pursued, that investigation ultimately leads to the assumption of an *epistemological unconscious* and a *physiopsychological* or *"structural"* unconscious. In Descartes' account of his dreams the *creative unconscious* puts in its appearance, that subliminal faculty which attends to the clarification of problems, the ripening of plans, the fleshing out of mental sketches. We must not confuse the creative unconscious with that realm which Freud called the *preconscious* or *latent consciousness* and which includes everything that is not yet conscious but "admissible to consciousness" and which "barring special resistance and upon fulfillment of certain conditions, can become an object of consciousness."[28] (As early as 1883 Francis Galton in his *Inquiries into Human Faculty* spoke of an "ante-chamber" of consciousness in contrast to the "presence-chamber.") We may include in the preconscious the entire stock of memory, insofar as it is not subject to inhibition; the stock is essentially stable and static, for all that it can be enormously increased. The creative unconscious, on the other hand, is a working, advancing capacity.*

A great deal of evidence, from all ages and peoples down to the present day, testifies to the operation of certain "parapsychological" forces in dreams or dreamlike states (premonitions, second sight, telepathic contacts). There is such a wealth of evidence, and so much of it serious, that it cannot be simply dismissed without being looked into. C. G. Jung, encouraged by his own clinical experiences, has studied such transcausal and "synchronistic" occurrences.[29] It seems likely that there also exists a *magical, "parapsychological"* unconscious. (And who is able to guess, as yet, what regions of the unconscious may be detected by further inquiries into "psychedelic" experiences.)

All such forms of the unconscious are born in darkness; we deduce them from their specific effects. Others, we see distinctly springing from personal or social circumstances. Each of us has no doubt encountered in his dreams certain remnants of the day, indeed fragments of life, representing continuations of *incomplete*

---

* Jacques Maritain in his Mellon Lectures (*Creative Intuition in Art and Poetry*, Bollingen Series XXXV, No. 1 [New York, 1953], Ch. III)—and much earlier Ernst Bloch, the German philosopher—discussed the preconscious as a province of the unconscious. Maritain identifies the preconscious with the function of poetic, or artistic intuition, a dynamic state, a surge *sur le rebord de l'inconscient*, "on the edge of the unconscious"; he calls it a "spiritual" or, in a Platonic sense, "musical unconscious," in contrast to the Freudian unconscious, which he terms the "automatic or deep unconscious, deaf to the intellect and structured into a world of its own, apart from the intellect." Conceived in this sense, the preconscious appears as a special, "musical" part of the creative unconscious. But in all our attempts at distinctions we should not forget that life is not compartmentalized, and that all its functions interconnect and interact.

consciousness, reliving of perceptions, experiences, preoccupations which in the waking state were not fully lived out, failed to cross into the territory of emotion. But even in the waking state we can see the formation of an unconscious which is nothing but *post-consciousness*—consciously strenuous operations which through practice are moved into the unconscious. When we set out to learn some athletic skill such as riding or skiing, we must carry out various movements and positions which could not possibly be coordinated in a purely conscious way; but after regular training, repetition automatizes our efforts and overcomes consciousness, the synthesis is completed and the skill is driven "under the skin," where it remains. In a similar way psychic and intellectual accessions of consciousness sink into the unconscious, forming and widening the "ante-chamber" from which consciousness constantly draws and with the help of which it forges on.

Similarly, the origins of the *reactive* and the *repressive unconscious* can be directly observed or systematically laid bare. Freud explained the highways and byways of the libido and the "death instinct," Adler those of the power drive. Jung—by extending Freud's observations—arrived at his theory of archetypes, which posits a realm beyond the individually based unconscious, a realm he called the "collective unconscious." This term seems to me misleading; what Jung presents is not a collective but a *generic unconscious*—primal images, primal attitudes, which became established in primordial, mythic ages and repeatedly arise in the psyches of generation after generation. Thomas Mann, in his *Joseph* novel and in the Freud lecture connected with it, gave a graphic picture of the pre-temporal, time-foreshortening life-in-myth, in which the whole of life is *imitatio*.

This terminological amendment is all the more important because in our collectivized, organizational society a truly *collective unconscious* has indeed developed. It is made up of residues of certain clichés, slogans, elements of standardized modes of thinking and acting, which sink in from outside, from modern collective life below the threshold of consciousness, and imperceptibly affect men's characters. In this collective unconscious there is gradually building up a power that fights the generic unconscious, or at any rate weakens it. Jung's discovery of archetypal legacies in the psyche made him, like Carus, confident that the unconscious itself could develop healing powers if it were set free. But it seems to me that today's wholly novel superpressure of the collective upon consciousness, and its forcing of material from consciousness into the unconscious, poses a serious threat to these healing powers. The falsifications and distortions produced in both the general and the individual unconscious by this collective pressure can be combatted only in consciousness, by the correcting of our social conditions.

Finally, the shattering of all faiths and the panic-stricken confusion of mind and emotions in our time has shown how much man needs some transcendental security. Only its loss has revealed the value of its ancient protection, has shown that its place in the psyche is the base on which all existence hitherto rested. An extremely deep stratum of the unconscious then becomes uncovered and is brought to consciousness by philosophical and psychotherapeutic analysis, a stratum in which abide the fear of death and life, the fear of death as fear of life. This is the *existential unconscious*. It is most repressed by the hurly-burly of everyday life; indeed, it is the most repressed of all parts of the unconscious; and yet it is operative in the hectic character of all phenomena and activities, in the stubborn, irrational clinging to discredited doctrines and ersatz ideologies, in the mania for proving oneself by acts of brutality. This inexpressible, unarticulable region of the unconscious is the most remote that we have penetrated to; and even as our consciousness has extended its range to this boundary, it is simultaneously shattered by the contact.

The present attempt at an anatomy of the unconscious must, however, never make us forget that the unconscious in itself and in its relation with consciousness is an enormously intricate whole, a living circulation of elements constantly flowing into one another. Its many shadings of types and characteristics show a certain similarity to subatomic particles; more and more new ones are constantly being detected, and yet more and more they distinctly betray the fundamental kinship among them all.

Our little life is rounded with a sleep, not only beyond but also within the boundaries of our existence—insofar as conscious life can be regarded as highest, essential life. Although our consciousness today extends farther than ever before, it nevertheless seems more powerless than ever before. This is because it has collectivized, "depersonalized" itself, and thus become intangible. We tend more and more to be astonished that there is such a thing as consciousness at all.

Rational man believed arrogantly in his autonomy. But in the meanwhile the inner dikes, the psychic walls have been broken down; the id has swelled mightily, has stormed the ego from the rear; ego and world have once more become one, object and subject merge with one another. But these powers which reach into the human psyche are no longer divine or mythic ones, residing outside the self; the power pressing upward is an "it" within man, an object *in* the subject, within the very self of the individual. Even the mythic powers appear to be archetypically incorporated in this self. Thus today consciousness has become a problem for us even more than the unconscious. We have every reason to be modest. Starting from the vast reaches of the unconscious, we must explore consciousness, must seek to attain and to cling to a consciousness of our present human situation.

[1961–1962]

Translated from the German
by Richard and Clara Winston

The Disintegration of Artistic Form

I The Forms of Form

1

ART IS a mode of human expression, a special manifestation of human existence. Art, therefore, just as life itself, is not compartmentalized, and what happens to artistic form seriously affects the human form, the form of man.

I speak of artistic form and of human form. This calls for an initial clarification of what precisely is to be understood by "form," a term which is commonly used very loosely and vaguely. Commonly, form is identified with *shape*. In this broadest, most palpable sense, anything bounded would have some form, and "form" would be equivalent to discernible bounds. But this, it would seem to me, is a very superficial, purely external conception of form. Shape may be the outer aspect of form, but in itself it is not form; it has to be sharply distinguished from form. Only inasmuch as shape constitutes the outer appearance of a *structure*, that is, of an inner organization, an inner organizational coherence of a bounded entity, it is an ingredient of form. *Form*, accordingly, can be defined roughly as structure manifesting itself in shape.

A lake, for instance, has shape, but it has no structure, and it is therefore, in my view, incorrect to speak of the "form of a lake." But any organic body, any living creature has form, indeed *is* form.

161

And the human being, which extends far beyond physical existence into the realms of psychic, intellectual and spiritual reflection, and thus, through memory and awareness of identity, also historically, into the dimension of time is, up to this point, the most highly structured being, the most advanced natural form. In this sense of a being, coherent beyond physical perceptibility, coherent through a reflective awareness that encompasses his psychic, cultural, and temporal existence, we can speak of *the human form*. This concept applies not only to the human individual, whose shape is, at least in part, physically perceptible, it applies also to the *genus humanum as a whole*, as a specific organic form which, if we believe the most recent prehistoric findings, has made its appearance about two and a half million years ago, and whose development has come to transcend its purely physical, and physically perceptible bounds, whose structure and shape can therefore be grasped only by intellectual means. I am fully aware that with such a view I am in striking conflict with the scientistic exclusive reliance on sensory validation and verifiability of facts, as it is overwhelmingly predominant today. It is, however, noteworthy that even in the basic sciences sensory verification has to be achieved in a more and more indirect, indeed abstractly instrumental way, and at certain points it has arrived at apparently impenetrable limits.

The present paper deals primarily with *artistic form* and its implications in regard to the human form. Artistic form is structure and shape created by a human act. This may indeed be accepted as a preliminary distinction of art: *art is form created by a human, intellectual act.*

But if we want to explore the meaning of the present trends in the arts and to establish the criteria indispensable for such a task, we have to delve a little deeper into the nature of form; and for such an endeavor, it seems to me, we cannot find a better point of departure than the first, classical, standard of form established by Aristotle in his *Poetics*. In doing so, we may disregard as irrelevant for our purpose Aristotle's thesis that the motive and function of art consist in imitation, however his concept of *mimesis* may be interpreted. Nor does it seem to me required any longer to dispose of the old aesthetic dichotomy of *form* and *content*. It may be taken for granted after all that "content" and "form" are but two aspects of one and the same thing—the *what* determines the *how*, and, conversely, the *how* does not exist without the *what* which it is meant to show. This is by no means invalidated by the observation that more recently the problem how to render the bewildering complexity of our reality has become the very subject matter of certain works of art. Such apparent "formalization" does not actually mean a prevalence of "form" over "content," it means the presentation in the work of art of the artist's struggle with his task, and of the problem of the possibility of rendering such complexity artistically—a kind of artistic epistemology. Besides, we shall see that it ultimately leads to the dissolution not only of what has been considered as "content," but of artistic form altogether. "Form" breaks down with its substratum, for it is inseparably one with its substratum.

In the passage of the *Poetics* that concerns us here, Aristotle speaks of beauty, but we may, I think, legitimately substitute for it the perfection of form. "Beauty," he says, "depends upon these qualities, size and order. Hence an extremely minute creature cannot be beautiful to us, for our view (of the whole) is confounded when it is formed in an almost infinitesimal moment of time. Nor could a creature of too vast dimensions be beautiful to us . . . for in that case our view could not take all of the object in at once and we do not see the unity of the whole. In the same way, then, as an inanimate object . . . or a living creature must be of such a size that the whole may be easily taken in by the eye (*eusynopton einai*), just so must the plot of a tragedy have a proper length, so that the whole may be easily embraced by the memory. . . . As in the other arts, so in poetry the object is a unit; therefore, in a tragedy, the plot, representing an organically unified action, must be an identical whole, the structural order of the incidents being such that transposing or removing any one of them will dislocate and disorganize the whole; for a thing whose presence or absence makes no perceptible difference is not an organic part of the whole."[1]

For Aristotle, then, a work of art is a closely coherent and consistent whole; it is, or rather should be, what Socrates in Plato's *Phaedrus* correspondingly demands of the discourse: a unit "like a living creature." It is, we may conclude, *a living thing, created by a human, intellectual act*. From the Aristotelian insistence on strict unity and closedness of artistic form, generations of poets and critics deduced the well-known rule of unity of place and time in tragedy.

This classical standard of artistic form has preserved its validity throughout the ages; it has been followed by Dante, by the French classicists and symbolists, by Goethe, by Heinrich von Kleist.* It has been, with increasing flexibility and complexity, the aim of conscious artistry in the last century. It is this form, the pursuit of which made "the joy and the agony" of Flaubert: it is what Henry James called "the sublime economy of art." It is what Flaubert meant when he said, *"les chef-d'oeuvres sont bêtes,"* "masterpieces are dumb," that is to say, they are so self-centered, so at rest in themselves, so rounded and closed, that nothing can enter and affect them from without. It is what Yeats had in mind when he said: "Our words must seem inevitable"; what dominates the work of Cézanne, of Matisse. "In a picture," Matisse says, "every part will be visible and will play the role

---

* Indeed, recently, a pre-Aristotelian, somewhat ritualistic structure of the *Iliad*, corresponding to geometric art, has been demonstrated by Cedric H. Whitman in his beautiful study, *Homer and the Heroic Tradition*, 2nd ed. (Cambridge, 1963). And, in a still more awakened, personally more independent state of human consciousness, Vergil seems to have built his *Aeneid* according to a rigorous structural order. George E. Duckworth, who discovered this order, calls the *Aeneid* "one of the most consciously planned and carefully constructed poems of world literature. . . . [It] reveals a conscious attention to various structural devices: alternation, parallelism by means of similarities and contrasts, concentric framework patterns, tripartite divisions; these appear both in the epic as a whole and in the individual books." ("Mathematical Symmetry in Vergil's *Aeneis*," *Transactions and Proceedings of the American Philological Association*, Vol. XCI 1960). Cf. also the same author's more elaborate work, *Structural Patterns and Proportions in Vergil's Aeneis, A Study in Mathematical Composition* (Ann Arbor, 1962).

conferred upon it, be it principal or secondary. All that is not useful in the picture is detrimental"; "[every drawing] will have a necessary relation to its format" and "When I have found the relationship of all the tones, the result must be a living harmony of tones, a harmony not unlike that of a musical composition." Cézanne's recommendation to "treat nature by the cylinder, the sphere, the cone, everything in proper perspective so that each side of an object, or a plane, is directed towards a central point" corresponds exactly to Tolstoi's demand that every work of art "should have a kind of focus." And this focus must not be completely explainable in words: "the content [of a true work of art] can in its entirety be expressed only by itself."[2] Chekhov's stories, Ibsen's plays, little as they may outwardly show it, reveal themselves upon a closer look as prodigies of meticulous construction. Finally, are not novels like Joyce's *Ulysses*, Thomas Mann's *Doctor Faustus*, Hermann Broch's *Tod des Vergil*—each of them the result of years of intent labor, of weighing and balancing every move and word—are they not vastly expanded and amplified paradigms of the Aristotelian concept of artistic form? There are among such works some whose strict organization bears more of a musical character, others whose order is rather of a pictorial kind; some unfolding their organic sequences and correspondences within the stretch of absolute time, that is, within one homogeneous time, others, more recent ones, in which time itself has become an element of artistic interplay, in which different relative modes of time mingle and intertwine, so as to convey a sense of transcending simultaneity, of a supratemporal space.

In music, accomplished form is evident in the manifold, more and more complex, dialectically dynamic, and yet supratemporal, coherence of compositions. Another requisite of artistic economy, conciseness, has been stressed by the modern composer Anton von Webern: "By art," he writes, "I understand the capacity to put an idea into the clearest, simplest, and that is, most graspable (*fasslichste*) form. . . . [Thus], Beethoven drafted the main theme of the first movement of his 'Eroica' so many times as to get it finally to a degree of simplicity comparable to a sentence of the Lord's Prayer."

2

There are, however, and there always have been, works which are recognized and admired as works of art although they do in no way fit into this classical concept; whose creators, either by disregard or by intent, have transgressed the basic standards of rounded form. Think of the modern novel in its beginnings, the boundless novels of the Baroque, *Don Quixote, Gargantua, Simplizissimus*; of the great English novels of the eighteenth century, and later, the profuse narratives of Balzac, of Dickens, of Proust. Think of the paintings of mannerism, or of Bosch and Breughel. And how about some of the greatest, yet somehow loose, lopsided Shakespeare plays? Or romantic, expressionist, surrealist poetry? Are we to consider all such works just faulty, unfinished, fragmentary endeavors which failed to attain to true form? But in most of them we do not even discover a conscious intention to achieve a closed form. Their creators simply let go, or deliberately go beyond any restrictive bounds. And yet we feel compelled to regard these creations as great works of art. Now what is it, we must ask, that compels us to do so?

To satisfy, or rather evade, this query, the term "open form" has been invented, as far as I can see by the Swiss art historian Heinrich Wölfflin in his book, *Kunstgeschichtliche Grundbegriffe*, 1915—"open form" in contradistinction to "closed form." The concept of open form, however, vague as it is, raises some basic problems. "Closed form" has only one distinct meaning, so precise, in fact, that it seems a redundancy. Being closed within itself like an organic being implies the perfection of form; and, as applied to artistic work, it indicates an effort toward the perfection of form which is by definition artistic. But a work composed in open form is not necessarily a truly artistic one; all sorts of extraneous aims may prevail in it, emotions, purposes, conventions, rhetorics of persuasion, or simply an uncontrolled enjoyment of depiction and narration. So a work constituting an open form requires an additional specification, as to whether and how far it may be considered artistic, and what it is that makes it artistic. When we look carefully we shall find that even in works with "open form" it is some conscious or half-conscious effort toward the perfection of form, i.e., closed form, that makes them artistic.

Any work of art has more than one dimension. Its artistic quality makes itself felt in the spatial dimensions of breadth, length, and depth, and indeed even in the dimension of time—whereby I do not mean "time" merely as an internal, structural element, that is, the rhythmical proportions of the work, but "time" as the medium of the work's evolutional effect, its pioneering capacity.

The structure, the inner coherence of a work of art extends, with its ramifications and correspondences of motifs, first of all, on its more manifest level, in the dimensions of *breadth* and *length*. The dimension of *depth* takes it to other levels, and that implies additional fields of correlation, and a no less essential attribute of the work of art: its *symbolic quality*, its *moving simultaneously on different levels*.

It is this quality which Thomas Hardy seems to have had in mind when he said: "The whole secret of fiction and the drama—in the constructional part—lies in the adjustment of things unusual to things eternal and universal. The writer who knows exactly how exceptional, and how non-exceptional, his events should be made, possesses the key to the art."

Hardy, quite rightly, I think, is saying that the essence of literary art consists in a relationship between two levels of existence. But I would argue that it is neither the relationship of "exceptional" to "non-exceptional," nor the "adjustment" of the "unusual" to the "universal" that makes the difference; it is rather the relationship of the *specific*, be it exceptional or non-exceptional, to the *universal* and it is not an adjustment, but an identity of the particular with the general. No single event has artistic value unless it has generally human relevance. The true artist reaches beyond the phenomenal level, the surface level, on which both the usual and the unusual take place; he drives an occurrence or a situation into a depth of intensity where it is every human being's concern and potentiality. (The commonly "usual," "non-exceptional" is by no means coincident with the humanly universal; it is more often its very opposite, a specific peripheral conventionality, like a ritual, a national custom, a class standard, a fashion.)

Both the commonly usual and the quite unusual, may, in the grasp of an artist, assume a general import. The classical example of the first case is Flaubert's *Un coeur simple*, a story in which something quite ordinary becomes *the* ordinary par excellence. A most trivial course of events, a most inconspicuous character and destiny, are raised to a paradigm of sublimity of the humble, more Christian than anything explicitly so. This is achieved by *symbolic concentration*, and accordingly this story is, like all other works of Flaubert, a *model of closed form*; it is so closely knit, it is done with such perfect accuracy and interaction of parts that not the minutest detail is superfluous or out of place. Here it is the concentration of closed form itself that constitutes the symbolic quality, the identity of two levels of existence.

Just the opposite in every respect are the stories of Balzac, which depict exceptional, indeed eccentric happenings, characters, careers, in a rather loose and prodigal manner. They are, on the phenomenal level, the surface level, striking instances of *open form*. But by their emotional intensity and by their very affluence, even prolixity of description, they achieve what masters of the closed form achieve through the perfection of artistic economy: symbolic depth, and that means, broadly human relevance. They show how within open form, one could even say *by means* of open form, a symbolic conformity, a conformity between two levels of existence can be attained that equals the artistic effect of a completely rounded form.*

The contrast between closed form and such open form as achieves an interlevel, symbolic conformity is exemplified in poetry

---

* There is no particular connection between the narration of the exceptional and open form. Edgar Allan Poe's stories, dealing particularly with extraordinary events, are constructed in the strictest, most calculated fashion.

by the conciseness of the verse of Baudelaire, Mallarmé and Hopkins as against the impetuous flow of Walt Whitman's free rhapsodies.

This interlevel, symbolic conformity is *one* mode of artistic form that occurs within an open form. There are others. Let us take an extreme case of open form, Henry Miller's *Tropic of Cancer*, which, as a whole, is certainly a chaotic book, exceptional in this respect even among the generally ebullient and unorganized narratives of this great author. What makes it artistic, what raises it beyond its entirely private records and sheer obscenities, is the rendering of a scene, a scenery, an atmosphere, with a passionate, sweeping vigor of truth; it is its showing in every instance and instant the multiformity of life with its harsh contrasts, the funny with the wretched, the blooming in the decay, the spark of love and charm in the whore. There are, within the wild flux of effusion, islands of wholeness, such as this:

> Wandering along the Seine at night, wandering and wandering, and going mad with the beauty of it, the trees leaning to, the broken images in the water, the rush of the current under the bloody lights of the bridges, the women sleeping in doorways, sleeping on newspapers, sleeping in the rain; everywhere the musty porches of the cathedrals and beggars and lice and old hags full of St. Vitus' dance; pushcarts stacked up like wine barrels in the side streets, the smell of berries in the market-place and the old church surrounded with vegetables and blue arc-lights, the gutters slippery with garbage and women in satin pumps staggering through the filth and vermin at the end of an all-night souse. . . .*

Such impression and expression of the many-shaded totality of existence, such delight in its newly-felt sub- and suprarational coherence is an achievement of the rarified sensibility of our age. Wherever it appears, even in the midst of entirely uncontrolled narrative, there is artistic form of a closed and rounded nature.

* Henry Miller, *Tropic of Cancer* (New York, Grove Press, Inc., 1961).

This may lead to the paradox of accomplished form made up of the very amorphous, of the debris of our fragmented life, as it appears in recent collages and assemblages, or in lyrics like those of the exquisite, most form-conscious German poet, Gottfried Benn. His poetry conveys, is intended to convey, a feeling of the disruption of organic being, of the shambles of our individual existence—and to convey it in an impeccable form. The very strictness of stanza, meter, and rhyme serves to accentuate the harsh disruptions they tell. Benn's whole work, a despairing attempt at integration of unresolved discord, may be seen implied in his poem *Schutt*, ("Rubble"). I quote two stanzas:

Schutt, alle Trűmmer	Wreckage—all the rubble
liegen morgens so bloss	lies at morning so bare
wahr ist immer nur eines:	true is only and always:
du und das Grenzenlos—	you and the boundless are there—
trinke und alle Schatten	drink, and all the shadows
hăngen die Lippe ins Glas	hang a lip in your glass
fűtterst du dein Ermatten—	if you feed your weakening—
lass—!	leave it and pass—!
Komm, und drăngt sich mit Brűsten	Come, if last life hankerings press into tête-à-tête
Eutern zu Tête à tête	with chest's and breasts' nipples,
letztes Lebensgelűsten,	
lass, es ist zu spăt,	leave it, it is too late.
komm, alle Skalen tosen	Come, all the scales rumble
Spuk, Entformungsgefűhl—	ghosts, sense of decay—
komm, es fallen wie Rosen	come, like roses tumble
Gőtter und Gőtterspiel.	gods, and the gods' play.

Generally, in recent poetry and in certain novelistic works of the twentieth century, form, expressing the totality of existence, be it in a positive, negative or neutral vein, reaches the fastest, transrational concentration: all elaborative, explanatory bridges are broken. "Sometimes," T. S. Eliot remarks in his preface to Djuna

Barnes' *Nightwood*, "in a phrase the characters spring to life so suddenly that one is taken aback, as if one had touched a wax-work figure and discovered that it was a live policeman." The flash-like abruptness of metaphorical connections opens a depth and subtlety of precision such as has never been attained before. Here are from *Nightwood*, a few examples of characterization of a woman:

> Her movements were slightly headlong and sideways: slow, clumsy and yet graceful, the ample gait of the nightwatch. . . . She was gracious and yet fading, like an old statue in a garden, that symbolizes the weather through which it has endured, and is not so much the work of man as the work of wind and rain and the herd of the seasons, and though formed in man's image is a figure of doom. [Or this:] When she touched a thing, her hands seemed to take the place of the eye. . . . Her fingers would go forward, hesitate, tremble, as if they had found a face in the dark. When her hand finally came to rest, the palm closed; it was as if she had stopped a crying mouth. . . .*

In passages like this the innermost nerve of a human being is touched with subtle marksmanship, a layer of truth is reached on the frontier of expression.

But such artistic feats of elucidation occur not only in the realm of art proper, where all the transrational faculties of language, magical, metaphorical, musical, can be applied. They can also appear in the rational domain, wherever a thinker, scholar, or scientist penetrates beyond the jargon of restrictive research and achieves a presentation of a broader coherence, a clarification of a comprehensive entity or problem. In all such cases a congruity of reality and expression, a rounded form, is accomplished. Often, the attempt to verbalize a problem, to assemble and connect its various aspects from a transcompartmental vantage point, discloses a new range and depth of insight. It is because of this capacity of verbal clarification, of unfolding in a non-specialized language a broad

* Reprinted by permission of the author and New Directions Publishing Corporation.

complex of reality, that thinkers like Bergson, Freud, Teilhard de Chardin have been called "artistic."

A well-built sentence whose elements—articulation, meaning, imagery, rhythm—are set in the right proportions, in a balance serving clarity and melos at once and as tightly as possible, is itself a microcosm of closed form. Even in a wordless mathematical demonstration with its "elegant" short cuts we may see the perfection of closed form.

3

Up to this point we have dealt with closed form in its various manifestations: as an integrally finished work, or as embedded in open form, be it through symbolic conformity of two or more levels of existence, or by a lucidly synoptic rendering of a character, a situation, a problem, a totality of existence.

It happens, however, that an open form as such has artistic validity. There is, apart from organic integrality in the dimensions of breadth, length, and depth, still another indispensable property, another *sine qua non* of art, namely, as has been indicated before, its creative extension in the dimensions of time, that is, its *evolutional capacity*. Any genuine artistic effort operates on the frontier of the expressible, conquering the hitherto untouched, ungrasped, unrevealed. A work lacking this ultimate effort is stale and without artistic value. Hence novelty, in this sense of initiatory creation, is an essential constituent of a work of art.

Now novelty, of necessity, opens traditionally closed form, it breaks through the forms which have been established before. Whenever new spheres, new depths of existence are disclosed by a thrust into the unknown, these new differential experiences will have to be integrated into a further, completed whole in order to reach a new and broader perfection of form. To be sure, our experience of the fundamental dynamism of reality has shown us all closed form to be a mere temporary halt on the road of endlessly moving processes. And yet, lest all efforts be lost in chaotic discontinuity and singularity, new discoveries have to be related with extant realizations; again and again the wholeness of existence must be re-established, a new, wider and more complex wholeness must be apprehended. This is true of the body of our scientific and scholarly knowledge; it is most particularly true of art whose very principle rests on the creation of form, which means, of wholeness.

In this perpetual situation of art between the breaking and the completion of form, it happens that certain experimental ventures, not having reached a settling integration, appear unbalanced, lopsided by extravagance and overemphasis of their new vistas. They point to a future, still imaginary supplementation. Open, fragmentary forms that they are, they are nevertheless artistic by virtue of their exploratory quality, their seeking a deeper truth, a deeper congruence with reality. Take as an example *Tristram Shandy*, this revolutionary work par excellence, which was intentionally created as an open form, to be continued and added on to indefinitely, as long as the life of its author would last. Its probes and innovations —disruptive in their time—have been integrated into closed form by the artists of our own epoch.

II The Triumph of Incoherence

1

More recently, however, a boundless predominance of this exploratory function of art has led to a critical point, where the survival of art as it was known through the millennia is in jeopardy. We are witnessing ventures which in their search for an expression of new reality have lost the sense of formal coherence altogether. Reality, to them, is so hopelessly disrupted that no consistent whole seems conceivable any longer. They either resort to a scornful presentation of the bare fragments of our existence, or deviate into sheer abstraction, confounding form with mechanical construction.

These experiments, to be sure, reflect the condition of our world and, most particularly, the condition of our psyche. As a result of complex developments, which cannot be followed up here in greater detail, the processes of the unconscious have come to prevail over the acts of consciousness. More and more, since the rise of irrationalism and romanticism in the eighteenth century, the outer world, the world of happenings and actions was seen as a reflection of the inner world of the psyche. In the nineteenth century, under the influence of the great Russian novelists, and increasingly in our century, the unconscious has become the object of artistic scrutiny. Phenomenal reality, pervaded by rationality as it is, was felt to be a fictitious surface reality, and true reality receded to ever deeper subliminal levels until it finally appeared unfathomable.

Nathalie Sarraute describes this process in her essay *De Dostoiewski à Kafka*:[3]

> The time had passed when Proust could venture to believe that "by pushing his impression to the utmost limit of penetration [he could] attempt to reach that ultimate bottom where the truth, the real universe and our authentic impression rest." But after all, informed by successive delusions, everybody was well aware that there was no ultimate ground. "Our authentic impression" had been revealed to consist of multifold layers of depth, and these depths extended ad infinitum. The depth that Proust's analysis had uncovered, turned out to be just another surface. The still deeper depth that the inner monologue, on which such legitimate hopes were placed, had brought to light, proved a surface again. And the immense leap of psychoanalysis, sweeping all stages and traversing several levels of depth in one stride had shown the inefficiency of classical introspection and makes us question the absolute value of all methods of research. So, the *homo absurdus* was the dove of the arch, the messenger of deliverance.*

A related process is apparent in the visual arts. The portraits of Van Gogh, of Kokoschka, of Beckmann no longer render the im-

* Nathalie Sarraute disregards the fact that each of these thrusts into the psychic underground has conquered for our consciousness a stage of reality, a level of being that has its lasting place in the expanse of existence. Existence, to be sure, is bottomless, it reaches into unfathomable grounds of emergence. But this in no way nullifies the reality and validity of the various gradations of psychic depth, as apprehended by artistic and scientific explorations. Something irrevocable happened through these explorations: they vastly extended the field of consciousness.

mediate, physiognomical appearance of a person—this the masters of the Renaissance and since have already exhausted. Their vision reaches beyond these surfaces; they seek "the bridge from the visible to the invisible," as Beckmann put it, for the psychic aura of a human being. Even their landscapes bare, animistically as it were, a psychic quality of the sceneries. In further pursuits artists were led to exploring the structure of phenomenality as such, and thereby to the analytical decomposition of the world of objects. The counterpart of the *homo absurdus* in literature may be seen in certain surrealist creations.

But this is only one branch of a complex, centrifugal process that issued from the ascendancy of the unconscious. Another turn of developments produced different results. The unconscious no longer remained a mere *object* of conscious acts exploring hidden regions of the psyche or depths of phenomenality. It seized upon the artistic act itself and emerged as the very *enactor* of artistic creation, as we see it at work in "beat" literature and "action painting." Nor did developments stop at this stage for any length of time—in our days they grow ever more rapid and hectic. Another conclusion was drawn from the condition of existential insecurity, again brought forward by Nathalie Sarraute: "Modern man, body without soul, tossed about by hostile forces, was ultimately nothing else but what he appeared from outside." Indeed all of reality came to be seen in this way. The despair of ever being able to gain a firm stand in the unconscious and to cast an anchor in the immense anarchy of our world turned people back to the presentation of the crudest surfaces of things, to pure, immediate materiality. "It looks," the former dadaist Hans Richter writes, "as if people today needed the instantly palpable material object to hold on to as a confirmation of their presence in this world; as if man could find himself substantiated only through his contact with his five senses, since in him all is broken up and uncertain. An inner void seems to force him outward, an urge to convince him of his existence by way of the object, because the subject, man himself, got lost. . . . Our generation has become so greedy of presence that even the lid of a w.c. is holy to us, we are not satisfied with seeing it pictured, we want to *have* it altogether, bodily."[4]

The pop artist Jim Dine, who exhibits "self-portraits" in the shape of empty bathrobes surrounded by tools and other objects, told an interviewer that having seen an advertisement of a bathrobe in the *New York Times* he first intended to use it at will when it suddenly looked to him as if he himself were in it. A striking correspondence to this notion we find in the French *nouveau roman*, particularly in the novels of Robbe-Grillet. Here man is left vacant amidst his prevailing surroundings, he appears as a hollow existence, only functionally reflected in surreally protrusive objects and behavioral responses. "Instead of [the] universe of 'signification' . . . ," Robbe-Grillet writes, "we must try . . . to construct a world both more solid and more immediate. Let it be first of all by their *presence* that objects and gestures establish themselves, and let this presence continue to prevail over whatever explanatory theory may try to enclose them in a system of references, whether emotional, sociological, Freudian or metaphysical. In this future universe of the novel, gestures and objects will be *there* before being *something*; and they will still be there afterwards, hard, unalterable, eternally present, mocking their own 'meaning,' that meaning which vainly tries to reduce them to the role of precarious tools, of a temporary and shameful fabric woven exclusively—and deliberately— by the superior human truth expressed in it. . . . Henceforth . . . novels will gradually lose their instability and their secrets, will renounce . . . that suspect interiority which Roland Barthes has called 'the romantic heart of things' . . . not only do we no longer consider the world as our own, our private property, designed according to our needs . . . but we no longer even believe in its depth."* It seems not to have occurred to Robbe-Grillet that the

* Alain Robbe-Grillet, *For a New Novel, Essays on Fiction*, trans. by Richard Howard (New York, Grove Press, Inc., 1965), pp. 21–24. The same trend may be gathered from a comparison of Rilke's aspiration for acting as the "mouthpiece of things (*der Mund der Dinge*)," which means voicing, through animistic empathy, a thing's imaginary soul, with Francis Ponge's *parti pris des choses*, "siding with the things," i.e., professing thingness as such, indeed seeing the human being as a thing. (Cf. his sketch *La Jeune Mère*.)

universe closely surrounding our life consists predominantly and increasingly of man-made objects, objects constructed for human purposes. More and more, nature, i.e., objects and beings that are genuinely independent of man, give way to artifacts in which human "significances," human conditions and changes are indelibly contained, and which certainly will not be there afterwards any more than they have been there before. On the contrary, they prove more transitory, more temporary than even man himself. This whole transformation of the surroundings and circumstances of our life, this externalization of our universe, expressed in the *nouveau roman* itself, and in Robbe-Grillet's thesis, indeed *means* something, it indicates something more than its surface presence, namely a transformation of man himself, his transition from individual to collective existence.

The new novelists' radical attention to sheer materiality involves, however, its very reversal. The subtly constructed works of Robbe-Grillet show the inherent connection of the extreme of quasi-tactual phenomenalism with the opposite extreme of acutest abstractness, in fact, the turn of one extreme into the other. The completely objectified rendition of a more and more externalized world and the total elimination of human motivation and sentiment, this is an artistic proceeding of utmost reduction; it can be undertaken only by means of keenest analytical pursuance of a factuality that is unreal in its not only imperceptible, but actually imaginary minutiae. The flow of actuality is dissected into slightest particulars. It leads to a formalism, a skeletal form, in which all vital substance has faded away. A ghostly consciousness is confronted with itself.

2

A closer scrutiny of these processes may further clarify the intrinsic movement from the prevalence of the unconscious to the functional isolation of consciousness through the loss of human substance, and finally to the disruption of reality and our means of communication.

Any artistic work has its ultimate roots in the unconscious. In creating his work, the artist always partly moves in his psychic underground; and even in the most strained efforts of artistic consciousness a residue of unconscious process inheres. No artist has ever been able fully to comprehend and control the scope of his work. After its completion the work starts on a life of its own, and only then it unfolds its whole meaning and effect unknown to its author. Picasso has stressed the role of the unconscious in his working. "When I paint," he said, "my objective is to show what I have found and not what I was looking for. In art, intentions are not sufficient. . . . I go for a walk in the forest of Fontainebleau. I get 'green' indigestion. I must get rid of this sensation into a picture. . . . A painter paints to unload himself of feelings and visions. . . ."[5] Similarly, Kafka, in his conversations with Gustav Janouch, said that his story *The Stoker* was the reminiscence of a dream, that *The Judgment* was a nightmare which had to be recorded, "stated" as a measure of defense and protection. "One pictures things in order to banish them. My stories are a manner of closing the eyes." And "the dream reveals a reality that our imagination cannot reach. Hence the terrifying quality of life— the heartrending quality of art." These sentences afford a clue to the whole work of Kafka.

Both these artists, however, have given the greatest conscious care to the form of conveying their experiences. Such scrupulous control, the working of a long-trained meditative sensibility is apparent in their creations; it is also explicitly attested. Picasso tells us of his procedure which he calls "a sum of destructions," but which actually is true abstraction, as exemplified by that sequence of drawings in which he gradually divested the figure of a bull of its naturalistic detail until the very essence of its structure lay bare. "In my case," Picasso says, "a picture is a sum of destructions. I do a picture— then I destroy it. . . . It would be very interesting to preserve photographically . . . the metamorphoses of a picture. Possibly, one might discover the path followed by the brain in materializing a dream. . . . You must always *start with something*. Afterwards you

can remove all traces of reality. There's no danger then, anyway, because the idea of the object will have left an indelible mark. It is what started the artist off, excited his ideas and stirred up his emotions. Ideas and emotions will in the end be prisoners in his work."[6]
Kafka's diaries give evidence of his constant struggle for the utmost precision in describing a phenomenon, of "the frightful strain and joy"—almost the same words as Flaubert's—"how the story developed before me, how I moved ahead in troubled waters. Several times during this night [when he wrote *The Judgment*] I bore my own weight on my back." This is what distinguishes the true poet: writing, he has to bear his own weight, the weight of his life on his back.

So these two great artists are fully aware of the unconscious sources of their creations. They consciously include the unconscious, they acknowledge the part it plays in their creation; yet they guide it, they work it out.

In the products of tachism, of "action painting," of "beat" literature and of a certain phase of multiform Dadaism, however, the unconscious is unleashed as sheer raw material, it is released intentionally, programmatically. Thus a peculiar, inorganic conjunction of consciousness and the unconscious takes place. In painting, it began with the revolt against the frame—the last buttress of form. (The impressionists had already cut off segments of the thematic, "objective" text of paintings—figures, movements, scenery—in favor of purely pictorial concordance.) The action painters' concern is no longer the finished work so much as the *act* of painting, which is supposed to guide the painter in his quest for identity.* A disciple of Mark Rothko (Okada) prescribes explicitly:

* With Edward Albee the creative process appears, in a certain sense, parallel to Picasso's and Kafka's or rather transitional to what could be called "action writing." "When I was writing *Tiny Alice*," he declared in an interview, "to a certain extent I didn't have any idea what I was doing. When I write plays, the writing of the play is an act of discovery for me. I find out what I was thinking about. I find out what was bothering me. And a certain time after the play I can say to myself, 'Ha! That is what I intended.' " The difference from the action painters consists in that here not the identity of the artist, but the identity of the artistic intent is supposed to be revealed by the creative act.

"Start painting with nothing and let it grow" [italics mine]. This results in whole walls of aggressive line and color whirls full of ebullient vitality, or shaded color squares, divided by horizontal or vertical lines. The effects on devotees consist, as Rothko himself once indicated, in a kind of mystical communication and ecstasy, similar to those aroused by the *musique concrète* and the frameless, static dynamism of jazz.

Such displays of the unconscious are, however, often supplemented by efforts of consciousness, that is, commentaries, interpretations, titles, which are affixed to the exhibited paintings. Indeed, with some of these painters such interpretations appear retroactively as original intentions revealed by the creative process. The exposition of an apparently incoherent or accidental arrangement is presented as "abstraction."

True abstraction is brought about by an act of concentrating an entity, a process, an impression, an argument, to the point where their essence is laid bare. In abstract expressionism, however, nothing is recognizable wherefrom these products may have been abstracted. They lack a substratum of abstraction and accordingly also that trace of creative origination and effort that can be sensed in any former work of art or thought, be it ever so accomplished in itself.

So what produces such paintings is not abstraction, but rather reduction. To be sure, reduction can also be seen as a kind of abstraction, an inverse abstraction, an abstraction into the concreteness of bare material, a divestment of substance.* Action

---

* The Museum of Modern Art has acquired a huge canvas, a paradigm of total reduction, which its originator, Ad Reinhardt, calls "Abstract Painting" and explains as follows: "A square (neutral, shapeless) canvas, five feet wide, five feet high, as high as a man, as wide as a man's outstretched arms (not large, not small, sizeless), trisected (no composition), one horizontal form negating one vertical form (formless, no top, no bottom, directionless), three (more or less) dark (lightless), non-contrasting (colorless) colors, brushwork brushed out to remove brushwork, a mat, flat, free-hand painted surface (glossless, textureless, non-linear, no hard edge, no soft edge) which does not reflect its surroundings—a pure, abstract, non-objective, timeless, spaceless, changeless, relationless, disinterested painting—an object that is self-conscious (no unconsciousness), ideal, transcendent, aware of nothing but art (absolutely no anti-art)."

painters still feel compelled to attribute to their works some extra-pictorial, metaphysical substance. But that pictorial reduction, that "abstraction" into the material elements of painting, leads as a consequence straight into "pop art," the abandonment not only of all pictorial substance, but of painting altogether, the display of material objects as such, or better, of fragments of objects or objects *as* fragments of our overcrowded and disrupted world.

In turn, such fragments of our world are brought into some extraneous relation, indeed sometimes into an exquisite formal balance, by an artistic consciousness we find at work in certain collages and assemblages which render the coexistence of the wildly contrasting residues of our daily life: relics of nature with pieces of technology, the closely familiar with the oddly rotten. Hovering over them one senses a mood of melancholy irony, of aimless rebellion, as vocalized in the manifestations of the "beat" movement.

This movement follows Allen Ginsberg's call: "Unscrew the locks from the doors! Unscrew the doors themselves from their jambs!" Here again, emotions, impressions, day and night dreams, and scraps of knowledge are let loose in rapturous medley. Ginsberg's and Kerouac's master, William Burroughs, declares: "I write about what is in front of my senses at the moment of writing. I do not presume to impose 'story' or 'plot' or 'continuity.'" Again, contrasts are deliberately sharpened.

But with the "beats" the intentional incoherence takes place in the domain of *language*, where the disjunctive tendencies carry into the very heart of the human constitution.

3

The problematic nature of language and, implicitly, the uncertainty of human communication has troubled people's minds for more than two and a half centuries. The awareness of it dawns in Locke's inquiry into the "Imperfection of Words," it manifests itself in *Tristram Shandy* and in *The Sorrows of Young Werther*. It grew with the increasing complexity of Western man's life and psychic condition, and more rapidly with the development of the collectivizing, instrumentalizing, functionalizing apparatus of our daily subsistence, which estranges man from man, and parts inner truth from compelling actuality.

The scrutiny of language issued from different sources: literary, philosophical and, last but not least, psychological. It grew into a widespread process, in which the various trends and effects interact. In the domain of letters it led to art questioning itself, its own function, methods, capacity of expression; and in a more advanced stage of the process, this inquiry into the communicative medium merges with the motif to be conveyed; experimental techniques prevail over and finally become the very subject matter of works of art. In true art, as it was said before, "form" and "content" are only two aspects of one and the same thing: the *what* determines the *how*. Recently, however, the order is reversed: the *how* not only determines, it downright constitutes the *what*. "The medium is the message," as McLuhan's timely slogan puts it. This medium concept—at least with regard to the "mass" aspect of media—corresponds to the physical field concept and reflects our collectivizing functionalism.

Let us follow up the development. It starts from the poetic incentive of Mallarmé, whose innovation appears as the ultimate source of recent linguistic experiments. What actuated Mallarmé's theory was, above all, a reaction against the preceding styles—for a full understanding of a literary movement it is always necessary to consider its epochal position and opposition. The French *poésie pure* arose from repugnance against the time-worn "philosophical" poetry of Romanticism and Classicism, as well as against the unpoetic, descriptive aim of Naturalism, hence against ideas or facts as poetic motives and motifs. The new poets' weariness of a mode of expression made hollow by sentimentality and rhetoric drew their creative attention to the body of language, to the self-contained effects of words: "The work of art in its complete purity implies the disappearance of the poet's oratorical presence. The poet leaves the initiative to the words, to the clash of their mobilized diversities. The words ignite through mutual reflexes like a flash of fire over jewels. Such reflexes replace that respiration [of the poet] perceptible in the old lyrical aspiration or the enthusiastic personal direction of the sentence."[7] This assertion shows clearly the turn against the previous declamatory style which was still prevalent at the time. More revealing is another statement which was intended to avert possible misunderstandings. "I do not see," Mallarmé writes, "—and this is my intense opinion—that anything that was beautiful in the past could ever become extinct. I remain convinced that in most cases the grand tradition whose preponderance stirs ever anew the classical capacity for genius will always be followed. But, to be sure, this will be achieved only if the venerable echoes are not disturbed for the sake of a puff of sentimentality, or for the sake of a narrative. Every soul is a melody which has to be re-vivified ever anew, and this is what everyone's flute or fiddle is for."[8] Just as Flaubert wants the novel to be strictly objective and rejects any personal intervening of the author, so, correspondingly, Mal-larmé insists that the "enthusiastic" poet disappear from the fin-ished poem. Yet, in his poems Mallarmé never gave up the coherence of meaning and the poet's control.

Mallarmé's suggestion was realized by Joyce in *Finnegans Wake*, but in a very different sense. With him, the ignition of words through confrontation has given way to their quasi-autonomous association through sound, producing a concentration of meanings. This is used as a means to render a vast symbolic network of motifs.

It was Dadaism which actually came to practice a completely free, undirected assemblage of words and linguistic sounds, as pre-luded by Rimbaud, for whom this was plainly jocose nonsense (*connerie*), by Futurist ventures (Marinetti), and by Apollinaire's principle of coincidence. Dada, this exuberantly inventive move-ment, uncommitted, flexible, humorous, using all imaginable means of provocation, anticipated everything that today is carried on by pedantic bores. In Dada we still sense the prime freshness of militant protest and behind it the groping for a new order, dis-persed later in different directions, according to the various tem-peraments of the members of the group. Richard Huelsenbeck, one of the founders of Dadaism in 1916, describes their common motivation as follows: "The Dadaists—far ahead of their time—were people whose peculiar sensibility made them aware of the approaching chaos and who tried to overcome it. . . . [They] were creative irrationalists who understood (unconsciously rather than consciously) what the chaos signified. . . . They loved the non-sensical without, however, losing sight of the sensible."[9] For them, too, non-sense remained nonsense.

In the meantime chaos has fully erupted, extending into suprahuman dimensions. The "beat" poets, while still revolting, seem to have settled down in it, and indeed to overstress it. In the poetry of Ginsberg, Gregory Corso, and others of the movement, the boundless rhapsodizing of Walt Whitman, reversed into disillusionment by the experiences of our age, is kept in motion through psychic, visual, and verbal free association.

4

Clearly, the literary development since the end of the nineteenth century shows a growing tendency toward dissolution of linguistic form. Syntactic and rational coherence is broken up, construction gives way to contraction or fragmentation. Yet, in all the works we have considered so far, language still remains human discourse. Human beings speak to human beings, be it to themselves.

With the present avant-garde movements, however, spreading all over the countries and continents of the West, language has ceased to be human communication. Just as the objects crowding around us are no longer implements of man, but have been given by subservient man an autonomous, overbearing character, so language is being dealt with as an external object, detached from its human manifestation and meaning. This does not prevent, on the contrary it makes all the more possible, its free intellectual manipulation. The isolation of words from their significative coherence— this started with Marinetti's "free words," *parole in libertà,* 1912 —is equivalent to their severance from their substance, i.e., human expression, and what remains is a devised free association of linguals, or a promiscuity of fractured, defunct meanings, corpses of meaning. It is paralleled, on the level of actuality, by the performance of random, discordant "happenings" per se. The inanimate word has nothing left to keep it from further disintegration into its components, into syllables and letters; indeed the letters themselves do not subsist any longer as form units, they break asunder into parts of their linear figurations, and what started as poetry ends up in typography. It thereby passes over into the sphere of the visual arts, where the wordless and so also the worldlessly transobjective is legitimate: matters beyond verbal expressibility, subtle balances, proportions, spatial forms and transcendencies, indeed most delicate psychic messages find here their accomplished expression—as originally with Mondrian, Klee, Braque, Miro, among others, and today, to quote only a few examples, with Nicholson, Manessier, Vieira da Silva, Gabo, Bissier. And the alphabetical leavings of post-lettristic writers meet with the imaginative letter paraphrases of artists like Mark Tobey and Tomlin, which derive from what Tobey called "the calligraphic impulse."

This is the process we are witnessing. It obviously corresponds to the developments leading to pop art—and op art in its stereotypically reductive variety—to "punctual," "concrete," and unintegrated electronic music; indeed, since Futurism, the borderlines between the various arts had become fluid. The same uncertainty about human communication, the same distrust of the language of meanings can be found in the attempts of analytical and linguistic logic to establish most rigorous conceptual delimitations, efforts that produce even more dissection and paralyzing insecurity. The heroic struggle of that dangerous genius, Wittgenstein, to rid us of problems ended up in unanswerable questions. All these contemporary endeavors are pervaded by a longing for the safety of the mathematical formula, which, however, can warrant such safety only when applied to models, theoretical or mechanical constructions, or statically circumscribed physical areas, but will never be able fully to comprehend the dynamically variable conditions of human existence.

The avant-garde movement has taken hold of all artistic domains, and under the fanfares of thrilling innovations, sounding everywhere, from Brazil to Iceland, literature fades away, not only into graphics, but into sound associations and mechanistic regimentation. There are "pop poems," "audiopoems," "machine poems," "concrete," "visual" and "phonic" poetry. An "audiopoem" (Henri Chopin) is a flux of natural and mechanical sounds (spoken and recorded by the poet) ranging from breathings, grunts, clicks, and whistles to dentist's drills, circular saws, ship's horns, and distant planes. Inasmuch as this performance is meant to be accompanied by a simultaneous show of illustrative drawings, it is an example of what is proclaimed as "spatial poetry," connecting phonetic and visual dimensions (Henri Garnier). We have poetic ventures called "topographies," "articulations," "combinations," "constellations," "demonstrations," "tautologies," "paralinguistic modes of communication," "permutational art." We have the "electronico-lyrics" of the Portuguese school, the lettristic "mecha-aesthetics, integral and infinitesimal," we have a "programming of beauty," characterized as "precise pleasures" (Max Bense).

5

Many people, including intellectuals, are inclined to consider these movements as vogues of folly that will pass. But it seems to me that they are to be taken very seriously. They are the outcome of an evolutional trend, a consistent artistic and broadly human development that I have tried to delineate. Let me recall: the overwhelming preponderance of collectivity with its scientific, technological and economic machinery, the increasing incapacity of individual consciousness to cope with the abstract anarchy of its environment, and its surrender to the collective consciousness that operates anonymously and dispersedly in our social and intellectual institutions—all this has shifted the center of gravity of our world from existential to functional, instrumental, and mechanical ways of life. At the same time, the hypertrophy of rationalization has produced an overcompensating irrationality, reversing to the bodily concrete or spiraling to the absurd. Hence the products of the avant-gardes display a strange blend of imaginative vagaries with technological and pseudo-scientific aspirations. Fragments of unconscious and sensory experience are in a ghostly manner treated with an exactitude derived from rational consciousness.

Let us look a little closer into the arguments, programs, and experimental practices of the recent "language" operators.

We are faced with the basic question: What is language? what is it for?

No human time is known to us when language was anything else but a more or less articulate mode of expression of the human being, expression of human feelings, experiences, thoughts, aims and desires, to be communicated to other beings. We shall never be able to trace the actual genesis of human language, but there can hardly be any doubt that it was the urge to express and to communicate, one passing into the other, that brought language forth. Today, for the first time in human history, language is being divorced from its human source and treated as a separate, independent thing.

Among the linguistic experiments of the avant-gardes three trends and evolutionary stages are distinguishable, although they mingle and blur in the process—there is much enthusiastic confusion. What all of them have in common is the isolation of linguistic material, which means getting rid of what is seen as content. The movement started with the elimination of sentiment, of all "emotional encumbrances," which are said to "deform and misuse the words." The word is supposed to constitute pure information "whose meaning is disclosed through the constellation,* i.e., the experimental combination with other words."[10] The aim is "getting behind the mirror" (*attraversare lo specchio*), as one of the Italian

---

* "By constellation I understand the arrangement of a few, diverse words, in such a way that their mutual relationship does not come about primarily through syntactical means, but through their material, concrete co-presence in the same compass." Eugen Gomringer, *Material* I (Darmstadt, 1958), quoted in Franz Mon, ed., *Movens: Dokumente und Analysen zur Dichtung, bildenden Kunst, Musik, Architektur* (Wiesbaden, 1960), p. 112.

innovators, Alfredo Giuliani, puts it,[11] the "mirror" being human expression. "There exist," he declares, "certain modes of that mechanical esperanto of imagination . . . which in themselves cannot be considered negative or positive, but simply factual; they form part of the material of that 'heteronomous semanticity' which the epoch offers to the writer. . . . It is . . . archaic to attempt using a *contemplative* language, which pretends to preserve, not so much the value and the possibility of contemplation, but its unreal syntax."[12] According to Giuliani, imagination itself in our days is discontinuous, "schizomorphic," and calls for "asyntactism" (*asintattismo*). A German experimentator, Helmut Heissenbüttel, is even more explicit. He contends that the old "withered" syntactical model *subject-object-predicate* is obsolete and no longer capable of conveying the new, the not-yet-graspable that is forming in our age. Therefore he wants to "penetrate into the innermost of language, to break it up and to sound out its remotest, most concealed relationships."[13]

Since the word combination of a regular, syntactic sentence is formed to express a content, that is, a substratum deriving from a human source and "encumbered" by uncontrollable personal overtones, by sentiments, sensibilities, experiences and contemplations, only combinations of originally incoherent words must appear capable of warding off such interferences. But, apart from the unescapable fact that even single words carry, indeed consist of nothing else than fragmented residues of some human significance, it is hardly conceivable how such combinations of incoherent sense-fragments could ever establish meaningful information. And where is "the new, the not-yet-graspable" to be registered, if not in the experiencing human mind? Where can we expect a new language to issue, if not from an extreme human effort to form an expression of new experience?*

This perverted "information theory" leads up—or rather down,

* The studies of Benjamin Lee Whorf have shown that linguistic forms, syntactive structures derive from the mental constitution of peoples, and vice versa. How could it be possible to do away with the syntactic structure of a language without abolishing the whole ethnic experience and the mental and psychic attitude toward reality of a particular people, and in our case of the Indo-

as we shall see—to the second stage of the avant-garde movement, which may be gathered from the theses of another German writer, Franz Mon: "The language of instantaneous composition [i.e., composition disregarding communicative meaning] is achieved through purely physiological articulation, in contrast to the language of communication that is made an efficient instrument by the repetition necessary to it. In the former, it is possible to reduce the meaning-values to such an extent that the articulatory process itself becomes a sign of intrinsic gesticulatory value, whereas the articulatory process disappears in communication. In instantaneous composition, the next step follows spontaneously from the constellation immediately preceding. The organs of articulation move of themselves from one position to the next."[14] This is further explained in another statement:

> Immediately at the threshold of articulation, noticeable in the particular chewing motion of the speech organs, lie the elementary words (*Kernworte*), which, this side of imagery, already penetrate under our skin; in them erotic and pre-erotic elementals are quite concrete; words are stimulatory forms of a reality that we often can reach only with their help. . . . Speaking, right at the threshold of articulation, is dance of the lips, the tongue, the teeth, articulated, and therefore accurate motion; words, the basic figures of the dance, carry along with them, to be sure, meanings, relations, shadows of images, but slurred into a distinctive motion that is directed solely by itself. . . . Long before all speech, lips, tongue, and teeth have performed the movements of appropriation, destruction, love and lust, they are informed by these experiences when they begin to form for speaking. Inevitably, the gestures of speaking will blend with

---

Germanic family of peoples? A fresh start would have to come from a level inaccessible to man's volition. "The tremendous importance of language," Whorf writes, "cannot, in my opinion, be taken to mean . . . that nothing is back of it of the nature of what has traditionally been called 'mind.' My own studies suggest to me, that language, for all its kingly role, is in some sense a superficial embroidery upon deeper processes of consciousness which are necessary before any communication, signaling, or symbolism whatsoever can occur" (Benjamin Lee Whorf, *Language, Thought and Reality* [Cambridge, Mass., paperback ed. 1964], p. 239).

the traits of those elementary movements . . . to this end, they avail themselves of the most fleeting stuff, the air, squeezing, pushing, sucking it to probe the elementary gestics the world abounds with. Here, we are dog, pig, bull, and rooster. . . .[15]

In this concept, the attempt to reach beyond the language of meanings takes us to a prehuman, animal level, a sphere below an unconscious—since the unconscious presupposes consciousness —a sphere also below imagery, a sphere where language consists of gestures. The physiological process of speech-forming, as described in the passage quoted, is not meant to represent just a stage of human evolution, it is assumed to go on perpetually in the human being, to form the basis of human language where meanings undeniably exist, but are seen as irrelevant. From this conjectural actualization and perpetuation of the evolutional process it is concluded that meanings, "shadows of images," no longer control a sentence, they are carried along, "slurred" into a motion that of itself determines its sense. We have arrived at the lowest conceivable level of association, association no longer of images of the unconscious, no longer of conceptual word images—"mutual reflexes like flashes over jewels"—nor through sound linkage of meanings, but association through "gestics," motion per se.*

Now human language is not an oral ballet. It starts, whatever may be said, with "imagination," forming of images, signs, meanings, with the simplest grasp of connections, with all that makes it possible to be something more than dog, pig and rooster, to put oneself in another's place, and thus establish a relationship with a psychic and mental opposite. Human language springs from incipient consciousness and aims at a responding, corresponding consciousness. By expressing something it implicitly tends to move

* To be sure, language *is* inherently gesture as much and as far as it is action. It is gesture in a sublimated, elaborated, "articulated" form. In his beautiful essay *Language as Gesture*, Richard Blackmur has shown how at the height of intensity, so often in poetry, language *becomes* gesture, "gains the force of gesture." Indeed, sometimes the primordial gesture breaks out beyond the words, "out of the native soil of feeling." Gesture in this sense is very different from the "gestics," the physical emotionless motions to which language is reduced in Mon's imaginary concept.

someone to some effect. Hence, it can never be shoved along by a sheer self-directed motion; it is always directed by the urge or the will of a human being.

The following is a demonstration of Franz Mon's conception of the beginnings of articulation, entitled *From What You Evolve* (*Aus was du wirst*):

```
rakon   tsiste   himil   kokard   reche   chrest   sukzess   arb
    hakon   tris   umir   kott   ädre   rest   kukt   abe
        acre   dress   umsens   gorf   eder   kest   schuga
            kran   drett   rums   gror   dree   kir   sus
                krakä   dreis   rirn   grett   erd   rich
                    kras   erk   ir   egs   rnd   re
                        kars   ese   rir   rd   r
                            hare   ids   urnd   hn
                                arr   drie   odt   runn
                                    tror         unds
                                        tar      usd
                                           drustar
```

The geometrical arrangement of this piece shows the transition to the third, lettristic and typographical, stage of the avant-gardes' movement. Its sequence and diverse manifestations can best be seen from an article by the Rumanian Isidore Isou that appeared in the second "Changing Guard" issue of the *Times Literary Supplement* in London, September 3, 1964:

Considering that the use of words in poetry has already been exhausted, our movement has propounded a purer and more profound element of versification—*the letter*. By totally and ruthlessly separating phonetic poetry from the poetry that uses words, by making the new and autonomous category into an irrevocable form which . . . has to be explored in all its sectors (the amplic and dissecting, the conscious, the automatic and the destructive) . . . we have established the most important school of poetry since the Surrealist school. . . . Our movement has propounded the *aphonic*, or *mute* system, in which the particles uttered are *inaudible* or *silent*. . . . Our movement has propounded *aes-*

thapeirism, or *infinitesimal aesthetics,* a discipline . . . where
each element *exists in so far as it allows one to imagine another
element which is either non-existent or possible.* . . . Considering
that after the linguistic juggling of *Finnegans Wake* the words
used in prose have become threadbare, our school has revealed
metagraphy or hypergraphy, which, in the course of a sentence,
replaces phonetic terms by "designs," thus introducing into
alphabetic writing not only the art of painting, but also the
graphisms of all peoples or social categories past or present, as
well as the graphisms or antigraphisms of every individual imagination. And then the new form is enriched by graphology [?],
by calligraphy, by all types of riddles and picture puzzles, by
photography, by the possibilities of superimposed printing. . . .

This document is a compendium of all the different experimental avenues envisaged by the vanguards of the avant-garde.
The products of their projecting theories hardly add anything substantial to the neologistic proclamations, they actually coincide
with them. And in following up this movement from stage to
stage, we realize how consecutive reduction turns into regression;
progression consists in regression. The detachment of language
from its human source leads, through the shrinking of verbality
to "gestics," through the gradual decomposition of language into
its components, and its merging in its phonic and graphic adjuncts,
to its final evaporation in silence and the void.

In the typographical arrangement of avant-garde texts the empty
space has a prominent role. It is the area, the "world," in which
the "gestic" dislocations of words and letters take place. The words,
word particles, letters are irregularly distributed over the surface,
on different levels, in different distances and positions, and in the
empty interspace between them associations, or rather infinite
potentialities of associations, are felt dormant, in suspense. Indeed,
not even the last remnants of literality appear to be needed for
such imaginary figurations to happen. "A scrap of paper," Mon
suggests, "hit by a few splashes of water, is already a reading field;
the delicate shadows, the tiny traces on the surface are enough to

make it readable. . . . They suffice to put us on the scent of un-known, suggestive articulations. During the concentration of read-ing, this piece of paper represents 'the whole,' the world . . . a coordination that, with its left and right, above and below, tight and wide, curved and straight . . . reflects the orientation of our body. . . ."[16]

This notion brings to mind Taoistic thinking and painting, where also a particular capacity is attributed to emptiness. It is clarifying to compare the two concepts. In Chinese paintings of the Sung period, the voids likewise dominate the scene, they "have become more important than the solids,"[17] indeed in a sense they create the solids. But this quality of the voids, which can be sensed in Chinese paintings, this "non-existent in which the existent is," issues from a cosmic principle: "There was something formless yet complete that existed before heaven and earth, without sound, without substance, dependent on nothing, unchanging, all-pervad-ing, unfailing. One may think of it as the mother of all things under heaven. Its true name we do not know. Tao is the by-name that we give it." And "though all creatures under heaven are products of Being/Being itself is the product of Non-Being."[18] So here the void represents "the creative entirety and potentiality of primeval origins."[19] In our modern situation, however, no creative whole, no cosmic origin, no substantive meaning is seen behind the void. The void is what it is, sheer emptiness. And the associative possibilities, infinitely indefinite, dissolve into the vacuum that is supposed to create them.

6

The avant-gardes declare their movement to be the only one fitting our technological age, and they may be right in maintaining that. For indeed their unbounded functionality equals that of a dominant technology that pursues its unending ends of constructing and refining abstract objects without giving much thought to their human, i.e., non-functional implications. It follows a line of con-duct common to all the dissipated activities of our society.

It has always been the task of art to express the true, unrecognized reality of its age and to make people aware of it. But the novel thing about the present avant-gardes is that they do not elucidate our reality, they simply belong to it, they are its victims. They do not, as former avant-gardes did, keep a stand beyond and superior to what they show, they no longer lead, they follow the trend; and what they produce are symptoms rather than creations. This seems to spell the end of what has been known as art throughout the ages. As far as present avant-gardes are avant-gardes at all, they are, with their various novelties, part of formations which we find everywhere at work today. I do not venture to predict what it is that is helped into being, aimlessly and unawares. Quite evident, however, appear to me the dangerous consequences of these developments for the future of humanity: they constitute an ultimate threat to human communication, or better, to the human element in the communication between man and man.

For a long time, human communication could be seen shifting from a discourse between the centers of inner life, that is, between people as human beings, to dealings between their functional peripheries, their occupational concerns. This has been noticeable in the ever growing preponderance of specialized activities and endeavors, which extends into daily life. What it involves may be gathered from the example of the transformations of reason. The commonly human faculty of reason, popularized in the term "common sense," has been expanded and rarefied into manifold scientific and technical rationality to a point where original reason and functional rationality have become sheer opposites; and in this process functional rationality has gained the upper hand so as to displace human reason. Scholars and scientists who in their studies control the most meticulous rational operations, may be seen sometimes lacking all sense of reason in their private lives, or when faced with issues of general human purport. Physical and chemical engineers who work on the refinement of nuclear or biochemical weaponry, military planners who have calculated all rationally foreseeable circumstances and tell us that, given adequate protective measures, not the whole nation would perish in a third world war but only a mere sixty to a hundred million people, that therefore a nuclear war is "feasible," such experts, if confronted with the question of broadly human consequences, would answer, with the pride of their professional amorality: "these matters exceed our competence. What we are concerned with are purely technical, rational problems." Limitation to strictly specialistic concerns has become a foremost academic virtue, and thus technical rationality serves universal possibilities which human reason is bound to regard as patent madness and a monstrous crime against humanity.

Now the avant-gardes by their methodical severing of language from human expression, not only work in the same direction, they make what is unwittingly done quite explicit, they make it a program. As indicated before, human language by conveying some human impulse, be it a sentiment, an experience, or a thought, tends to effect something, to affect human beings. Expression and aim are one. Hence, if language is divorced from human expression, it ceases to serve human aims. The experiments of the avant-garde neither convey nor aim at anything human. They have established a new kind of artless, scientifically tinged *l'art pour l'art*. And even more radically than other intellectual activities they contribute to the atrophy of human concerns in human beings.

7

Let us finally give brief consideration to the condition and the prospects of *poetry*, this most intense form of human communication, in the circumstances of our age. The avant-gardes rarely use the word "poetry" any longer, and rightly so. Their products go under a variety of names, the most common among them is "texts." However, poetry, true poetry still exists, apart from and in spite of the recent tendencies to dissolve non-functional language. To be sure—and how could it be otherwise—poetry also is affected by the general disintegration of form and devaluation of human sentiment.

Poetry is based on feeling. Even its rendering of very concrete experience, or of very abstract contemplation, even its most in-

tellectual formulations, must be borne along by feeling to move
its audience to the specifically poetic effect, that intense illumination of existence, "that heightened, that excited sense of being"—
as Richard Blackmur put it—from which it sprang. Now the
radical extraversion, the phenomenal and psychic complexity of
our life, and hence the manifold jargonization and trivialization
of language have brought about a scattering of human sentiment
into multifarious peripheral sensibilities, a kind of subtle analytical
sentience. Those who are sensitive to language, to whom the magic
of the spoken word is quite real, are repelled by overused and mis-
used words, by clichés that have become too flat to express a
unique personal experience in a unique human situation. The
devaluation of the words reflects on the feeling behind them, and
in this way sentiment comes to be identified with sentimentality,
which actually is inflated, corrupted, conventionalized sentiment.
The uncertainty of language often produces an uncertainty of
feeling: Do I really feel? Is it worth feeling?

This is the process that compels what there is of real sentiment
to escape into the anonymity of the factual, to disperse into
minute sensibilities kindled by incidental experiences; or to flow
hidden in satire or in cryptically remote and compressed meta-
phorics. Of course, any genuine poem is cryptic, venturing as it
does at the frontiers of the expressible. But the new kind of
metaphoric contraction is cryptic through the remoteness of sensibility, which is the result of ineluctable linguistic fastidiousness,
and emotional reserve.

We see poetry degenerate into sheer factual statement, the narratives cursed by Mallarmé, and into hacked prose—bad prose at
that, since such fettered prose is prevented from following its own
peculiar rhythms. Not only inept scribblers resort to such misuses,
but occasionally even true, important poets like Robert Lowell:

> One afternoon in 1922,
> I sat on the stone porch, looking through
> screens as black-grained as drifting coal.
> Tocky tock, Tocky tock

clumped our Alpine, Edwardian cuckoo clock,
slung with strangled, wooden game.
Our farmer was cementing a root-house under the hill.
One of my hands was cool on a pile of
black earth, the other warm
on a pile of lime. All about me
were the works of my Grandfather's hands:
snapshots of his *Liberty Bell* silver mine;
his high school at *Stuckert am Neckar*;
stogie brown beams; fools-gold nuggets;
octagonal red tiles,
sweaty with a secret dank, crummy with ant-stale;
a Rocky Mountain chaise-longue,
its legs, shellacked saplings. . . .*

This certainly renders the atmosphere and flavor of Lowell's home scene. But why did it have to be versified? Let us not forget what a poem is, what distinguishes poetry from prose: not meters, not lines cut by enjambements, but a different kind of language. A poem is, and always has been, a communication which a genuine urge, the immediate impulse of experience, be it a flash of lucidity, delight, or suffering, raises quite naturally to a language more intense, more concentrated, more vibrant than prose. It is a language never belying its musical, "lyrical" origin, a language creating its own rhythms, of which meters are just the appropriate divisions. Such sublimation of language has nothing to do with loftiness, uplift, verbal rarefication. The elevated tone may carry day-to-day, even slangy language, and even in its most rarefied creative innovations it must remain the authentic expression of the poet, an essentialization of his normal speech, or, to put it in reverse, the poet must in his daily life be innately capable of such elevation. The authenticity or falseness of the tone shows unmistakably.

The poetic form is not arbitrarily applicable to any "content." What can be said in prose should not be forced into verse. Only

* Reprinted from *Life Studies* by Robert Lowell (New York, 1959), by permission of Farrar, Straus and Giroux, Inc.

something that cannot be said otherwise than poetically is worthy of verse, indeed produces real verse, which is but the form of expression of heightened experience. What determines poetry is the poetic urge.

This does not mean that such an indispensable urge is all that is needed to create a true poem. The full realization of a poem requires work, hard work, sometimes. "The lord and master," Valéry said, "has given you the spark, it is your task to make something out of it." The problems of this "making"—methods and style—have to be pondered and discussed, but, should poetry remain true poetry, the "making" should never predominate in the poem, poetry should never become professional, as it tends to be so frequently today.

We have still among us, in all countries, genuine, even great poets, voices of humanity in a confused and corrupted world. But given the all-pervading blind emulation of science and technology, which tend to monopolize the human purpose without being capable of establishing a purpose, of providing guidance for the general conduct of our life, we may seriously question whether poetry will be able to maintain itself much longer amidst "ultra-intelligent machines," how long it will be left time and space and a natural soil to grow from in the young. We see the poetic urge arise from inner revolt in oppressed countries, we still sense it breaking through the intellectual thicket in the distress and rebellion of Western poets. But it is high time, I believe, to warn our youth of a grave and vital danger: the overall dominance of scientism, i.e., scientistic mentality (to be distinguished from science itself, its inestimable value, though not limitless validity); to warn them of that common inclination to see all our life, indeed all reality, as a complex of detectable, and ultimately predictable and reproducible "mechanisms."

We live in a chaotic world, overcrowded with people, objects and techniques, torn by conflicts and corruptions, overshadowed by perils of unprecedented dimensions. The general anarchy is increased by boundlessly proliferating analysis all over our life, part of which is what appears to be the most futile of all, the methodical wrecking of human language. We are confronted with an ever increasing mass of unmastered life-material, without and within ourselves. What we have to do today above all is, it seems to me, to assemble all our resources for the mastery of our world, which means directing our efforts toward establishing, rather than dissevering and dissecting, coherences. The sciences find it difficult to make such an effort in their own way. They cannot help becoming more and more specialized, they are forced in their research to proceed analytically. Advance of material knowledge calls for analysis. The sciences would have to enlist the aid of the synoptical faculties of art, whose function has always been to concentrate, to lift the essence out of phenomenality, to seek integration through intuitive vistas, to see things in perspective, and as wholes. From new experiences, from the exertion to express them with utmost and inmost accuracy ever new language evolves.

Mastery means form. Form, developing from whatever material through unhurried, laborious care is the last sanctuary of human expression, our last defense against the onslaught of technocratic slogans, against the boundless analytical arguings that threaten to smother the human voice.

[1962–1965]

The True, the Good, and the Beautiful

I

To RESOLVE the nature of the three basic values of humanity—
the true, the good, and the beautiful, with their manifold premises
and effects—within the confines of a brief essay; to resolve thus
a complex of problems on which the greatest thinkers of the
world have exercised their wits, and on which innumerable books
have been written—such an attempt must indeed be considered
foolhardy.

But the purpose of my undertaking is of necessity a more modest
one. From the outset, I shall refrain from dealing with the subjective part of the matter, that is to say, with the effects and quan-
daries which these values have produced in people of various
times and places. I will also exclude the logico-linguistic approach
to the problems in question, an approach which is in vogue
today. This aspect is being taken care of by the vast majority of
academic philosophers in England as well as in this country.
Brilliant and enlightening as some of their analyses are, they mostly
do not reach beyond the formal prolegomena, to the substance
of the matter, the very nature of these values. Or rather, the substantive meaning of these terms has come to be identified with
their complex logico-linguistic premises; it fuses with these premises. Meaning threatens to dissolve into the casuistic complex-

200

ities of logical or grammatical distinctions and of individual attitudes. This is in fact a general feature of our present stage of intellectual life. We find it in literature, in the visual arts, in music. Everywhere the essential, "thematic" problems have become one with those of their formal expression. In other words, what was commonly distinguished as "form" and "content," two quasi-parts of an intellectual entity which were always only two aspects of the same thing, have by now become one and the same aspect.

There is, of course, an evolutional consequence in this development on which I do not want to dwell any further here, since what I propose to do in this essay runs in a way counter to this trend. While recognizing its historical necessity and partial validity, I believe that, in the case of these basic values, it is also necessary, humanly necessary, not to lose sight of general criteria by which we may orient ourselves, criteria objectively valid beyond the intricacies of logical premises and individual situations. I also believe that human language contains more than what can be grasped by grammatical, logico-linguistic, and even purely stylistic analysis; that it is loaded with emotional, contemplative, and intercommunicative elements, evolutionally variable elements, which easily escape a formalistic view.

So what I want to do is simply examine what these three basic values, the true, the good, and the beautiful, taken substantively, can signify for us today, in our present human situation; in what respect they have changed their meaning since the time when they arose millennia ago, and in what respect they have preserved a core of meaning throughout the ages and can therefore be considered as valid for man as a whole, indeed, as constitutional in man.

Until the nineteenth century, these values were seen as stable *noumena*, and what thinkers were searching for from their different viewpoints was the essential meaning of these everlasting values. Then the findings and experiences, mainly of anthropologists, but also of more penetrating historians, gave rise to the great relativistic revolution, which resulted in the general tendency to view values as mere empirical *phenomena*, that is, as multifarious and variable expressions of different cultures and stages of culture. Something similar happened to what the Crusades effected in regard to religion, when the close contact with another religion, claiming the same universality as the Christian, was one of the basic determinants of incipient secularization. In our case, it was the new scientistic neutrality, *Wertfreiheit* ("value freeness"), of investigating explorers and historians which had this relativizing effect on values.

In the twentieth century, the growing social complexity and anarchy, finally the frightful regression of humanity from an apparently safe overcivilization to a savage barbarism—all the more savage since it availed itself of the very achievements of civilization: science and technology—all this contributed its share to the ruin of basic values. The ensuing "total suspicion of ideology" (*der totale Ideologieverdacht*), as Karl Mannheim put it, and the refinement of logical and logico-linguistic analysis did the rest. This is where we have arrived today, when all of these values are considered what has been termed "open concepts."

To be sure, we cannot annul our experiences, we can never go back to a stage which the process of history has abandoned. We certainly have to acknowledge the fact that values, even basic values, have proven to be radically different in various societies and that it is the social structure on which values greatly depend. We have to recognize further, that ours is a dynamic world; that in all fields of human endeavor we have undergone the irrevocable experience of fundamental change, and that there exist no comfortably stable absolutes in the old sense of the word, no clear-cut, neatly palpable eternal certainties which we can carry with us like a talisman. Finally, we have learned from the flux of our social and existential situations the subtle variables in our relationships and in our attitudes.

Granted all this, I still venture to contend that within the confines of human nature, as far as we agree that there *is* such a thing as human nature—that is, a specific quality distinguishing man from other organic forms—and within the confines of human history—which is the display of human nature in time—within these confines not all is pure change. There is an element of constancy running through the perpetual change, interwoven with it like a musical motif. The trouble is—and this makes the great, disturbing difference between the old views and ours—that we cannot separate the constant from the changing, that we cannot distill it from the live historical compound. The constant occurs only in inextricable conjunction with the changing. This holds good for the particular qualities and values of nations just as it is true of what we call the character of a person, and, I maintain, it is equally true of man as a whole, of man as an organic form.

It is commonly recognized that any individual, any one of us, has a characteristic identity implying particular ways of behavior, predilections and aversions, habits and lines of conduct. An individual in his lifetime goes through different ages and stages; he is not quite the same as an adolescent, as an adult and as an old man, and he also changes through experiences and the perpetual encounter with reality, indeed through the intercreation, I would say, of an inner being with its outer reality. But through all these changes, his identity persists. Every one of us acts and feels and thinks within an arena of latent memory which forms and informs his consciousness, his feeling of self. If he loses this identity and this feeling of self, he is mentally sick, indeed, according to recent findings, actually physically sick.

Now if this is said of an individual person, everybody will readily accept it. The problem begins when we consider a nation. And why? Because we are brought up with positivism and scientism, with a view which takes for granted only what we can, directly or indirectly, touch with our senses.

We can grasp an individual sensorily, that is, immediately, simultaneously: we see him, we hear him, we communicate with him, he exists on our own level as a person among persons, he is one of us. But a nation we cannot grasp immediately as a whole being, and therefore it is widely questioned whether a nation can be considered as a real entity or whether it is a mere abstraction, a *nomen*; and this, in spite of the fact that we constantly speak of and experience national characters, their particular ways of life, customs and values, that we recognize, glorify or loathe, particular traditions, which are nothing else than a communal form of feeling of identity. This refusal to accept as real anything that cannot be grasped or in some way verified by our senses is what I would call *sensuomorphism* or—not to couple a Greek with a Latin form, which is a sin—*aesthetomorphism*, a special kind of anthropomorphism, in which we are still mentally confined.

The difficulty increases when it comes to man as a whole. Although we cannot avoid referring to "human nature," although we know that the genus Homo sapiens came into existence in an approximately identifiable period of life, although we distinguish it as a specific organic form by clearly established physical and mental characteristics, although there exists a corresponding background of generally human identity, namely history, without which, little aware of it as people in our days may be, none of our institutions could carry on, still man is commonly seen as a sheer abstraction.

The concept of history as a consistent career of man, as a coherent evolution of the human form, is widely in disrepute. It has been discredited by historicism itself and the overgrowth of newly discovered factual details which have blurred the broad lines of general developments and bewildered the minds of historians. It has been discredited by the scientistic tendency of historical theorists to split the stream of human evolution into histories of isolated cultures and to derive from certain phenotypical parallels among them rather uncertain "laws of history." Finally, the continuity of human evolution has been lost sight of as a consequence of a current anti-historism that runs through the various fields of our cultural endeavor.

All this was made possible by the disregard of a simple fact, too simple apparently to be noticed or taken cognizance of in our intellectual turmoil: the fact of change from Neanderthal man to figures like Socrates and Jesus, like Buddha and Confucius, like Dante and Shakespeare—let alone the rational intricacies and rarefied abstractions of our modern intellectuality, in contrast with the sensuous animism of early conceptions. A comparison irrefutably tells us that some evolution must have taken place in the human constitution since the time of its inception. Or what else can we call this stupendous change?

If we grant this—and how can we avoid granting it!—it seems to me plainly nonsensical to consider all the various "cultures," —"the overcivilized" or "the underdeveloped," "the advanced" or "the retarded," or "the arrested," (whatever term we may use will inevitably be evolutional)—on the same level, as merely different cultures with different values, a view widely held by modern anthropologists and historians. Such a view is just as valid as if we would equate the behavior of children, who move within a narrowly restricted area of environment and whose inclinations and aversions, shifting moods and habitual arrangements fit the limited scope of an ego in the first stages of formation, if we would equate such behavior with the comparatively wide and abiding and organized sphere of an adult consciousness. We have, I contend, *a perfectly reliable criterion of evolution*, not only of human evolution, but of evolution in general—that is: *extension of scope, extension of range of being*—with all the increasing differentiation, organization, concentration, with all the variation and intensification of experience that goes with it.

Every individual grows, which means he expands his range of being, up to a certain point, which we call maturity. This is the peak, the pivotal point in anybody's life; from then on, the expansion of, or rather the capacity to expand, his range of being slowly fades out.

With lower organic forms, the vegetal and the animal, the range of being is purely physical. Once the individual, the species, the genus has developed physically, development and evolution stop. Man, however, is not a purely physical being; his mental, spiritual,

intellectual grasp reaches beyond his capacity of physical realization. This happens with individuals, it happens with nations, it
happens with man as a whole. Human life, in individuals, in
national communities, in humanity proper, sends out experien-
tial and experimental outposts, tentacles, antennae as it were,
to feel ahead, to feel forth the broader reality to come, and sometimes, alas, not to come, or not yet to come, for this particular
form of being. What we call ideas, projects, designs are such
antennae in individual minds. What we call great men, historical
men, "men of vision," are such antennae in the life of nations,
and of humanity.

Here is the core of human evolution, and also of human tragedy.
By means of these spiritual and intellectual antennae man was
carried to the peak of his psychic potentiality, and beyond. Something happened that is a stringent confirmation of the reality and
the development of human nature. Four cultures, four branches
of humanity, reached, at the point of their own particular maturity,
a degree of expansion of scope which at the same time can be
considered as the standard of generally human maturity; that is
to say, they arrived at *the self-awareness of man.* In all of these
four cultures men arose whose visions, although deriving from
different ethnic and environmental conditions, converged on
certain commonly basic values, which, to be sure, are expressed
in different fashion according to their different origins, but which,
all of them, derive from one common visional experience: the
conception of man as a whole, of humanity pure and simple,
beyond specific ethnic communities and not identified with them.
Such self-awareness, self-conception of man evolved within the
Judaeo-Christian sphere with the Jewish prophets and Jesus; it
evolved within the Greek orbit with Plato and ultimately the
Stoics; in India with Buddha; in China with the Great Sages. This
basic spiritual concept has not attained its realization anywhere,
but it has created the concept of a human community of values,
and it has produced, in the course of history, a variety of versions
and formulations of these common values, which have helped

individuals, communities and classes in their specific circumstances and in their attempts to broaden the perspective and the conduct of their lives.

What I am driving at with these apparently digressive introductory remarks is a preliminary confirmation of the fact that there is an element of constancy pervading not only every individual and communal form, but also the human form as a whole, a constancy within its organic limits; that there is a certain constancy of basic values which, at a certain point of maturity, emerged into broadly human consciousness and subsequently, in the process of history, blended with changing forms according to changing circumstances.

So while our experiences have shattered our belief in integral absolutes, that is to say, in entities and values that are valid for all times and in all places, entities and values high above our lives, eternally fixed and loftily detached like stars—which, correspondingly, also have lost their immutability and aloofness—while these firmly established, *real absolutes* have vanished from our intellectual sky, there still subsist for us certain "*relative absolutes*," valid within the confines of a particular human form and so within the confines of man as a whole; absolutes which are not actual "absolutes" in the literal sense of the word and in the ancient sense of the concept, but which appear always in inextricable conjunction with changing conditions, and form and re-form out of these changing conditions. They are in every respect limited and dynamic absolutes.

When I speak of the true, the good, and the beautiful, what I have in mind are such relative absolutes moving and changing along with the changes and ranges of our human condition. And what I propose to do is to examine precisely what residue of generally *human* absolute has remained for us in these three terms, and what metamorphosis this residue of absolute has undergone in the conditions of our age.

I will speak first about the good and last about the true, because truth is the supreme value.

II

Let me start from what I indicated before: these basic values of man emerged at a certain point of human maturity, in a stage of expansion of scope where an actual self-awareness of man was attained, the awareness and the concept of humanity pure and simple, not identified with a specific ethnic community. Within the orbit of our Western civilization, such an awareness appeared first in the projected form of the universal, spiritual and invisible, imageless and nameless, non-mythological God of the Jews, who is not just *one* god, *a* god, but plainly God. I cannot, in the present context, go into a detailed documentation of this statement. Suffice it to recall the foundation and the consequences of the Jewish concept of God. The conclusion of a covenant between God and the patriarchs and leaders of Israel implies that God is originally the God of all peoples. The special relation between Him and the people of Israel was established through a formal agreement that reads like a legal contract (cf. Deuteronomy 26: 16–19): an elevation is granted in exchange for a mission. Israel is a "chosen" people insofar as it is to be a "holy" people, a model people, a "light to the Gentiles" with all the hardships and suffering this involves (Exodus 19:6 and Isaiah 49–51). Likewise the story of the Tower of Babel is based on the explicit assumption of one common humanity, originally speaking the same language under one universal God. This is the foundation. The conclusion is contained in the basic commands: "Love thy neighbor as thyself" (Leviticus 19:18), and the more explicit one, "The stranger that dwelleth with you shall be unto you as one born among you and thou shalt *love* him as thyself" (Leviticus 19:34). This command is one of the oldest parts of the Old Testament. And in it we have not only the clear distinction and transcendence of ethnic particularities, distinction *in order* to transcend these particularities, since it implies that both the Jew and the stranger are equal human beings; but we have at the same time the first general interpretation of *goodness*, of goodness beyond all specific hieratic, social, or practical purposes, a concept of goodness that has continued as the basis of true Christianity throughout the following ages.

This, however, was still a religious command. In a free, mundane form the three values of which I speak appeared in our Western world as purely human values first among the Greeks. And there are two most important circumstances which are noticeable in this genesis. First, *the three values appear in unison, they are indeed one*; and an ethical overtone hovers over all of them. Secondly, they are not only one in themselves, but they are *also one with the cosmic quest*, the quest for the nature of nature. In fact, *they originated in the cosmic problem*. Here we can clearly observe the impulse from which the awareness of human values has arisen; the roots of the ethical motive lie bare.

The Greeks were an extremely lively, curious, worldly people, whose senses were wide open to the variety of experience. They were, however, still under the primeval spell of religion. In fact, their paramount historical achievement as a people may be seen in the loosening of the human mind from religious bonds. And the first act of this loosening was the pre-Socratic transformation of the religious into a cosmic absolute. In pre-Socratic philosophy we see the new observation of natural diversity, the new experience of change in human life, clashing with the deep-rooted need of a stable, eternal order. Pre-Socratic thought was essentially concerned with the conciliation of this discrepancy between the eternal and changeless being which was seen as the underlying truth of all existence and the manifest shift and multiplicity of life which was taken only as an outward appearance and delusion of the senses, indeed as sin and guilt (*adikia*) of the mortal creature. The particular and the temporal were felt to be an apostasy of the physical being; and the search for a comprehensive cosmic substance and for a principle connecting phenomenal variety and intrinsic unity, apparent change and true eternity, this search was an effort not only for true knowledge, but also for justification and salvation. We have here, on the one hand, a more mundane parallel to the problem of Jewish monotheism, the struggle to conform the incipient freedom, the incipient humanity of the human individual to the unity and harmony of the divine order; on the other hand, we find in pre-Socratic thought all the basic problems of modern philosophy, modern science, and modern ethics, in an undeveloped, primevally combinative form.

In these concepts the true and the good are one and the same, and they are conceived as immaculate, indelible absolutes. Euclid of Megara, a disciple of Socrates and founder of the school of Megara, identified the good with being, pure and simple, with oneness, with the basic and the immutable cosmic principle. For Plato it is the foundation of being, and as such the *megiston mathema*, the supreme subject of learning. The Idea of the Good, it is said in the *Republic*, is "what endows the things known with their truth and grants him who knows the power to know." It is "the source of knowledge and truth."[1] In the *Timaeus*, the *demiourgos*, the Creator himself, being given to goodness, "wants everything in the world to resemble him as much as possible."[2] These conceptions reach down to the Stoa and Cicero; and in Neoplatonic and later in medieval Christian thought, the good and the true are again, in the old religious manner, embodied in God, in His mind and in His will.

So the *first*, the initial meaning of the good in a mundane form, is the absolute per se, the *quality of absoluteness*, that is, of oneness, immutability, and essentiality.

With Aristotle the relation between eternal stability and change became more complex and flexible. It was seen as a kind of interpenetration in which, however, the primacy and intangibility of the divine was still preserved. In Aristotle's theory of entelechy (*entelecheia*), the substance of all existence is form. Form is the innate principle, the divine origin, and at the same time the aim and the end of any particular being. Any human being carries in himself potentially his characteristic form and has to make it real, bring it to perfection in his life.[3] Manifold differentiation set in, and an elaborate hierarchy of goods emerged from the good of the individual, which is the perfection of his specific nature, up to the supreme and divine good, the highest of all attainable goods (*to panton akrotaton ton prakton agathon*). And in this hierarchy the general good takes precedence over the particular. A good is more valuable, it is more of a good, the more permanent and the more general it is.[4] This implies that the psychic and the spiritual precede the physical good.

Here we have a *second* meaning. The good is *the general, the ever more general, up to the completely general,* the good of all. This notion of Aristotle implies what I indicated before: that evolution, a rise in grade, is identical with the expansion of scope.

But Aristotle's theory yields even more new meanings of the good. The Greeks did not as yet speculate for speculation's sake, but with a pragmatic intention, in order to find a direction of conduct, to find out how to live propitiously, prosperously, desirably. Even the *vita contemplativa,* the life spent in contemplation, which was praised as the highest form of life, by no means signified what today is called "a life devoted to the search of knowledge." It was the highest form of life because it released all human faculties for the seeking of meaningful life, for "the working of the soul" (*psyches energeia*). Thus, from the outset the good was to the Greeks at the same time the *chresimon,* the *ophelimon,* as Socrates has it, the literal translation of which would be "the useful, the wholesome"; this, however, does not render the Greek meaning at all. It is rather what we would call "the good life," "the right way to live." To the Greeks and most particularly to Aristotle, the "good life" was a life in the sense of *eudaimonia,* which again, basically, does not mean our "happiness," but a life in accordance with one's own personal destiny and disposition, with one's God-given form which everybody has to bring to perfection, and, ultimately, in accordance with the cosmic order, the reasonable order of divine nature.*

This, then, is the *third* meaning of the good: *conformance,*

---

* "For that which is most peculiar (*oikeion*) to somebody is also the best and most agreeable for him; and for the human being it is evidently a life according to the spirit (*nous*), inasmuch as spirit is the most human attribute. Therefore, such a life will be the most propitious (*eudaimonestatos*) for him" (*Eth. Nicom.* X 1178 A). "If the spirit is divine in relation to man, life according to the spirit is divine in relation to human life" (*loc. cit.* X 1177 B).

harmony with one's own essential nature, and of personal nature with the order of nature as a whole. And this version again continues through the ages: we find it expressed not only by the Stoics, by Seneca and Marcus Aurelius, whose concept of *autarkeia*, of self-sufficiency, reflects a similar notion of inner harmony and wholeness; we find it expressed in the Middle Ages, by Albertus Magnus, by Thomas Aquinas, and later by Suarez; we find its traces among the Italian thinkers of the Renaissance (Patrizzi and Bruno), in Leibniz, and in Shaftesbury.

Just as the Jews imagined the One and Everlasting, the "eternal God," as integrally spiritual and opposed to sensuous shift and variety, so, correspondingly, for the Greeks the substance of the universe, the principle of cosmic order, was spiritual and not to be grasped by the senses. Yet, with the Greeks, "spirit" came to assume the character of "reason," which was the result of a fully, that is, mundanely developed consciousness of self. The God of Israel was still an unconscious projection of an urge toward a unified humanity, an incipient concept of the identity of man. The Greek concern for an all-embracing spiritual absolute arrived at a conscious, elaborate investigation of the working of the human mind that was seen as a microcosmic reflection of the universe. The search for the spiritual consistency of the cosmos was one with the search for the consistency of human thinking, its capacity to reach the truth, through Socratic *maieutic*, Platonic dialectic, and Aristotelian logic.

The Christian repudiation of terrestrial and bodily life enhanced the sway of the spirit, and gradually, when the supremacy of dogma crumbled, human Reason took over from divine Spirit the rule and guidance of the world in the minds of men. The good, accordingly, was identified with the rational. In Spinoza's *Ethics*, for instance, the good rests solely on reason. Good is what leads us to higher cognition, what promotes and strengthens a rational way of life, the only way of life worthy of a human being.* "By

* *"Nihil certo scimus bonum aut malum nisi id quod ad intelligendum re vera conducit, vel quod impedire potest, quo minus intelligamus"* (Eth. IV, Prop. XXVII).

good I understand," Spinoza says, "that which we know for sure to be a medium for our approximating more and more our ideal (*exemplar*) of human nature . . . what furthers our being and our capacity to act."* In other words, good is *what promotes a humanly worthy and productive life*. In this, Spinoza anticipates a modern interpretation of Erich Fromm, to whom also the good is identical with the vitally productive. And this is a *fourth* significance of the good.

His particular stress on a rational conduct of life leads Spinoza to introduce in his concept of the good a *new social connotation* —a *fifth* meaning of the good—which in fact is an early, non-imperative, formulation of Kant's categorical imperative. Good is, he says in another passage in his *Ethics*, "what anyone seeking virtue desires not only for himself, but would also desire for the rest of humanity."** In Kant's famous wordings of the imperative (there are several) we have finally the modern version of Aristotle's interpretation of the good as "the general, the more and more general," which is implicitly the rational. What among the Greeks could still be seen as an innate desire of the human being, a desire of his innermost being, what even Spinoza still formulated as a desire, has now become a duty imposed by a moral law: "Act in such a way that the maxim of thy will could at any time serve as the principle of a general legislation" (in another version it even reads: "of a law of nature").[5] This reflects the modern rift between the natural and the rational, between the individual pursuing his private material aims and the fully developed "collective," the state. The Greek *polis* was not a collective, it was a community, and a small community at that; and although there always existed a discrepancy between the ends of the individual

---

* "Per bonum . . . intelligam id, quod certo scimus medium esse, ut ad exemplar humanae naturae, quod nobis proponimus, magis magisque accedamus" (Eth. IV, Praef.). "Id bonum aut malum vocamus, quod nostro esse conservando prodest, vel obest, quod nostram agendi potentiam auget vel minuit, juvat vel coercet" (loc. cit., Prop. VIII).
** "Bonum quod unusquisque qui sectatur virtutem, sibi appetit, reliquis hominibus etiam cupiet . . . " (loc. cit., Prop. XXXVII).

and the ends of the community, the Athenian or Spartan had a much greater and a much deeper share in his community than a modern citizen has in his collective state.

This difference between the Aristotelian and the Kantian formulation discloses both constancy and change in the meaning of the good. It shows us that not all has changed, that something has persisted, but that it could not persist in a stable, immutable form. Indeed all the diverse meanings of the good that I have enumerated here—and they are really the essential interpretations that have been conceived from antiquity up to now—all these different meanings have something in common, or rather, converge on one single motif.

Let me recall them. They were: 1) the religious command of *love* among human beings as plain human beings, which implies peace, kindness, generosity, commiseration; 2) *substantiveness, essentiality, oneness*; 3) *generality*, the furtherance of all, which implies the increase of scope, and hence the use of the higher rational faculties of man, without which there would be no expansion of scope; 4) *eudaimonia*, harmony with and within one's self and with the order of nature as a whole; and 5) *productivity*, furtherance of life. All of these meanings of the good, expressing different shades and aspects as they do, show a tendency toward the same fundamental meaning: *oneness, wholeness, harmony of life*. And, in point of fact, the teaching of Buddhism, original or Zen, and the Chinese conception of Tao are, in one way or another, closely related to this basic meaning.

This is what has persisted. But very much has changed; indeed, what has persisted can only be valid for us in a changed form. When we ask: What does goodness signify to us today, in what form can it be valid for us today? we have to detach the concept from both its emotional and its overintellectual, overanalytical aspects. The first, the emotional, is too vague, and the second dissolves the value into mere casuistry.

Love is certainly a boon and a blessing, it is in fact the best we can have on earth. And yet, in itself we cannot call it the good.

Even in former periods, when the issue was predominantly one of relationship between individuals, love was too much to be asked and not enough in itself to fulfill the good. It is the *aim* of love that could be seen as the good, not love itself which is a feeling and escapes all command and direction of the will. If we take Alyosha Karamasov as the model of loving goodness, of a man who is naturally kind enough and personally detached enough to love the human being as a human being, beyond personal attraction and beyond individual flaws, we can see in this model of a Christian, how much knowledge, understanding, sensibility, and capacity of experience is needed, even between individuals, to make love really good.

But in the meantime, goodness has ceased to be an issue merely between individuals or even between the individual and a real community of individuals, which has become rather scarce. A crucial change has occurred in the structure of our society, cutting deep into the nature of human relationships. The same evolutionary expansion of scope that raised man to the peak of personality drove him on, further, to collectivity, which threatens to destroy personality. In this age, when the individual as a human being is confronted with overpowering collectives which split him apart and imperil his very existence, the good is more than ever an aim that calls for an effort of the intellect. The predominant issue is to create conditions in which a human being is allowed to be a human being. The good is still identical with the general and the whole, with a vantage point of the widest scope, but this implies today, besides peace and harmony, a difficult process of transformation of a world of self-contained, function-minded collectives into a human community. To seek the good today, requires that one be more than a kind man; it requires an impulse toward the general and the whole, combined with the mental clarity and capacity to *grasp* the whole. It means a sustained effort to penetrate through the intricacies of forms and impediments, to beware of being completely submerged by the overwhelming perplexities of collective life and by the functional exigencies of our specialized work; in short, to keep ourselves perseveringly concerned about the human condition, to feel responsible for it, to care.

III

As I stated before, the three human values which we are considering were for the Greeks basically one: the good was the true, the good was the beautiful. The good implied oneness, wholeness, harmony, harmony with one's self and with the order of the cosmos. And we have to remember that the term "cosmos" indicates not simply the universe, but at the same time order as such, form, adornment (the roots of "cosmic" and "cosmetic" are the same).

Accordingly, the human ideal of the Greeks, the Greek ideal of a "gentleman," as Werner Jaeger puts it—somewhat anachronistically, I would think—was *kalokagathia*, beauty-goodness, the "highest unity of all excellences."

While the concept of the good, notwithstanding its intrinsic coherence throughout the ages, has been expressed in a great variety of ways, the concept of *beauty* as an objective value has been represented essentially only in three versions, which again point to one and the same basic meaning. The *first* is harmony pure and simple, *"taxis, symmetria kai to horismenon,"* as Aristotle termed it in his *Poetics*, "order, symmetry, and the bounded," which cannot be transgressed, or altered in any detail, without undoing the whole. The *second* was set forth by Plato who, besides also emphasizing harmony and symmetry,* characterized beauty as "the transparence of the idea in the sensuous appearance."[6] Hegel paraphrased this interpretation by calling beauty "the sensuous shining of the idea" (*das sinnliche Scheinen der Idee*).[7] The first version, we could say, stresses *harmony in the dimension of breadth*, that is, harmony among the apparent parts within a whole, the second stresses *harmony in the dimension of depth*, harmony between the phenomenal appearance of the whole and the inmost, essential being behind it. Throughout European tradi-

* *Metriotes kai symmetria* (*Philebus* 51).

tion, up to the nineteenth century, beauty has been defined as harmony, however differently paraphrased.* Harmony, the correspondence and interdependence of all parts within a whole is nothing else than the principle of the organic, and as such equivalent to oneness and wholeness.

But there is a later, *third* version, which emphasizes the activating effects of the other two and thus mobilizes, dynamizes the old concepts. This version is phrased best by Goethe who says that we find the beautiful "wherever we see the order of life (*das gesetzmaessig Lebendige*) in its highest activity and perfection, an experience which makes us on our part feel intensely alive and moved to highest activity."[8] This emphasis on the life-enhancing, creative quality of beauty somehow corresponds to Spinoza's interpretation of the good as a life-promoting, productive force, as that which "furthers our being and our faculty to act."

These three essentially related meanings of beauty have been blurred by the indiscriminate common use of the word "beautiful" for everything that pleases us in nature, in art, in everyday life, without any awareness of what the word actually stands for. People speak for instance of a "beautiful steak," and what they have in mind is the promise of its massive tastiness. Or they call a dress beautiful because of its lustrous color or thrilling shape. This is not to deny that a dress *can* be really beautiful if it subtly reveals and thereby enhances the charm of a body and of more than a body, the personality of a person. In such a way a dress can be an extension, an accentuation, of the character of a body or a face, which in itself may be called beautiful not simply by virtue of a certain regularity, or due proportion, of its features, but because of the expression of an inner life and feeling that vibrates in every line of it; in other words, to follow Plato's inter-

* A few examples of such variants: Thomas Aquinas calls beauty *integritas sive proportio*, integrality or proportion, and *proportio sive consonantia*, proportion or consonance (*Summa Theol.* I 398 C); Kant defines it as *Zusammanhang des Mannigfaltigen zu Einem*, concurrence of the manifold toward One, and *Zweckmässigkeit ohne Zweck*, purposiveness without purpose (*Kritik der Urteilskraft* § 16). Schelling (in his *System des transzendalen Idealismus*) sees it as *das Unendliche endlich dargestellt*, the infinite in finite representation.

pretation, because of "the transparence of the idea of the person in the sensuous appearance."

In contemplating *nature*, what we call beautiful is by no means the harmony of a scene, it is on the contrary sometimes precisely the *dis*harmony, the romantic excessiveness and expressiveness, the elemental grandeur of a natural scene. In general, the vague popular sentiment of "beauty" in the face of nature abounds with emotional overtones. Some people, in some particular mood, harassed by inner troubles or just the turbulence of modern city life, will find a calm, idyllic scene "beautiful"; others may want to lose and loosen themselves in a feeling of infinity, and will be inclined to call natural phenomena "beautiful" just because of their mysterious, disproportionate immensity.

But it is not only this careless use of the word that has obscured the original meanings of beauty, it is also a profound change in our experience since the classical and classicistic periods. Our experience, as reflected and projected in art, has broken through the traditional symmetries, it has extended its scope in width and depth. In proportion as a world of individuals and individual relations has given way to a world of supra- and transindividual dimensions, the reality with which art has to deal has outgrown the reality of our plain senses; it has waxed far beyond the level of the shapes and objects of our phenomenal life. The exploratory advance into the depths of the human psyche and into the breadth of modern collective life and, further, into the nature of phenomenality and tonality has brought into the picture ever more and more diverse elements of reality, and this has meant by necessity dissolution of the old harmony, hence *dis*harmony.* In the accelerated rhythms of our contemporary life we feel more inspired by these new dynamic disharmonies and the insights and emotional

---

* Gertrude Stein reports a dictum of Picasso: "Picasso said once that he who created a thing is forced to make it ugly. In the effort to create the intensity, and the struggle to create this intensity, the result always produces a certain ugliness, those who follow can make of this thing a beautiful thing because they know what they are doing, the thing having already been invented, but the inventor because he does not know what he is going to invent inevitably the thing he makes must have its ugliness."

penetrations which they open up for us than by the old static harmonies. Beauty, for us, is no longer static, it has become dynamic. The meaning of beauty that has come to prevail is the one expressed by Goethe, according to which we find the beautiful wherever the experience of the order of life makes us feel more intensely alive and moves us to highest activity.

But even so, while enjoying the vital expressiveness of the pioneering creations, we feel those works of art to be superior in which the disparities and dissonances are correlated into a new system of correspondences; in which the disharmony has been brought to rest in a richer and deeper, more comprehensive harmony. Think of achievements like Joyce's *Ulysses,* like certain most finished realizations by Van Gogh, by Matisse, or Braque, or Picasso. Indeed such creations of Joyce and Picasso (particularly those of the Guernica period) and related works of other artists have unfolded a *new dimension of harmony,* an *interlevel harmony,* harmony between different levels of existence, a new kind of transparence of the idea in the sensuous appearance, whereby the phenomenal world has come to assume a metaphorical character as it were. This interlevel harmony has been effected by a new mode of *symbolization,* a more multifold and complex symbolization.

IV

We finally come to the *true,* which also consists in a kind of harmony or rather in various kinds of harmony: harmony, or conformity, between thinking and being, between thinking and experience, between thinking and itself; or between appearance and reality, language and reality, propositions and reality—these are, approximately, the interpretations of truth underlying philosophical theories from antiquity up to now. There has been considerable disagreement on whether truths exist as objective, timeless absolutes, independent of our mind and of our thinking them, or whether any truth exists only insofar as we are able to comprehend it in our mind. The notion of absolute, timeless verities has of

course been held by all thinkers who believed them instituted by
God. In our secularized era the problem has assumed a purely
epistemological character. The absolute existence of truth, the
last bastion of the absolute, has been defended by Bolzano, Hus-
serl, and Nicolai Hartmann. But in general, the nominalistic, relativistic, formalistic concepts of truth are the more modern ones.

There are views intermediate between the two extremes, like
that of Aristotle, to whom truth resides in our thought, but is not
made true by our thinking—we rather think it because it is true.
This view derives from the initial, pre-Socratic notion that the
true is identical with the absolute being, with substantive existence
itself, which we are able to grasp only by the faculty of thinking.
Later, similarly, Descartes assumed that the eternal, basic verities,
the mathematical axioms, or *notiones communes*, are founded by
God, yet abide in our mind.

I cannot go further into these controversies. I must confine myself to summarizing four distinct forms of truth which seem to
me the essential ones; and let it be emphasized in advance that to
my mind truth is more than a mere factually empirical relationship, more also than the purely formal, logical or linguistic, relationship to which it has shrunk in the prevailing thought of our
days; it is, beyond all that, an existential condition, and it is this,
primarily, that makes it a value.

There are *four forms* in which truth asserts itself. First, *correctness*, conformity of a statement with a fact: Abraham Lincoln
was born on the 12th of February, 1809, and was assassinated by
a man called John Wilkes Booth on the 14th of April 1865. The
second is *logical coherence*, consistency of one proposition with
another within a given system, or of a mathematical theorem with
its demonstration; or, in the Kantian sense, accordance of thinking with the aprioristic structure (or laws) of thought. A simple,
the simplest, syllogistic example: An animal that gives birth to
living young and nourishes them with milk is a mammal. The
whale gives birth to living young. Therefore the whale is a mammal. It is of course a far cry from this elementary example to the

intricacies and paradoxes of modern logic, which have made it more than ever doubtful whether this plainly logical mode of truth is at all real, or, rather, whether this plainly logical mode of search is capable of helping us to grasp the real, dynamic complexity of truth. The third form of truth is *authenticity, genuineness*, conformity of the appearance of an object, an utterance, a being, with its origin. Here, the meaning of truth begins to exceed a purely formal relationship. We may still call it a formal relationship when we speak of pure gold, an authentic document, a genuine Rembrandt. But the implication reaches much deeper when we apply the criterion of authenticity to the human being, to his looks, his bearing, his language, and, beyond that, to style and artistic expression. In these connections, truth takes on a substantive, existential significance; it becomes a quality, and a value. The way a person looks, expresses and carries himself bears on his very nature, and whether his appearance and expression conform with his feelings and with his being, this affects all his faculties, it tinges, inspires or corrupts them. What I am speaking of is not, or not necessarily, a matter of intention, even unconscious intention; the question is not simply whether a person is a *liar*, the question is whether he is a *lie*. He may be perfectly reliable as to statements of fact, but what is crucial is whether he has enough vitality to sustain the purity, the immediacy and directness of his sensibility, or whether he has to resort to the suggestions of convention and circumstance.

This applies to all intellectual levels. But in this age of ours it comes easier to completely naïve persons to be existentially true, that is, true to themselves. Children—if only they are allowed to remain children and are not stimulated to affectation by the ambition of their parents—are naturally true (as are animals) because they live fully in the moment, uninhibited by memories, projects and regards; they live *spontaneously*, close to the sources of life, from which they derive themselves ever anew. We may also find such existential truth among simple peasants in the backwoods who are not as exposed as sophisticated people to the overwhelming interferences of a complex civilization. Much more vital power is needed to maintain the integrity of personal responses against the pressures and influences of our urban and intellectual life. These pressures have grown so strong that they sometimes lead to the complete obliteration of the self to which a person would have to be true. A friend of mine, a psychotherapist, told me that time and again in his practice a patient confronts him with the horrifying question: "What am I supposed to feel?"

We have a subtle yardstick of authenticity in language, which is inventive and creative only on the lowest and on the highest intellectual level: among children and, sometimes, simple folk and, on the other hand, among great artists and poets. What distinguishes a real artist from epigones is not, in the first place, the quality of his style and imagery as such; it is above all the immediacy and originality of his language, originality in the literal sense of the word, which indicates his natural possession of a language of his own. Such originality is the result of a strong and undisturbed personal response to experience. A true artist's capability of doing what he has done rests on his incapability of doing otherwise.

It is obvious how the value of what I call existential truth is connected with the aesthetic and moral values. It is what is left of the ancient *eudaimonia*, the life in accordance with one's own God-given form which everybody has to bring to perfection, and in which likewise the true, the good and the beautiful converge.

But *eudaimonia* meant not only accordance with one's own personal disposition, it meant also accordance with the cosmic order, which was assumed to be a stable absolute. The cosmic order, however, has ceased to be such an absolute for us; indeed it has been questioned whether the universe is a coherent order at all. I do believe that it somehow is because otherwise any coherent existence is hardly conceivable. At any rate, the universe cannot be seen as a *stable* order any longer, it has proven to be a dynamic order, and what we may assume to know about it is equally dynamic and subject to continuous change. This affects the character of truth profoundly inasmuch as it calls into question the stability of facts—at least of their meaning in relation to their context. Knowledge is more than an assemblage of incoherent and passing data, knowledge is comprehension of coherence, comprehension of a whole of reality; and reality, taken as a coherent complex and a subject of knowledge, has revealed its shifting and receding nature. Our knowledge is constantly on the move, and truth appears to be identical with the extreme frontier to which our knowledge of the world and of our self has advanced at a particular time. Thus, it seems to be tied to an epoch, a generation, indeed to the momentary state of a collective consciousness, for no single mind is capable today of encompassing the whole fluctuating complexity that constitutes our knowledge at any moment.

Therefore, conformity with the cosmic order, the ultimate measure of truth, is not attainable for us any longer, which is a tragic predicament. So all that seems to be left to us of existential truth is personal authenticity. However, apart from religious verities, the "verities of faith"—if we are ready to accept this term—two alternative criteria of transpersonal truth have been offered to us: one by the existentialists, who have reduced all available certainty to our feeling of sheer existence, existence of the lone, forsaken human being, which is the last, shrunken remains of the ancient absolute, the Eleatic absolute being; and another one, set forth by the pragmatists who, by dynamizing, functionalizing truth, adjusted it to the dynamic character of our knowledge. "Truth and error," says F. C. S. Schiller, "both become incidents in the progressive growth of knowledge, and are no longer opposed to each other in implacable enmity."[9] Hence, according to Ralph Barton Perry, "an idea is true when it works; that is, when it is successful, when it fulfills its function or performs what is demanded of it."[10] In this way, truth has become a collective instrument, a "working value" as the instrumentalists put it. This seems to me the last abdication of the majestic existential significance of truth. The only relativistic interpretation of truth that preserves its existential quality—though only in a subjectively restricted sense—is that of Goethe: "When I know my relationship to myself and to the outside world," he says, "I call it truth. So everyone can have his own truth and yet it is always the same."[11] This is a profound insight, perfectly valid in regard to personal authenticity, but it leads further to the following conclusion, which sounds like an anticipation of the pragmatist concept: "I have made the observation that I hold true an idea that is fruitful for me, that ties up with my whole way of thinking and at the same time furthers me."[12] "What is fruitful, creative, that alone is true (*Was fruchtbar ist allein ist wahr*)."[13] This concept of truth strikingly corresponds to Goethe's idea of beauty as a life-enhancing force. But as applied to truth, the same idea can prove extremely dangerous inasmuch as the existential meaning of truth is apt to be confounded with its factual significance: the personal authenticity appears to justify a claim to suprapersonal validity by implying the converse: true is what furthers me, humanly or intellectually.

In this way, a dogma to which a person, by inclination or exigency, adheres, may claim general acceptance that would help guarantee its believer's *eudaimonia*. There are catholics by nature and puritans by nature, persons in whom a peculiar religious constitution has come, through genealogical tradition, to shape their whole mentality and way of life. By being true to themselves such persons feel themselves in accord with the suprapersonal doctrine that formed them, that protects and "furthers" them. In our age, however, in which rationally guided empiricism has established itself as a basic factor of generally acceptable knowledge, all dogmas have assumed a subjective character. "Verities of faith" have become particular suppositions, they rest upon beliefs that do not submit to the criterion of concordance with the present state of intellectual experience. Whenever a belief is compelled to elude some part of reality, this belief has lost its general validity, and if it usurps a sweeping authority, it can, in conflict with prevailing reality, jeopardize the existential truth of its believers. It may even, as in the case of Nazism, compel them to commit outrageous horrors and to unleash a universal cataclysm.

Such claim to unwarranted authority reveals a *fourth* meaning of truth: truth is also a *social condition*. Anyone who has lived in a totalitarian state has experienced what it means to live in an atmosphere of lies. And even here in America, in our present social situation, we are surrounded by lie and fraud. It is exceedingly difficult to preserve one's existential truth, one's personal authenticity, if one does not live in social truth, but under overwhelming economic or ideological pressure inducing him to serve a lie.

V

In conclusion, let us give brief consideration to the *interrelation between the three values*, the true, the good, and the beautiful. They started in union, as we have seen, so close that it was almost perfect unity. But not only in antiquity, even in our modern era certain thinkers and poets affirmed the unity, or at least the close interconnection of some, or all three, of these basic values. Shaftesbury and Schiller emphasized the unity of the three; Kant and poets like Keats and the German romanticist Novalis linked beauty with truth.

All three values have sprung from the search for the substance and order of the cosmos, for the true nature of being. This primacy of truth has persisted throughout; truth still appears as the arch-value, the mainstay of all values.

There is no goodness without truth. This is not to deny that in certain circumstances it may be good and humanely necessary to tell a lie. But never can a lie remain the basis for a good life and a life for goodness. The doctrinaire Gregers Werle in Ibsen's *Wild Duck* wrecks the life of the family by destroying Hjalmar Ekdal's "existential lie." But the intention of the play is by no means a vindication of the existential lie. For it is not the pricking of the lie which caused the tragedy, it is the lie itself, the falseness and incapacity for love of pompous, self-pampering Hjalmar; it is the shakiness and sterility of a life built on a lie. The connection of the good with the true is in fact the pivot of Ibsen's work:

the moral agony and perplexity of truth in his age, and of the avenging lies. In our present human situation particularly, when goodness is no longer plainly identifiable with kindness toward the fellow individual, but demands knowledge and understanding of general conditions, it is impossible to be good without seeking the truth.

The relation between goodness and beauty has proved more problematic. The beautiful and the good, seen as one by the ancients, have been turned into sheer opposites by modern developments. The Protestant residue of Christianism in moralistic enlightenment, the fossil conventionality of the nineteenth century middle class, and finally the melting away of values in the wars and crises of the twentieth century—this chain of conditions has generated a sequence of intellectual revolts. It started with the romantic cult of the "poetic," offering an escape from bourgeois drabness. A reaction against faded and no longer genuine romanticism took shape in the various movements of l'art pour l'art, realistic or symbolistic, as professed by Flaubert and Baudelaire, Mallarmé and Oscar Wilde, Walter Pater and Swinburne, Stefan George (in his early period) and Gottfried Benn.

Such exalting of beauty was countered by a passionate emphasis on goodness, all the more impressive since it issued from particularly form-conscious artists: Tolstoi, Brecht and Broch. Each of them in his peculiar way rejected the pursuit of beauty and asserted man's duty actively to care for the good of his fellowmen.

In the last analysis, however, this division seems to me illusory. It is a result of the disruptive tendency of our age to drive human faculties and aims functionally apart. Extreme dedication to beauty may indeed alienate a person from the sense of goodness. But it should be clear by now that there is no absolute, i.e., stable, beauty. Any established harmony is but a stage of rest in an unending process of expanding experience, and he who tends to immortalize it is ineluctably shoved into irreality. Awareness of the ephemerality of all harmony makes the cult of absolute beauty a thing of the past. In the suprapersonal dimensions of the human and artistic integration that is demanded of our generation, the beautiful and the good no longer conflict.

There has been a near consensus, even among romanticists and adherents of *l'art pour l'art*, that beauty is based on truth. (Theories like Oscar Wilde's, who in his dandy period maintained that beauty issues from imaginative lie, are a rare exception.) Novalis asserted that "poetry is the genuine and absolute reality." Wordsworth declared in his Preface to the *Lyrical Ballads*, that the object of poetry "is truth, not individual and local, but general and operative; not standing upon external testimony, but carried alive into the heart by passion." Keats, contemplating his Grecian Urn averred that "Beauty is truth, truth beauty—that is all/ye know on earth, and all You need to know." This famous dictum, to be sure, is just a statement of sentiment—none of the various books and essays that have been written about it have been able to squeeze out of the few extant verses and sentences concerning this identity a clarification of the sentiment. What Keats expressed in this conclusion of his poem seems to be a conviction—somewhat similar to Gottfried Benn's in his later years—that "silent form," which "teases us out of thought," is the only untouchable confirmation of lasting existence.

For the two originators of the principle of *l'art pour l'art*, Flaubert and Baudelaire, the perfection of form, which means beauty, was inseparable from utmost precision, which is truth. Baudelaire, who in his *Fleurs du Mal* extolled beauty, insisted on what he called *une franchise absolue*, "an absolute candor." He was in fact the first to break through the barriers of classical aesthetics by drawing the ugly and even the decaying into the compass of form, thereby submitting it to beauty. Art is a peculiar kind of comprehension, and its ever transforming, ever expanding realization is what alone may be called beauty today.

But we need not go very far to verify the fact that beauty rests on truth. We only have to look around us. There we can see at every step the aesthetic ravages committed by falsity. We see plastic pretending to be marble, or wood, or leather. We find, on houses, on cars, on objects, all sorts of twisted, perplexed ornaments, perplexed because they have nothing to say or to mean. (Ornaments were beautiful as long as they evolved from something real, paraphrased a natural form, like the meander or the lotus, or carried symbolically some ritual, or traditional, or emblematic meaning.) There are "indoor lawns" made of plastic, there are roses or carnations dyed purple or green, just because nature did not want them that way. We see old ladies with blue hair, and people wearing parrots around their neck as neckties, or Egyptian friezes on their shirts; such clothes are designed for faceless figures —which people actually become as a result of standardization— since they do not, as they should, emphasize a personal face, but push it aside like something negligible.

We see faces and hands which could be beautiful if they had not been uglified by beautifying, by the commercial imagination of beauticians. These people cover the face with a conventional surface, they efface the real face with its sensibility and imprint of experience. They ruin the character, the personality of a hand by that horrible fashion of red claws. Indeed, the new invention of contact lenses enables women to change their eyes from day to day, in order to match them with their varying dresses and makeup. This is the ultimate reversal of beauty through lack of truth: the face serves the dress instead of the dress serving the face.

Wistfully we recall the Platonic and Hegelian definitions of beauty as "the transparence of the idea in the sensuous appearance," "the sensuous shining of the idea." How can there be beauty when the "idea" of a person, what once was called the "soul," has vanished under the fraud of appearance.

I summarize what our survey has shown us.

We have found an intrinsic relationship and correspondence between the three basic values, not only in their origin, but throughout the ages. All three aim, in their characteristically different ways, at harmony, oneness, and the furtherance of life. Whether *the good* is understood as love, or as the more and more general, or as conformance with one's own and with the cosmic nature, whether *the beautiful* is seen as harmony in breadth, or as harmony in depth, whether *the true* assumes the significance of correctness, consistency, or authenticity—the ultimate meaning is the same, it is concord, unity, wholeness, reflecting the order of organic form.

Two motifs stand out particularly among others, again various aspects of one common postulate. One is the ancient concept of *eudaimonia* which, in the sense of propitious accordance with one's own nature and with the order of the cosmos, is sought as the good, which in the sense of transparence of the idea in sensuous appearance, is seen as constituting the beautiful; and which in the sense of authenticity is identical with existential truth. The other motif is the pervading conception, indeed the feeling, of a *creative, life-inspiring capability* of goodness, truth, and beauty alike.

We have seen that the change of circumstances, dimensions and proportions in human life, most particularly the expansion of the range of being and the scope of knowledge, have profoundly modified the significance of these values. We have noticed the turn from stability to dynamism, from the eternal absolute to what I have called the "relative absolute"; we have come to realize that what is constant in human matters is inextricably interwoven with move and change. The crucial change has occurred with the shift of the center of gravity from the individual to the collective, which means that the technological and intellectual scope of humanity has advanced far beyond the capacity of the individual mind—an incongruity that carries the gravest dangers for the human values and for humanity itself.

We have seen all these fundamental changes. But we have also seen that something of the original meaning of the basic values has survived. It was, indeed, the purpose of these remarks to demonstrate that, contrary to appearances, the true, the good, and the beautiful have not altogether perished from the earth; that, secretly, clandestinely, they are still there.

Whenever and wherever we aim at coherence and integration: when we seek new artistic forms, when we work for peace and understanding among the nations and for the establishment of a world order, when we mind first and foremost the human being and reject the vainglory of nationalism and the choice between two camps for which good means what is good for capitalism or what is good for communism—in brief, whenever, in the face of unprecedented perils, we are resolved to attempt unity, these three values come to life again, a last stronghold of humanity that is left to us.

[1959]

References

Culture and Evolution

1. For a more elaborate account of this process see my study, *The Meaning of History* (New York, 1964).

2. Edgar Dacqué, *Urwelt, Sage und Menschheit* (Munich, 1924).

3. For general information about the new concept of nature (not quite up to date, but adequate in the main) I refer to the book by the German physicist, Carl Friedrich von Weizsaecker, *The History of Nature* (Chicago, 1949).

4. George Gaylord Simpson, *The Meaning of Evolution* (New Haven, 1951), Pt. II, Ch. XV, pp. 240*ff*.

5. *Ibid.*, p. 246.

6. *Ibid.*, Pt. II, Ch. XVII, pp. 285*ff*.

7. *Ibid.*, p. 286.

8. T. H Huxley and Julian Huxley, *Touchstone for Ethics 1893–1943* (New York and London, 1947), p. 133.

9. *Ibid.*, p. 146.

10. George Gaylord Simpson, *op. cit.*, Pt. II, Ch. XV, pp. 257*ff*.

11. A. L. Kroeber, "The Concept of Culture in Science," *The Nature of Culture: Collected Essays* (Chicago, 1952), pp. 120*ff*.

Science and History

1. Geoffrey Barraclough, *History in a Changing World* (Norman, Oklahoma, 1956), p. 2.

The Persistence of Myth

1. Karl Kerényi, *Die antike Religion* (Amsterdam, 1940). The anonymous quotations refer to a passage in Thomas Mann's *Freud and the Future.*
2. Thomas Mann, *Freud and the Future.*

The Nature of the Symbol

1. Sigmund Freud, "Symbolism in Dreams," *Introductory Lectures on Psychoanalysis,* 2nd ed. (London, 1949), Tenth Lecture, pp. 128*ff.*
2. Carl G. Jung, *Modern Man in Search of a Soul* (New York, 1933), pp. 27*ff.*
3. Heinrich Zimmer, *Myths annd Symbols in Indian Art and Civilization* (New York, 1946), p. 62.
4. Cf. *The Logic of Hegel,* trans. by William Wallace (Oxford, 1874), Ch. II, pp. 46*ff;* Heinrich von Kleist, "Essay on the Marionettes," *Vertical: A Yearbook for Romantic-Mystic Ascensions,* ed. by Eugene Jolas (New York, 1941).

What Is Art?

1. *Journal of Aesthetics and Art Criticism,* Vol. XV, No. 1 (Sept. 1956); reprinted, together with the present reply, in *Problems in Aesthetics, An Introductory Book of Readings,* ed. by M. Weitz (New York, 1959).
2. G. G. Simpson, C. S. Pittendrigh, and I. H. Tiffany, *Life* (New York, 1957), pp. 427*ff;* 2nd ed., 1965, p. 479.
3. Cf. the articles "Ars" and "Art," *Thesaurus Linguae Latinae;* Grandsaigne d'Hauterive, *Dictionnaire des racines des langues européennes* (Paris, 1949); H. C. Wyld, *The Universal English Dictionary* (London, 1952).

Varieties of the Unconscious

1. For proof of the existence of the unconscious cf. *The Psychology of Invention in the Mathematical Field,* by the French mathematician

Jacques Hadamard (Princeton, 1944), especially Ch. II: "Discussions on Unconsciousness."

2. E. L. Margetts, "The Concept of the Unconscious in the History of Medical Psychology," *Psychiatric Quarterly* 27 (1953).

3. *Confessions* X.30.

4. *Ibid.,* X.8.

5. *Ibid.,* X.10.

6. *Ibid.,* X.11.

7. *Ibid.,* X.13.

8. *Ibid.,* X.16.

9. Cf. *Oeuvres de Descartes* (Paris, 1908), Vol. X, pp. 180–188.

10. Quoted in Lancelot Law Whyte, *The Unconscious Before Freud* (New York, 1960), p. 95. (A highly instructive book which contains a quantity of material, unfortunately arranged only in chronological order, not by subject.)

11. Printed in Otto Jahn, *W. A. Mozart* (Leipzig, 1858), Pt. I, pp. 496*ff.* This letter was originally published by Rochlitz in 1815. Since the original manuscript cannot be located and much of the data in the text does not correspond with facts known from other sources, the authenticity of the letter has been challenged. It is, however, so significant and describes with such unusual clarity the process of musical creation to the point of auditory vision, that I cannot believe it a complete forgery. If it were, the writer himself must have been an unusual person who had experienced this process. A friend in the field, the composer Roger Sessions, whom I have consulted, agreed with this view.

12. *Bulletin de la Société Française de Philosophie,* 28e Année, No. 1 (1928).

13. From Otto Loewi, "An Autobiographic Sketch," *Perspectives in Biology and Medicine,* Vol. 4, No. 1 (Autumn 1960). Reprinted by permission of the Univ. of Chicago Press.

14. *Observation on Man,* quoted by Whyte, *loc. cit.*

15. Quoted in Wilder Penfield and Lamar Roberts, *Speech and Brain Mechanism* (Princeton, 1959). More information on electrical stimulation experiments will be found here.

16. "*C'est une grande erreur de croire qu'il n'y a aucune perception dans l'âme que celles dont elle s'aperçoit.*" Cf. Kurt Joachim Grau, "Die Entwicklung des Bewusstseinsbegriffes im XVII. und XVIII. Jahrhundert," *Abhandlungen zur Philosophie* 39 Heft (Halle, A. S. 1916).

17. "Von den Vorstellungen, die wir haben, ohne ihrer bewusst zu sein," *Anthropologie* §5 (1798).

18. *The New American Painting* (New York, 1959), p. 64.
19. Selden Rodman, *Conversations with Artists* (New York, 1957), p. 82.
20. *Ibid.*, p. 93.
21. *Ibid.*, p. 108.
22. *System der Phychologie* I (Leipzig, 1855), p. 97.
23. *Psyche* (Stuttgart, 1851), pp. 95*ff.*
24. *Ibid.*, p. 100.
25. "Der Mann Moses und die monotheistische Religion," *Gesammelte Werke*, XVI, p. 224.
26. "Die Frage der Laienanalyse," *Gesammelte Werke*, XIV, p. 254.
27. Cf. Ernest Harms, "Simon-André Tissot, the Freudian before Freud," *American Journal of Psychiatry* No. 112, 9 (1956), p. 744.
28. "Das Unbewusste," *Theoretische Schriften (1911–1925)* (Vienna, 1931), p. 106.
29. Cf. *Naturerklärung und Psyche: Synchronizität als ein Prinzip akausaler Zusammenhänge* (Zurich, 1952); "Synchronicity: an Acausal Connecting Principle," *Collected Works of C. G. Jung*, Vol. 8 (New York, 1960).

The Disintegration of Artistic Form

1. The English version of the *Poetics* used here is the one by Lane Cooper (rev. ed., Ithaca, 1947).
2. Robert Goldwater and Marco Treves, eds., *Artists on Art* (New York, 1945), pp. 410*ff.*
3. *L'ère du soupçon* (Paris, 1952), pp. 10*ff.*
4. Hans Richter, *Dada–Kunst und Antikunst* (Cologne, 1964), pp. 210*ff.*
5. Goldwater and Treves, eds., *op. cit.*, pp. 416*ff.*
6. *Ibid.*
7. Stéphane Mallarmé, *Crise de vers* (Paris, 1951), p. 366.
8. *Ibid.*, p. 363.
9. Richard Huelsenbeck, *Dada, eine literarische Dokumentation* (Hamburg, 1964), pp. 9*ff.*
10. From a review of a German avant-garde book in the *Frankfurter Allgemeine Zeitung*.
11. Introduction to *I Novissimi* (Milan, 1961), p. xiv.
12. *Ibid.*, pp. xvii*ff.*

13. Helmut Heissenbüttel, "Voraussetzungen," in Hans Bender, *Das Gedicht ist mein Messer, Lyriker zu ihren Gedichten*, 2nd ed. (Munich, 1961), pp. 89*ff*.

14. Original English text, from *Movens, Dokumente und Analysen zur Dichtung, bildenden Kunst, Musik, Architektur* (Wiesbaden, 1960), p. 189.

15. Franz Mon, *Artikulationen* (Pfullingen, 1959), pp. 31*ff*.

16. *Ibid.*, p. 113.

17. George Rowley, *Principles of Chinese Painting* (Princeton, 1947), p. 72.

18. Tao Tê Ching, quoted by George Rowley, *Ibid.*, Ch. XXV, p. 5.

19. *Ibid.*, p. 77.

The True, the Good, and the Beautiful

1. *The Republic* VI. 505 A *ff*, 508 E–509 B.

2. *Timaeus* 29 D–31.

3. *De Anima* 414 A.

4. *Pol.* VII 1, 1323 B 16; *Top.* III 1, 116 A 13; *Eth. Nicom.* I 1, 1094 B 7, and I 8, 1098 B 12*ff*.

5. "Grundlegung zur Metaphysik der Sitten," 2. Abschnitt, Akademie Ausgabe IV, p. 421.

6. *Phaedrus* 250 B *ff*.

7. *Vorlesungen über Aesthetik* I (1835), p. 144.

8. *Kampagne in Frankreich* (Münster, 1792).

9. *Contemporary British Philosophers* I (1924), p. 402.

10. *Present Philosophical Tendencies* (1925), p. 204.

11. *Maximen und Reflexionen: Aus Kunst und Altertum.*

12. Letter to Zelter (31 December, 1829).

13. *Vermächtnis* (1829).

INDEX